ECCE HOMO

THE GREAT EVENTS

BY

FAMOUS HISTORIANS

A COMPREHENSIVE AND READABLE ACCOUNT OF THE WORLD'S
HISTORY, EMPHASIZING THE MORE IMPORTANT EVENTS, AND PRE-
SENTING THESE AS COMPLETE NARRATIVES IN THE MASTER-WORDS
OF THE MOST EMINENT HISTORIANS

NON-SECTARIAN   NON-PARTISAN   NON-SECTIONAL

ON THE PLAN EVOLVED FROM A CONSENSUS OF OPINIONS GATH-
ERED FROM THE MOST DISTINGUISHED SCHOLARS OF AMERICA
AND EUROPE, INCLUDING BRIEF INTRODUCTIONS BY SPECIALISTS
TO CONNECT AND EXPLAIN THE CELEBRATED NARRATIVES, AR-
RANGED CHRONOLOGICALLY, WITH THOROUGH INDICES, BIBLIOG-
RAPHIES, CHRONOLOGIES, AND COURSES OF READING

EDITOR-IN-CHIEF

ROSSITER JOHNSON, LL.D.

ASSOCIATE EDITORS

CHARLES F. HORNE, Ph.D.
JOHN RUDD, LL.D

With a staff of specialists

VOLUME III

The National Alumni

CONTENTS

VOLUME III

CONTENTS

LIST OF ILLUSTRATIONS

VOLUME III

AN OUTLINE NARRATIVE

TRACING BRIEFLY THE CAUSES, CONNECTIONS, AND CONSEQUENCES OF

THE GREAT EVENTS

(THE PERIOD OF THE ROMAN EMPIRE)

CHARLES F. HORNE

S O vast and wonderful a construction was the Roman world, so different from our own, that we are apt to imagine it as an arrangement far more deliberately planned, far more mechanically complete, than it appeared to its own inhabitants.

From a cursory glance, we may carry away wholly mistaken conceptions of its thought and purpose. Thus, for instance, the Roman Republic never assumed the definite design of conquering the world; its people had only the vaguest conception of whither the world might extend. They merely quarrelled with their neighbors, defeated and then annexed them.

At almost any time after Hannibal's death, Rome might have marched her legions, practically unopposed, over all the lands within her reach. Yet she permitted a century and a half to elapse ere Pompey asserted her sovereignty over Asia. It was left for Augustus to take the final step, and, by absorbing Egypt, make his country become in name what it had long been in fact, the ruler of the civilized world.

Thus, too, we think of Augustus as a kindly despot, supreme, and governed only by his own will. But his compatriots looked on him as simply the chief citizen of their republic. They considered that of their own free will, to escape the dangers of further civil war, they had chosen to confer upon one man, eminently "safe and sane," all the high offices whose holders had previously battled against one another. So Augustus was Emperor or Imperator, which meant no more than general of the armies of the Republic; he was Consul, or chief civil administrator of the Republic; he was Pontifex Maximus, high-priest of the Republic. He could have had more titles and offices still if he would have accepted them from an obsequious senate.

But the title of "king," so obnoxious to Roman taste, Augustus never sought, nor did his successors, who were in turn appointed to all his offices. For nearly three centuries after the one-man power had become absolute, Rome continued to call itself a republic, to go through forms of election and ceremonial, which grew ever more and more meaningless and trivial.

Augustus seems to have felt the tremendous weight of his position, and to have tried honestly to divide his authority. He invested the trembling senate with both power and responsibility. In theory, it became as influential as he. But the appointment of its members, and also the supreme control of the armies, remained always with the Imperator; and thus the senate continued in reality little better than a flickering shadow. Under the reign of a well-meaning emperor, it loomed large, and often dilated into a very valuable and honorable body. In the grip of a tyrant, it sank at once to its true aspect of helpless and obsequious submission.

THE "ROMAN PEACE"

To the outside world the reign of the emperors was welcome. The provinces were governed by salaried officials, whose conduct was seriously investigated. The hideous extortions and cruelties of the governors sent out in the earlier days of the Republic almost disappeared. This milder rule seemed happy in the contrast. An emperor might be a brute at home, but his personal cruelties could scarce spread over an entire world. Money for even the hugest extravagances of only one man, the provinces could supply. At first they scarce felt the drain.

For two entire centuries after Augustus had assumed power, the world flourished and apparently prospered under the

"Roman peace." The ruins of Pompeii, the tale of its destruction, show how well and how lazily the upper classes and even
the masses lived.[1] The legions were scarce needed except for
petty wars along the frontier. The defeat inflicted by the German barbarians was avenged, and the northern wilderness
seems to have come very near to sharing the fate of Gaul.[2]
But the long campaigns were costly and apparently valueless.
No taxes flowed into the treasury from the poor half-subjugated
savages; and the emperor Tiberius contemptuously declared
that he would leave them to fight among themselves. Another
frontier strife completed the subjugation of Spain. Another
added Britain to the Empire. Another made temporary conquest over Dacia and extended the Asian boundary. There
were minor revolts in Gaul.

Then the Jews, roused to sudden religious frenzy and believing themselves invincible, burst into rebellion.[3] Titus stormed
their capital and burned their Temple. But the lesson was
wasted on the stubborn, fanatical race, and sixty years later
they flared out again. Roman relentlessness was roused to
its fullest rage, and accomplished against them the destruction of prophecy. Their cities were razed to the ground, and
the poor remnant of the race were scattered abroad. Yet, apparently imperishable, refusing to be merged with other men,
they remained a people though without a country. They became what they are to-day, a nation of wanderers.[4]

One other tumult, more central and in that sense more
serious, intruded on the Roman system. Just a century after
the rise of Augustus, the tyrannies of his successor Nero
became so unbearable that even his own senate turned against
him; and he was slain, without having appointed a successor.
The purely military character of the Empire was at once revealed. Different armies each upheld their own general as
emperor. The claimants attacked one another in turn, and the
strongest won. The turmoil lasted for only a year or so, just
long enough for the distant legions to gather around Rome;

---

[1] See *Destruction of Pompeii*, page 207.
[2] See *Germanicus in Germany*, page 1.
[3] See *Siege and Destruction of Jerusalem*, page 150.
[4] See *Jews' Last Struggle for Freedom*, page 222.

xiv AN OUTLINE NARRATIVE OF

the bloodshed was nothing as compared to former ages; the helpless senate acquiesced in each new proclamation of each successful army; and the rest of the world, scarce even jarred in its daily course, flowed on as before.

On the whole, then, these two hundred years were one long period of peace. It was Augustus who for the first time in centuries closed the gates of the war-god's temple in Rome. He encouraged literature, and we have the "Augustan" age. He boasted that he found Rome built of bricks, and left it of marble. He and his successors did far more than that. They constructed roads extending from end to end of their domains. Communication became easy; a mail post was established; people began to travel for pleasure. The nations of the world intermingled freely, and discovered, for the first time on earth, that they were much alike. The universal brotherhood of man may be not even yet fully recognized and welcomed; but the first step toward its acknowledgment was taken under imperial Rome.

CHRISTIANITY

This brings us to a very solemn thought. Many earnest men have believed that they see a divine Providence running through the whole course of history, and nowhere more obvious than here. They point to the careers of both Greece and Rome as being a special preparation for the coming of the Christ. The mission of Greece, they tell us, was to arouse the mind of man, to make him capable of thought and sensitive to spiritual beauty; that of Rome was to teach him the value of law and peace, and yet more, to draw all men together, that all might have opportunity to hear the lessons of the new faith.

Certain it is that at any earlier date it would have seemed practically impossible for a religion to spread beyond a single people. Not only was communication between the nations faint and intermittent, but they were so savage, so suspicious of each other, that a wanderer had to meet them weapon in hand. He must have a ship to flee to or an army at his back. Now, however, under the restraint of Roman law, strangers met and passed without a blow. Latin, the tongue of law, was everywhere partly known. Greek was almost equally widespread as the language of art and culture.

The Hebrews, too, had done their share in the work of preparation. They had developed the religious sense, beyond any of the Aryan peoples. Their religion had become a part, the main part, of their daily lives. They believed it, not with the languid logic of the Romans, not with the sensuous pleasure of the Greeks, but fiercely, fervidly, with a passion that swept all reason to the winds.

Among them appeared the Christ, born in the days of Augustus, crucified in those of Tiberius.[1] His teaching was mainly the doctrine of love, which Buddha had announced five hundred years before, but which was new to the Roman world; and the promise of life beyond the grave, which many races had more or less believed in, but which never before had been made to carry a vision of such splendor and such glory. He also advocated non-resistance to enemies, a principle which the early Church obeyed, but which has found small favor among the masses of later Christians.

These teachings, then, were none of them wholly unconceived before; but they were enforced by a life so pure, a manner so earnest, as compelled respect. Converts became many; and one of these at least took literally the command of the Master, to proclaim the faith to all peoples of the earth. The apostle Paul, stepping beyond the narrow bounds of Judea, preached Christianity to mankind.[2]

Paul was the first great missionary. The earlier faiths of Greece and Rome had not sought to extend themselves, because they did not recognize the brotherhood of man. The new faith insisted upon this, insisted on our duty to our fellows; and so under Paul's leadership every Christian became a missionary, teaching, uplifting the downtrodden, giving them hope, not of this world, but of an infinitely brighter one. The faith spread faster than ever world conquest had been spread before. Scarce a generation after the Crucifixion it had permeated the Empire, and Nero, to divert from himself the suspicion of having burned Rome, accused the Christians.[3]

[1] See *The Crucifixion*, page 23.
[2] See *Rise and Spread of Christianity*, page 40.
[3] See *Burning of Rome under Nero*, page 108.

This led to their first persecution. They were tortured as a punishment and to extort confession. Most of them stood nobly by their doctrine of non-resistance, and endured heroically a martyrdom which they looked on as opening the gates of heaven.[1]

Their devotion drew to them the first serious notice of the Roman authorities. Hitherto they had been regarded merely as a sect among the Jews. But now, with reluctant admiration of their courage, there came also a recognition of their rapid growth and a suspicion of their motives. The Romans could not understand such devotion to a mere religion; and they always feared lest the faith was something more, a cloak for nameless crimes, or a secret conspiracy of rebellion among their slaves, who would some day turn and rend them.

Thus while Nero's attack on the Christians was in a sense an accident, the blind rush of a half-crazed beast, the later persecutions were often directed by serious and well-intentioned emperors and magistrates. The Romans were far from being intolerant. They had interfered very little with the religions of their subject races, and had, indeed, adopted more than one foreign god into their own temples. They were quite willing that the Christ should be worshipped. What they could not understand was that reverence to one god should forbid reverence to another.

It was the new religion which was intolerant, which, in the passionate intensity of its faith, attacked the old gods, denied their existence, or declared them devils. When a man was summoned before a Roman court on the charge of being a Christian, he was not, as a rule, asked to deny Christ; only, there being a general impression that his sect was evil, he was required to prove his honest citizenship and general good character by doing reverence to the Roman gods.[2]

In spite of persecution, some writers say because of it, Christianity spread. Toward the end of the first two hundred years of the Empire, it seemed about the only prosperous institution in a world which was beginning to go badly. During the reign of Marcus Aurelius, the last of the "good" emperors

[1] See *Persecution of the Christians under Nero*, page 134.
[2] See *Martyrdom of Polycarp and Justin Martyr*, page 231.

(161–180), troubles, some accidental, some inherent in the Roman system, were gathering very dark.

The curse of inaction, of wealth without liberty, of intellect without a goal to strive toward, had long been corrupting the upper classes. Now, a terrible plague swept the world from end to end, so that laborers became scarce, lands went untenanted, taxes unpaid. The drain of supporting Rome's boundless extravagance, in buildings, feasts, and gladiatorial displays, began to tell upon the provinces at last. Newer and ever harsher methods had to be employed to wring money from exhausted lands. Driven by their sufferings to cling to religion as a support, men thought of it more seriously; and a cry went up that earth was being punished for its neglect and insult of the ancient gods. The Christians were persecuted anew.[1]

THE PERIOD OF DECAY

The reign of Commodus,[2] son of Marcus Aurelius, marks the beginning of a century which sank almost into anarchy. He was murdered, and his guards auctioned the Empire to the highest bidder. Once more the legions fought against each other and placed their generals upon the throne. During ninety-two years there were twenty-five emperors fully acknowledged, besides a far larger number of claimants who were overthrown before Rome had time to hear of and salute them. The Imperial city was no longer mistress of the world; she was only its capital, as feeble and helpless as the other cities, which these unstable emperors began at times to favor in her stead.

The barbarians also, who through all these ages were growing stronger while Rome grew weaker, became ever a more serious menace. The internal disorder of the Empire left its frontiers often unguarded. The Germans plundered Gaul in the West, the Persians ravaged Asia in the East. In fact, so comparatively strong had the Persians grown that one emperor, venturing against them, was defeated and captured, and lived out his miserable life a Persian slave. Rome could not rescue him.[3]

[1] See *Persecutions of Christians in Gaul*, page 246.
[2] See *Beginning of Rome's Decline*, page 263.
[3] See *Eventful Reign of Sapor I, King of Persia*, page 277.

In the year 284 there came to the front an emperor "of iron," Diocletian. He did what Augustus had done three centuries before, re-formed and recast the government of the world. The last empty ceremonies of the Republic were discarded. Even the pretence of Rome's leadership was brushed aside. The Empire was divided into four districts, each with a capital of its own, and Diocletian selected three other generals to share its rule with him. He and his colleagues restored the long-lost peace. They chastised the barbarians. Diocletian's reforms saved the Roman fabric from what seemed inevitable extinction, and enabled it to exist in some shape for almost another two hundred years.

His system of division did not, however, save the Empire from civil wars. No sooner was his restraining hand removed than his colleagues fought among themselves, until Constantine overthrew his antagonists and once more united the entire Empire. Constantine became a Christian.[1]

It has been repeatedly asserted that his conversion was one of policy rather than belief; and there could be no stronger evidence of the changed position of the new faith. Diocletian had ordered a persecution against it, the last and most terrible which its martyrs suffered. But all that was best and most energetic and most living in the moribund Empire seemed to have gathered round the Church. The persecution did but emphasize its worth and influence.

Constantine did not force his followers to change their beliefs with him; but he encouraged and rewarded those who did. Under him was held the first general council of the faith. The bishops gathered from all the different cities of the world to compare ideas and settle more exactly the doctrines to be taught. Christianity stepped out from its hiding-place and supplanted paganism as the state religion of the Empire.[2]

As though the unimportance of Rome were not thus sufficiently established, Constantine abandoned the decaying capital altogether, and built himself a new city, Constantinople, at the junction of Europe and Asia. This became the centre of the changing world. Built upon the site of an old Greek col-

[1] See *Conversion of Constantine*, page 289.
[2] See *First Nicene Council*, page 297.

ony, it was almost wholly Greek, not only in the nationality of
the people who flocked to it, but in the manners of the court
which Constantine created around him, in the art of its deco-
rators, in the language of its streets.[1] The Empire remained
Roman only in name. The might of a thousand years had
made that name a magic spell, had sunk its restraining influence deep in the minds of men. It was not lightly to be
thrown aside.

Julian, a nephew of Constantine, who after an interval succeeded him upon the throne, abandoned the adopted religion of
his family, and tried to revive paganism.[2] Julian was a powerful and clever man; he seems also to have been an honest and
an earnest one. But he could not turn back the current of the
world. He could not make shallow speculation take the place
of earnest faith. Altruism, the spirit of brotherhood, which
was the animating force of Christianity, might and later somewhat did lose itself amid the sands of selfishness; but it could
not be combated by one man with a chance preference for
egotism.

Julian turned to a worthier purpose. He died fighting the
barbarians. These, held back for a time by Diocletian and
Constantine, were recommencing their ravages with renewed
force. And now a change comes over the character of the invasions. Hitherto they had been mere raids for plunder; but
now a huge, far-reaching, racial movement was in progress.

From the distant plains of Asia came the vanguard of the
Huns, a race of horsemen, whose swift steeds enabled them to
scatter or concentrate at will around slower-paced opponents.[3]
The Huns swept over Southern Russia, then occupied by the
Goths, the most civilized of the Teutonic tribes. The Goths,
finding themselves helpless against the active and fierce
marauders, moved onward in their turn. They crossed the
Danube, not as a raiding troop, but as an entire nation, and,
half begging, half demanding a place of refuge, they penetrated into the world of civilization. With them came fearful
stories of the Huns; but these latter, sweeping off in another
direction, failed for a while to follow up the fugitives.

[1] See *Foundation of Constantinople*, page 320.
[2] See *Julian the Apostate*, page 333.
[3] See *The Huns and Their Western Migration*, page 352.

As for the Goths, after they had defeated and slain one emperor, they were given lands and temporarily subdued by Theodosius the Great, the last ruler to hold the entire Roman domain. In 395 Theodosius, dying, divided his possessions, quite like a hereditary monarch, between his two sons, both mere boys.[1] To the elder he gave Constantinople and the East, to the younger Rome and the West. So instead of one kingdom there were two. Partly through its own disorganization, partly from the pressure of the barbarians, the Roman world had burst and fallen into halves. These proved two very helpless and feeble halves in the hands of their boy rulers; and the eager Teutons, finding themselves no longer withheld, began that remarkable series of plundering invasions by which they overwhelmed the ancient world.

[1] See *Final Division of the Roman Empire*, page 364.

[FOR THE NEXT SECTION OF THIS GENERAL SURVEY SEE VOLUME IV.]

GERMANICUS IN GERMANY

A.D. 13–16

TACITUS

When the Germans first became known to the Romans—about B.C. 112—they showed themselves as warlike tribes along the northern borders of Italy and in various parts of Gaul, where Cæsar afterward had frequent encounters with them, driving them across the Rhine into their own country. But Cæsar's knowledge of them was confined to those tribes whose dwellings were near the Rhine, beyond which he did not pursue them.

Augustus fortified against the Germans along the Rhine, and Drusus, his step-son, took command against them, defeating them in several expeditions (B.C. 13–9). As a reward, he received for himself and his posterity the surname of Germanicus, conqueror of Germany. He died at the age of thirty.

His son, Germanicus, born B.C. 14, was sent, in A.D. 12, to command the forces on the Rhine. After quelling serious mutinies among his legions he crossed the Rhine and attacked and routed some of the German tribes who had been actively aggressive against the Romans. During the following year he defeated other tribes, and after his return across the Rhine he was persuaded by Segestes to aid him against his son-in-law, Arminius (the Latin name for Herman), by whom Segestes was besieged and who, according to Tacitus, became in the end the deliverer of Germany from the power of the Romans. But before he was able to render this service to the German peoples he had many hardships to endure, and at the hands of Germanicus he met with severe reverses.

Arminius had defeated Varus, who, by reason of that disgrace, killed himself (A.D. 10), and the despatch of Germanicus to command the German legions was ordered in the first instance to revenge the overthrow of his predecessor. Although it required several campaigns, the work of Germanicus was so effectual that he withdrew in the end, at the command of Tiberius, with advantage on his side, and, returning to Rome, enjoyed a triumph (A.D. 17). His name is preserved in history, alike for his military talents and services, for his attainments in literary pursuits, and his nobleness of mind.

IN the consulship of Drusus Cæsar and Caius Norbanus a triumph was decreed to Germanicus; the war continuing. He was preparing with all diligence to prosecute it in the summer, but anticipated it by a sudden irruption early in the spring into the territories of the Cattians: for he had conceived a hope that the enemy was divided into opposite parties under Arminius and Segestes, both remarkable for perfidy or fidelity toward us: Arminius was the incendiary of Germany, but Segestes had given repeated warning of an intended revolt at other times and during the banquet immediately preceding the insurrection, and advised Varus "to secure him and Arminius and all the other chiefs; that the multitude, bereft of their leaders, would not dare to attempt anything; and Varus would have an opportunity to separate the guilty from the innocent." But fate decreed it, and he was slain by Arminius. Segestes, though drawn into the war by the universal agreement of the nation in it, yet continued to disapprove of it; his detestation being augmented by motives of a domestic nature, for Arminius had carried away the daughter of Segestes, already betrothed to another: the son-in-law hated, the fathers-in-law were at enmity; and those relations which are bonds of affection between friends fomented the animosities of enemies.

Germanicus therefore handed over to Cæcina four legions, five thousand auxiliaries, and some tumultuous bands of Germans who dwelt on this side the Rhine; he led, himself, as many legions, with double the number of allies, and erecting a fort in Mount Taunus, upon the site of one raised by his father, he pushed on in light marching order against the Cattians; having left Lucius Apronius to secure the roads and the rivers, for, as the roads were dry and the rivers within bounds—events in that climate of rare occurrence—he had found no check in his rapid march, but on his return apprehended the violent rains and floods. He fell upon the Cattians with such surprise that all the weak (through sex or age) were instantly taken or slaughtered. The young men swam over the Adrana and endeavored to obstruct the Romans, who commenced building a bridge; then, repulsed by engines and arrows and having in vain tried terms of peace—after some had gone over to Germanicus—the rest abandoned their cantons and villages and dispersed themselves into the woods. Mattium, the capital of the nation, he burned, ravaged the open country, and bent his march to the Rhine; nor durst the enemy harass his rear, which is their custom whenever they have fled, more from craft than fear. The Cheruscans had purposed to assist the Cattians, but were deterred by Cæcina, who moved about with his forces from place to place; and the Marsians, who dared to engage him, he checked by a victory.

Soon after arrived deputies from Segestes, praying relief against the violence of his countrymen, by whom he was besieged; Arminius having more influence with them than himself, because he advised war, for with barbarians the more resolute in daring a man is the more he is trusted and preferred in times of commotion. To the deputies Segestes had added Segimund, his son; but the young man hesitated from self-conviction; for the year when Germany revolted, having been created priest at the Ubian altar, he had rent the fillets and fled to the revolters: yet, induced to rely upon Roman clemency, he undertook the execution of his father's orders, was graciously received, and conducted with a guard to the Gallic bank of the Rhine. Germanicus thought it worth while to march back, fought the besiegers, and rescued Segestes with a numerous train of his relations and followers, in which were ladies of illustrious rank, and among them the wife of Arminius—the same who was the daughter of Segestes—with a spirit more like that of her husband than her father; neither subdued to tears, nor uttering the language of supplication, but her hands folded within her bosom, and her eyes fixed upon her teeming womb. There were, likewise, carried off the spoils taken at the slaughter of Varus and his army, and given as booty to most of those who then surrendered.

At the same time appeared Segestes himself, of vast stature, and undaunted in the consciousness of his fidelity. In this manner he spoke: "This is not the first day that I have approved my faith and constancy to the Roman people: from the moment I was by the deified Augustus presented with the freedom of the city I have chosen my friends and enemies with reference to your interests, and that not from hatred of my country—for odious are traitors even to the party they prefer —but, because the interests of the Romans and Germans were the same, and because I was inclined to peace rather than war. For this reason, before Varus, the then general, I arraigned Arminius, the ravisher of my daughter and the violator of the league with you. Put off, from the supineness of the general, and seeing there was little protection in the laws, I importuned him to throw into irons myself and Arminius and his accomplices: witness that night—to me I would rather it had been the last! More to be lamented than defended are the events which followed. However, I cast Arminius into irons, and was myself cast into irons by his faction: and now, on the first opportunity of conferring with you, I prefer old things to new, peace to turbulence; and at the same time I might be a fitting mediator for the German nation, with no view of reward, but to clear myself of perfidy, if they would rather repent than be destroyed. For the youth and inexperience of my son I implore pardon. I admit my daughter has been brought into this state by constraint; it will be yours to consider which should preponderate with you—that she is the wife of Arminius or the daughter of Segestes." The answer of Germanicus was gracious: he promised indemnity to his children and kindred, and to himself, as a retreat, a place called "Vetera," in the province; then returned with his army, and by the direction of Tiberius received the title of *Imperator*.

The account circulated of the surrender of Segestes, and his gracious reception, affected his countrymen with hope or anguish as they were severally prone or averse to the war. Acting upon a temper naturally violent, the captivity of his wife and the child in her womb subjected to bondage drove Arminius to distraction: he flew about among the Cheruscans, calling them to arms against Segestes, against Germanicus; nor did he refrain from invectives—"An excellent father! a great general; a valiant army, whose many hands had carried off one bit of a woman! That before him three legions fell, three lieutenants-general; for his method of carrying on war was not by treason nor against pregnant women, but openly, against armed hosts. That the Roman standards were still to be seen in the German groves, there suspended by him to his country's gods. Segestes might live upon the vanquished bank; he might get the priesthood restored to his son; but the Germans would ever regard the fellow as the guilty cause of their having seen between the Elbe and Rhine rods and axes and the toga. That to other nations who know not the Roman domination, executions and tributes were unknown; and as they had thrown them off, and as Augustus (he who was enrolled with the gods) had retreated without accomplishing his object, and Tiberius, his chosen successor, let them not dread an inexperienced stripling and a mutinous army. If they preferred their country, their parents, and their ancient possessions, to masters and new settlements, they should follow Arminius, who led them to glory and liberty, rather than Segestes, who conducted them to infamous servitude."

By these means not the Cheruscans only were roused, but the bordering nations; and Inguiomer, paternal uncle to Arminius, a man long in high credit with the Romans, was drawn into the confederacy. Hence Germanicus became more alarmed, and to prevent the war falling upon him with unbroken force, sent Cæcina with forty Roman cohorts to the river Amisia, through the territories of the Bructerians, to effect a division in the army of the enemy. Pedo, the prefect, led the cavalry along the confines of the Frisians; he himself, embarking four legions, sailed through the lakes; and at the aforesaid river the whole body met—foot, horse, and fleet. The Chaucians, upon offering their assistance, were taken into the service; but the Bructerians, setting fire to their effects and dwellings, were routed by Lucius Stertinius, despatched against them by Germanicus with a band lightly armed. And amid the carnage and plunder he found the eagle of the Nineteenth legion lost in the overthrow of Varus. The army marched next to the farthest borders of the Bructerians, and the whole country between the rivers Amisia and Luppia was laid waste. Not far hence lay the forest of Teutoburgium, and in it the bones of Varus and the legions, by report, still unburied.

Germanicus, therefore, conceived a desire to pay the last offices to the legions and their leader; while the whole of the army present were moved to deep commiseration for their kinsmen and friends, and generally for the calamities of war and the condition of humanity. Cæcina having been sent before to explore the gloomy recesses of the forest, and to lay bridges and causeways over the watery portions of the morasses and insecure places in the plains, they enter the doleful scene, hideous in appearance and association. The first camp of Varus appeared in view. The extent of ground and the measurement of the *principia* left no doubt that the whole was the work of three legions. After that a half-decayed rampart with a shallow foss, where their remains, now sadly reduced, were understood to have sunk down. In the intervening portion of the plain were whitening bones, either scattered or accumulated, according as they had fled or had made a stand. Near them lay fragments of javelins and limbs of horses. There were also skulls fixed upon the trunks of trees. In the adjacent groves were the savage altars, where they had immolated the tribunes and centurions of the first rank. Those who survived the slaughter, having escaped from captivity and the sword, related the sad particulars to the rest: "Here the commanders of the legions were slain; there we lost the eagles; here Varus had his first wound; there he gave himself another, and perished by his own unhappy hand. In that place, too, stood the tribunal whence Arminius harangued. How many gibbets he erected for the execution of his captives; what trenches he dug; and how, in proud scorn, he made a mock at the standards and eagles."

The Roman army which was on the spot buried the bones of the three legions six years after the slaughter: nor could anyone distinguish whether he buried the remains of a stranger or of a kinsman; but all considered the whole as friends, as relations, with heightened resentment against the foe, at once sad and revengeful. Germanicus laid the first sod used in raising a tomb, thus rendering a most acceptable service to the dead, and showing that he shared the sorrows of the living, a proceeding not liked by Tiberius; whether it were that upon every action of Germanicus he put a malignant construction, or that he believed that the impression produced by the sight of the unburied slain would dampen the ardor of the army for battle and inspire them with fear of the enemy. He also said that "A general invested with the office of augur and the most ancient religious functions ought not to have put his hand to the ceremonies of the dead."

Arminius, retiring into pathless places, was pursued by Germanicus, who, as soon as he reached him, commanded the horse to advance and dislodge the enemy from the post he had possessed. Arminius, having directed his men to keep close together and draw near to the wood, wheeled suddenly about, and to those whom he had hid in the forest gave the signal to rush out. Then the Roman horse were thrown into disorder by the assault of a new army, and the cohorts sent out to support them, broken in upon by the body of troops that fled, had augmented the consternation, and were now being pushed into the morass—a place well known to the pursuers, but dangerous to those unacquainted with it—had not Germanicus drawn out the legions in order of battle. Hence the enemy became terrified, our men reanimated, and both retired without advantage on either side. Germanicus, soon after, returning with the army to the Amisia, reconducted the legions, as he had brought them, in the fleet; part of the horse were ordered to march along the sea-shore to the Rhine. Cæcina, who led his own men, was warned that, though he was to return through well-known roads, yet he should with all speed pass the causeway called the Long Bridges. It is a narrow causeway, between vast marshes, and formerly raised by Lucius Domitius. The rest of the country is of a moist nature, either tough and sticky from a heavy kind of clay or dangerous from the streams which intersect it. Round about are woods which rise gently from the plain, which at that time were filled with soldiers by Arminius, who, by short cuts and quick marching, had arrived there before our men, who were loaded with arms and baggage. Cæcina, who was perplexed how at once to repair the causeway decayed by time and to repulse the foe, resolved to encamp in the place, that while some were employed in the work, others might begin the fight.

The barbarians, having made a vigorous effort to break through the outposts and fall upon those employed in the works, harass the troops, march round them, and throw themselves in their way. A mingled shout arose from the workmen and the combatants; all things equally combined to distress the Romans—the place deep with ooze, sinking under those who stood, slippery to such as advanced; their bodies were encumbered with their coats of mail, nor could they hurl their javelins in the midst of water. The Cheruscans, on the contrary, were inured to encounters in the bogs: their persons tall; their spears long, so as to wound at a distance. At last the legions, already giving way, were saved from defeat by the approach of night; the Germans not feeling fatigue on account of their success, without refreshing themselves with sleep, even then diverted all the courses of the springs which rise in the neighboring mountains into the plains; thus the ground being flooded, and the work, as far as they had carried it, overturned, the soldiers had all to do over again. Cæcina, who had served forty years, either under others or in command, was experienced in the vicissitudes of war, prosperous or disastrous, and thence undaunted. Weighing, therefore, all probabilities, he could devise no other expedient than that of restraining the enemy to the wood until he had sent forward all the wounded and baggage; for between the mountains and the marshes there stretched a plain large enough to admit a small army. To this purpose the legions selected were: The Fifth, for the right wing, and Twenty-first, for the left; the soldiers of the First legion to lead the van of the Twentieth to oppose the pursuers.

It was a restless night to both armies, but from different causes. The barbarians, with festive carousals, songs of triumph, or horrid cries, filled the vales below and echoing wood. Among the Romans were feeble fires, low broken murmurs; they leaned, drooping here and there, against the pales, or wandered about the tents, more like men wanting sleep than quite awake. The general, too, was alarmed by direful visions during his sleep; he thought he heard, and saw, Quintilius Varus, rising out of the marsh, all besmeared with blood, stretching forth his hand and calling upon him, but that he rejected the call, and pushed back his hand as he held it toward him. At break of day the legions, posted on the wings, whether from perverseness or fear, deserted their post and took sudden possession of a field beyond the bogs; neither did Arminius fall straight upon them, though they lay open to assault; but when the baggage was set fast in the mire and ditches, the soldiers about it in disorder, the order of the standards confounded, and—as usual at such a time—each man acting hastily for himself, when the ears are slow to catch the word of command, he then commanded his Germans to charge, exclaiming vehemently, "Behold! Varus and his legions again subdued by the same fate!" Thus he cried, and instantly, with a select body, broke through the mass, and chiefly against the horse directed his weapons. Floundering in their own blood and the slippery soil of the marsh, they threw their riders, overturned all they met, and trampled on those that were on the ground. The greatest distress was around the eagles, which could neither be carried against a shower of darts nor be planted in the slimy ground. Cæcina, while he sustained the fight, had his horse shot and, having fallen, would have been overpowered had not the First legion come up to succor him. Our relief came from the greediness of the enemy, who ceased slaying, to seize the spoil. And the legions, as the day closed in, by great exertion got into the open and firm ground. Nor was this the end of their miseries; a palisade was to be raised, an intrenchment digged; their instruments, too, for throwing up and carrying earth, and their tools for cutting turf, were almost all lost. No tents for the soldiers; no remedies for the wounded. While dividing among them their food, defiled with mire or blood, they lamented that mournful night; they lamented the approaching day, to so many thousand men the last.

It happened that a horse which had broken his fastenings and, as he strayed about, become frightened by a noise, had run over some that were in his way. This raised such a consternation in the camp—from a persuasion that the Germans had forced an entrance—that all rushed to the gates, especially to the postern,[1] as the farthest from the foe and safer for flight. Cæcina having ascertained that there was no cause for alarm, but unable to stop them or hold them back, either by his authority or prayers or even by force, prostrated himself on the threshold of the gate; and thus at length by appealing to their humanity—for if they proceeded it must be over the body of the general—he blocked the passage, and the tribunes and centurions satisfied them the while that it was a false alarm.

[1] There were four gates to a Roman camp. Livy says so in express terms: "*Ad quatuor portas exercitum instruxit, ut, signo dato, ex omnibus portubus eruptionem facerent.*" The several gates were the *prætorian;* the gate opposite to it, at the extremity of the camp, called the *decuman;* and two others, called the *right* and *left principals*, because they stood on the right and left sides of the camp, fronting the street called *Principia*.

Then assembling them in the court, and desiring them to hear him with silence, he warned them of their difficulties, and their duty under them: "That their sole hope of safety was in their valor, but that must be guided by counsel; that they must keep close within their camp till the enemy, in hopes of taking it by storm, came up nearer to them; then make a sudden sally on every side, that by this sally they might make good their way to the Rhine; but if they fled, more forests, deeper marshes, and the fierce attack of the foe still remained to them; but that if they conquered, honor and renown awaited them." He reminded them of all that was dear to them at home, and the rewards to be obtained in the camp, but suppressed all mention of defeat. He next distributed horses, first his own, then those of the tribunes and leaders of the legions, to all the bravest warriors, without any flattery, that these first, and afterward the infantry, might charge the enemy.

The Germans were in no less agitation from hope, eagerness, and the opposite counsels of their leaders. Arminius proposed "To let them march out, and to beset them again in their way when they got into marshes and difficult passes." Inguiomer advised measures more resolute and acceptable to barbarians—"To invest the camp; it would be quickly captured; there would be more captives, and the plunder uninjured." As soon therefore as it was light, they level the ditch, cast hurdles into it, attempt to scale the palisade, there being but few men on the rampart, and those who were, standing as if paralyzed by fear. But when they were hampered in the fortifications, the signal was given to the cohorts; the cornets and trumpets sounded at once, and instantly, shouting and charging, they poured down upon their rear, telling them tauntingly "that there were no thickets, no marshes, but equal chances in a fair field." The enemy, expecting an easy conquest, and that the Romans were few and half-armed, were overpowered with the sounds of trumpets and glitter of arms, which were then magnified in proportion as they were unexpected; and they fell like men who, as they are void of moderation in prosperity, are also destitute of conduct in distress. Arminius fled from the fight unhurt, Inguiomer severely wounded. The men were slaughtered as long as day and rage lasted. At length, at

night, the legions returned, and though distressed by the same
want of provisions and more wounds, yet in victory they found
all things—health, vigor, and abundance.

Meanwhile a report had spread that an army was cut off,
and a body of Germans on full march to invade Gaul; so that,
under the terror of this news, there were those whose cowardice would have emboldened them to demolish the bridge upon
the Rhine, had not Agrippina forbidden the infamous attempt.
This high-minded woman took upon herself all the duties of a
general, and distributed to the soldiers, gratuitously, medicines
and clothes, according as anyone was in want or wounded.
Caius Plinius, the writer of the German wars, relates that she
stood at the head of the bridge as the legions returned, and be-
stowed on them thanks and praises; a behavior which sunk
deep into the heart of Tiberius, for these attentions he thought
were not disinterested; nor was it against foreigners she sought
to win the army; for nothing was now left the generals to do,
when a woman paid her visits of inspection to the companies,
attended the standards, and presumed to distribute largesses;
as if before she had shown but small tokens of ambitious designs in carrying her child (the son of the general) in a soldier's uniform about the camp and desiring that he be styled
Cæsar Caligula. Already Agrippina was in greater credit with
the army than the lieutenants-general, or even the generals—a
woman had suppressed a sedition which the authority of the
Emperor was not able to restrain. These jealousies were inflamed and ministered to by Sejanus, who was well acquainted
with the temper of Tiberius, and supplied him with materials
for hatred, prospectively, that he might treasure them up in his
heart and draw them out augmented in bitterness.

Germanicus handed over the Second and Fourteenth of the
legions, which he had brought in ships, to Publius Vitellius to
conduct them by land, that his fleet, thus lightened, might sail
on the shoally sea, or run aground with safety when the tide
ebbed. Vitellius at first marched without interruption while
the ground was dry or the tide flowed within bounds. Presently the ocean beginning to swell by the action of the northwest wind upon it, and also by the influence of the equinoxial
constellation—at which season the sea swells most—the troops

were miserably harassed and driven about. The lands were completely inundated; the sea, the shore, the fields, had one uniform face: no distinction of depths from shallows, of firm from treacherous footing; they were overturned by billows, absorbed by the eddies; beasts of burden, baggage, and dead bodies floated among them and came in contact with them. The several companies were mixed at random, wading now breast high, now up to their chin; sometimes, the ground failing them, they fell, some never more to rise. Their cries and mutual encouragements availed them nothing; the noise of the water drowning them; no difference between the coward and the brave, the wise and the foolish; none between circumspection and hap-hazard, but all were involved in the sweeping torrent. Vitellius at length, having by great exertion gained the higher ground, withdrew the legions thither, where they passed the night without fire and without food, many of them naked or lamed, not less miserable than men enclosed by an enemy—for even such had the resource of an honorable death, while these must perish ingloriously. Daylight restored the land, and they marched to the river Unsingis, whither Germanicus had gone with the fleet. The legions were then embarked, while rumor reported that they were sunk; nor was their escape believed until Germanicus and the army were seen to return.

Stertinius, who had been sent before to receive the submission of Sigimer, the brother of Segestes, had now brought him and his son to the city of the Ubians; both were pardoned, the father promptly, the son with more hesitation, because he was said to have insulted the corpse of Varus. For the rest, Spain, Italy, and the Gauls vied in supplying the losses of the army, offering arms, horses, money, whatever each had at hand. Germanicus, applauding their zeal, accepted only the horses and arms for the war; with his own money he assisted the soldiers; and, to soften by kindness also the memory of the late disaster, he visited the wounded, extolled the exploits of individuals, and, looking at their wounds, with hopes encouraged some, with a sense of glory animated others, and by affability and attention confirmed them all in devotion to himself and to his service. Between the Romans and the Cheruscans flowed the river Visurgis. On its bank stood Arminius, with the other chiefs, inquiring whether Germanicus was come; and being answered that he was there, he prayed leave to speak with his brother. This brother of his was in the army, his name Flavius, remarkable for his fidelity, and for the loss of an eye under Tiberius. Permission was then granted. Flavius, advancing, was saluted by Arminius, who having removed his own attendants, requested that the archers ranged upon our bank might retire. When they were gone—"How came you," he asked his brother, "by that deformity in your face?" The brother having informed him where and in what fight, he desired to know "what reward he had received"? Flavius answered, "Increase of pay, the chain, the crown, and other military gifts"; which Arminius treated with derision, as the vile wages of servitude.

After that they began in different strains. Flavius urged "the Roman greatness, the power of Cæsar, the severe punishment inflicted on the vanquished; and the clemency vouchsafed to those who submitted; that neither the wife nor son of Arminius was treated as a captive." Arminius to this opposed "the claims of country, their hereditary liberty, the domestic gods of Germany; their mother, who joined in his prayer that he would not prefer the character of a deserter, and a betrayer of his kinsmen and connections, in short, of his race, to that of their general." From this they gradually proceeded to invectives; nor would the interposition of the river have restrained them from an encounter, had not Stertinius, running to him, held back Flavius, full of rage and calling for his arms and his horse. On the opposite side was seen Arminius, menacing furiously and proclaiming battle. For most of what he said in this dialogue was in Latin, having, as the general of his countrymen, served in the Roman camp.

Next day the German army stood in order of battle beyond the Visurgis. Germanicus, who thought it became not a general to endanger the legions in the passage without bridges and guards, made the horse ford over. They were led by Stertinius and Æmilius, one of the principal centurions, who entered the river at distant places to divide the attention of the foe. Cariovalda, captain of the Batavians, dashed through where the stream was most rapid, and was by the Cheruscans

—who feigned flight—drawn into a plain surrounded by woods.
Then starting up at once, and pouring upon him on every side,
they overthrew those who resisted, and pressed after those
who gave way, who at length, forming themselves into a circle,
were assailed by some hand-to-hand, by others were annoyed
by missiles. Cariovalda, having long sustained the fury of the
enemy, exhorted his men to break through the assailing bands
in a solid body; he himself charged into the thickest, and fell
under a shower of darts—his horse also being killed—and many
nobles fell around him. The rest were saved by their own
bravery, or by the cavalry under Stertinius and Æmilius, which
came up to their assistance.

Germanicus, having passed the Visurgis, learned from a deserter that Arminius had marked out the place of battle; that
more tribes also had joined him at a wood sacred to Hercules,
and would attempt to storm our camp by night. The deserter
was believed, the enemy's fires were in view, and the scouts,
having advanced toward them, reported that they heard the
neighing of horses and the murmur of a mighty and tumultuous
host. Being thus upon the eve of a decisive battle, Germanicus thought it behooved him to learn the sentiments of the
soldiers, and deliberated with himself how to get at the truth;
"the reports of the tribunes and centurions were oftener
agreeable than true; the freedmen had servile spirits; friends
were apt to flatter; if an assembly were called, there, too, the
counsel proposed by a few was carried by the clamorous plaudits of the rest. The minds of soldiers could, then, only be thoroughly known when, by themselves, free from all restraint, and
over their mess, they gave unreserved utterance to their hopes
and fears."

At nightfall, taking the path leading by the place of divina-
tion,[1] he went out with a single attendant, a deerskin covering
his shoulders,[2] and proceeding by a secret way where there
were no sentinels, entered the avenues of the camp, stationed
himself near the tents, and eagerly listened to what was said of
himself, while one magnified the imperial birth of his general,

[1] In the camp a place was set apart for taking the auspices, on the
right of the general's tent.
[2] He assumed this disguise in order to appear like a German soldier.

another his graceful person, very many his firmness, conde-
scension, and the evenness of his temper, whether seriously
occupied or in moments of relaxation; and they confessed that
their sense of his merits should be shown in battle, protesting
at the same time that those traitors and violators of peace
should be made a sacrifice to vengeance and to fame. In the
mean time one of the enemy who understood Latin rode up to
the palisades, and with a loud voice offered, in the name of Arminius, to every deserter a wife and land, and, as long as the
war lasted, a hundred sesterces a day. This affront kindled the
wrath of the legions. "Let day come," they cried, "battle should
be given, the soldiers would themselves take the lands of the
Germans, lead away wives by right of conquest; they, however,
welcomed the omen, and considered the wealth and women of
the enemy their destined prey." About the third watch [1] an attempt was made upon the camp, but not a dart was discharged,
as they found the cohorts planted thick upon the works, and
nothing neglected that was necessary for a vigorous defence.

Germanicus had the same night a cheering dream: he
thought he sacrificed, and, in place of his own robe besmeared
with the blood of the victim, received one fairer from the hands
of his grandmother Augusta. Elated by the omen, and the
auspices being favorable, he called an assembly, and laid before
them what in his judgment seemed likely to be advantageous
and suitable for the impending battle. He said "that to the
Roman soldiers not only plains, but, with due circumspection,
even woods and forests were convenient. The huge targets,
the enormous spears of the barbarians, could never be wielded
among trunks of trees and thickets of underwood shooting up
from the ground like Roman swords and javelins, and armor
fitting the body; that they should reiterate their blows, and
aim at the face with their swords. The Germans had neither
helmet nor coat of mail; their bucklers were not even strengthened with leather or iron, but mere contextures of twigs, and
boards of no substance flourished over with paint; their first
rank was armed with pikes, in some sort, the rest had only

[1] The Romans divided the night into four watches. Each watch was
on duty three hours, and then relieved by the next in turn. The third
watch began about the modern twelve at night.

stakes burned at the end, or short darts. And now to come to their persons, as they were terrific to sight, and vigorous enough for a brief effort, so they were utterly impatient of wounds; unaffected with shame for misconduct, and destitute of respect for their generals. They would quit their posts or run away before the enemy; cowards in adversity, in prosperity despisers of all divine, of all human laws; if weary of marches and sea voyages, they wished an end of these things, by this battle it was presented to them. The Elbe was now nearer than the Rhine; there was nothing to subdue beyond this; they had only to place him, crowned with victory, in the same country which had witnessed the triumphs of his father and uncle, in whose footsteps he was treading." The ardor of the soldiers was kindled by this speech of the general, and the signal for the onset was given.

Neither did Arminius or the other chiefs neglect solemnly to assure their several bands that "these were Romans; the most desperate fugitives of the Varian army, who, to avoid the hardships of war, had put on the character of rebels; who, without any hope of success, were again braving the angry gods, and exposing to their exasperated foes, some of them backs burdened with wounds, others limbs enfeebled with the effects of storms and tempests. Their motive for having recourse to a fleet and the pathless regions of the ocean was that no one might oppose them as they approached or pursue them when repulsed; but when they engaged hand-to-hand, vain would be the help of winds and oars after a defeat. The Germans needed only remember their rapine, cruelty, and pride; was any other course left them than to maintain their liberty, and, if they could not do that, to die before they took a yoke upon them?"

The enemy thus inflamed, and calling for battle, were led into a plain called Idistavisus. It lies between the Visurgis and the hills, and winds irregularly along, as it is encroached upon by the projecting bases of the mountains or enlarged by the receding banks of the river. At their rear rose a majestic forest, the branches of the trees shooting up into the air, but the ground clear between their trunks. The army of barbarians occupied the plain and the entrances of the forest; the Cheruscans alone sat in ambush upon the mountain, in order to pour down from thence upon the Romans when engaged in the fight. Our army marched thus: the auxiliary Gauls and Germans in front, after them the foot archers, next four legions, and then Germanicus with two prætorian cohorts and the choice of the cavalry; then four legions more, and the light foot with the mounted archers, and the other cohorts of the allies; the men were on the alert and in readiness, so that the order of march might form the order of battle when they halted.

As the bands of Cheruscans who had impatiently rushed forward were now perceived, Germanicus commanded the most efficient of his horse to charge them in the flank, and Stertinius with the rest to wheel round to attack them in the rear, and promised to be ready to assist them at the proper moment. Meanwhile an omen of happiest import appeared; eight eagles, seen to fly toward the wood and to enter it, caught the eye of the general. "Advance!" he cried, "follow the Roman birds; follow the tutelar deities of the legions!"

At once the foot charged, and the cavalry sent forward attacked their flank and rear, and, strange to relate, the two divisions of their army fled opposite ways; that in the wood ran to the plain, that in the plain rushed into the wood. The Cheruscans between both were driven from the hills; among them Arminius formed a conspicuous object, while with his hand, his voice, and the exhibition of his wounds he strove to sustain the fight. He had vigorously assaulted the archers, and would have broken through them had not the cohorts of the Rhætians, the Vindelicians, and the Gauls advanced to oppose him. However, by his own personal effort and the impetus of his horse he made good his passage, his face besmeared with his own blood to avoid being known. Some have related that the Chaucians, who were among the Roman auxiliaries, knew him and let him go; the same bravery or stratagem procured Inguiomer his escape; the rest were slain on all hands; great numbers attempting to swim the Visurgis perished either by the darts showered after them or the violence of the current, or, if they escaped these, they were overwhelmed by the weight of the rushing crowd and the banks which fell upon them. Some, seeking an ignominious refuge, climbed to the tops of trees, and, concealing themselves among the branches, were shot in sport

by the archers, who were brought up for the purpose; others
were dashed against the ground as the trees were felled.   This
was a great victory, and withal achieved without loss on our
side.

This slaughter of the foe, from the fifth hour [1] of the day
until night, filled the country for ten miles with carcasses and
arms.   Among the spoils, chains were found, which, sure of
conquering, they had brought to bind the Roman captives.
The soldiers saluted Tiberius as "Imperator" [2] upon the field of
battle, and, raising a mount, placed upon it, after the manner
of trophies, the German arms, with the names of all the vanquished nations inscribed below.

This sight filled the Germans with more anguish and rage
than all their wounds, afflictions, and overthrows.   They, who
were just now prepared to abandon their dwellings and retire
beyond the Elbe, meditate war and grasp their arms; people,
nobles, youth, aged, all rush suddenly upon the Roman army
in its march and disorder it.   Lastly, they chose a position
shut in by a river and a forest, the inner space being a confined
and humid plain; the forest, too, surrounded with a deep
marsh, except that the Angrivarii had elevated one side by
erecting a broad mound to part them and the Cheruscans.
Here their foot were posted; their horse were concealed among
the neighboring groves, that they might be on the rear of the
legions when they had entered the wood.

Nothing of all this was a secret to Germanicus.   He knew
their counsels, their stations, their overt movements and their
concealed measures; and turned their subtlety to the destruction of themselves.   To Seius Tubero, his lieutenant, he com-

[1] It appears that the battle was fought in July or the beginning of
August, *adulta jam æstate.*   If so, the *fifth* hour nearly agrees with our
nine in the morning.

[2] In the time of the republic, the title of Imperator was given by the
soldiers in the field of battle to the commander-in-chief.   The custom
ceased under Augustus, who annexed the title to the imperial dignity, the
prince being then generalissimo of all the armies of the empire.   The
name of Imperator, it is true, was afterward given to the general who
gained a victory; but that was not done without the special permission
of the prince.   The same rule was observed under the following emperors; and accordingly we find that Tiberius was saluted Imperator; but
the soldiers did not presume to do that honor to Germanicus.

mitted the horse and the plain; the infantry he so formed
that part might pass the level approaches into the wood, and
the rest force their way up the rampart; whatever was ardu-
ous he reserved to himself, the rest he committed to his lieu-
tenants. Those who had the even ground to traverse easily
forced an entrance; but they who were to storm the rampart
were battered from above, as if they had been assaulting a wall.
The general perceived the inequality of this close encounter,
and, drawing off the legions a small distance, ordered the sling-
ers and engineers to discharge their missiles and dislodge the
enemy. Immediately darts were poured from the engines, and
the defenders of the barrier, the more conspicuous they were,
with the more wounds were beaten down. Germanicus, having
taken the rampart, first forced his way at the head of the prætorian cohorts into the wood, and there fought, foot-to-foot.
Behind the enemy was the morass, behind the Romans the
mountains or the river; no room for either to retreat, no hope
but in valor, no safety but in victory.

The Germans were not inferior in courage, but in their
method of fighting and the nature of their arms; as their
vast numbers, hampered in narrow places, could not push forward, nor recover their immense spears, nor practise their
usual assaults and rapid motions, being compelled by their
crowded condition to adopt a stationary manner of fighting.
On the contrary, our soldiers, with shields fitted to their breasts,
and their hands firmly grasping their sword hilts, could gash
the brawny limbs and naked faces of the barbarians, and open
themselves a way with havoc to the enemy. Besides, the activity of Arminius now failed him, being either exhausted by a
succession of disasters or disabled by his recent wound. Nay,
Inguiomer, too, who flew from place to place throughout the
battle, was abandoned by fortune rather than courage. Germanicus, to be the easier known, pulled off his helmet, and
exhorted his men "to prosecute the slaughter; they wanted
no captives," he said; "the extermination of the people alone
would put an end to the war!" It was now late in the day
and he drew off a legion to pitch a camp; the rest glutted
themselves till night with the blood of the foe; the horse
fought with doubtful success.

Germanicus, having in a public harangue praised his victori-
ous troops, raised a pile of arms with this proud inscription:
"That the army of Tiberius Cæsar, having subdued the nations between the Rhine and the Elbe, had consecrated these
memorials to Mars, to Jupiter, and to Augustus." Of himself
he made no mention; either fearful of provoking envy or that
he felt satisfied with the consciousness of his own merit. He
next charged Stertinius with the war among the Angrivarians,
and he would have proceeded had they not made haste to submit; approaching as suppliants, and making a full confession
of their guilt, they received pardon without reserve.

The summer being now far advanced, some of the legions
were sent back into winter quarters by land; the greater part
Cæsar put on board the fleet and conveyed them along the
Amisia to the ocean. The sea, at first serene, resounded only
with the oars of a thousand ships or their impulse when under
sail; but presently a shower of hail poured down from a black
mass of clouds; at the same time storms raging on all sides in
every variety, the billows rolling now here, now there, obstructed the view and made it impossible to manage the ships.
The soldiers, too, unaccustomed to the perils of the sea, in their
alarm embarrassed the mariners, or, helping them awkwardly,
rendered unavailing the services of the skilful. After this, the
whole expanse of air and sea was swept by a southwest wind,
which, deriving strength from the mountainous regions of Germany, its deep rivers, and boundless tract of clouded atmosphere, and rendered still harsher by the rigor of the neighboring north, tore away the ships, scattered and drove them into
the open ocean, or upon islands, dangerous from precipitous
rocks or the hidden sand-banks which beset them. Having got
a little clear of these (but with great difficulty), the tide turned,
and, flowing in the same direction as that in which the wind
blew, they were unable to ride at anchor or bale out the water
that broke in upon them. Horses, beasts of burden, baggage,
even arms, were thrown overboard to lighten the holds of the
vessels, which took in water at their sides and from the waves
running over them. Around them were either shores inhabited
by enemies or a sea so vast and unfathomable as to be supposed
to be the limit of the world and unbounded by any land. Part

of the fleet was swallowed up; many ships were driven upon remote islands where, without a trace of civilized humanity, the
men perished through famine, or were kept alive by the carcasses of horses that were dashed upon the same shore. The
galley of Germanicus alone reached the coast of the Chaucians [1]
where, during the whole period of his stay, both day and night,
amid the rocks and prominences of the shore, he reproached
himself as being the author of such overwhelming destruction,
and was hardly restrained by his friends from destroying himself
in the sea. At last, with the returning tide and favoring gale,
the shattered ships returned—almost all destitute of oars, or with
garments spread for sails, and some towed by those which were
less disabled. He repaired them hastily, and despatched them
to search the islands. By this diligence the greater part were
recovered; many were by the Angrivarians (our new subjects)
redeemed from their more inland neighbors and restored; and
some, driven into Great Britain, were sent back by the petty
kings. Each according to the remoteness of the region he had
returned from recounted the wonders he had witnessed: "the
impetuosity of whirlwinds; strange birds; sea monsters of ambiguous form between man and beast"—things either seen or
fancied from the effects of fear.

Intelligence of this wreck animated the Germans with hopes
of renewing the war, which Germanicus, perceiving, resolved to
check. He commanded Caius Silius, with thirty thousand foot
and three thousand horse, to march into the country of the Cattians; he himself, with a greater force, invaded the Marsians,
where he learned from Malovendus, their general—lately taken
into our subjection—that the eagle of one of Varus' legions was
hidden underground in a neighboring grove kept by a slender
guard. Instantly two parties were despatched: one to face the
enemy and draw him from his position, the other to march
around upon the rear and open the ground. Success attended
both. Hence Germanicus, advancing toward the interior with
greater alacrity, laid waste the country and destroyed the effects
of the late disaster. The foe, wherever they engaged, were instantly defeated; nor (as was learned from the prisoners) were
they ever more dismayed. "The Romans," they exclaimed,

[1] The mouth of the Visurgis, or the Weser.

"are invincible; no calamities can subdue them; they have wrecked their fleet, their arms are lost, our shores are covered with the bodies of their horses and men; and yet they have invaded us with their usual spirit, with the same firmness, and as if their numbers were increased."

The army was thence led back into winter quarters, full of joy to have balanced, by this prosperous expedition, their misfortunes at sea; and by the bounty of Germanicus their happiness was increased; since to each sufferer he paid as much as he declared he had lost; neither was it doubted but that the enemy was tottering and concerting measures for obtaining peace, and that the next summer would terminate the war. Tiberius, by frequent letters, pressed him "to come home to the triumph decreed him." He urged also that he had experienced enough of events and casualties; he had indeed fought great and successful battles, but he must likewise remember his losses and calamities, which (however, owing to wind and waves, and no fault of the general) were yet great and grievous. He himself had been sent nine times into Germany by Augustus, and effected much more by policy than arms. It was thus he had brought the Sygambrians into subjection, thus the Suevians, thus King Maroboduus had been obliged to submit to terms. The Cheruscans, too, and the other hostile nations— now the Roman honor was vindicated—might be left to pursue their own intestine feuds. Germanicus besought one year to accomplish his conquest, but Tiberius assailed his modesty with fresh importunity, by offering him another consulship, the duties of which would require his presence; he added "that if the war were still to be prosecuted, he should leave materials for the fame of his brother, Drusus, who, as there then remained no other enemy, could acquire the title of *Imperator,* and earn the privilege of presenting the laurel in Germany alone." Germanicus persisted no longer; though he knew that this was all hypocrisy, and that through envy he was torn away from a ripened harvest of glory

THE CRUCIFIXION

A.D. 30[1]

FREDERIC WILLIAM FARRAR

The Crucifixion of Jesus Christ took place on Friday of the Passover week of the Jews, in the year A.D. 30. This day is known and now generally observed by Christians as Good Friday. Crucifixion, as a means of inflicting death in the most cruel, lingering, and shameful way, was used by many nations of antiquity. The Jews never executed their criminals in this way, but the Greeks and Romans made the cross the instrument of death to malefactors. The cross was in the shape either of the letter T or the letter X, or was in the form familiar in such paintings of the Crucifixion as the well-known representation of Rubens. It was the usual custom to compel the criminal to carry his own cross to the place of execution. The cross was then set up and the criminal was usually tied to it by the hands and feet and left to perish of hunger and thirst. Sometimes he was given a narcotic drink to stupefy him. In the case of the crucifixion of Jesus Christ the victim was fastened to the cross by nails driven through his hands and feet.

As Dr. Judson Titsworth has plainly pointed out, the men who were crucified with Jesus Christ were not thieves, but robbers (this is the term also used below by Farrar), or perhaps Jewish patriots, to the Romans political rebels and outlaws. They would then be classed with Jesus under the accusation that they were not loyal to the sovereignty of the Roman Emperor. During the procuratorship of Pontius Pilate there was a widely prevailing spirit of sedition and revolt among the Jews, and many rebels were sentenced to crucifixion. Such a rebel was the robber Barabbas, whom Pilate wished to substitute for Jesus as the victim of popular fury. The "robber" episode of the Crucifixion is treated by Farrar with a picturesque effect which heightens the vivid coloring in his account of the supreme event that marks "the central point of the world's history."

UTTERLY brutal and revolting as was the punishment of crucifixion, which has now for fifteen hundred years been abolished by the common pity and abhorrence of mankind, there was one custom in Judea, and one occasionally practised

---

[1] The disputed date of the Crucifixion of Jesus—long variously placed between A.D. 29 and 33—is definitely fixed by many later authorities at the year 30.

by the Romans, which reveal some touch of passing humanity. The latter consisted in giving to the sufferer a blow under the armpit, which, without causing death, yet hastened its approach. Of this I need not speak, because, for whatever reason, it was not practised on this occasion. The former, which seems to have been due to the milder nature of Judaism, and which was derived from a happy piece of rabbinic exegesis on Prov. xxxi. 6, consisted in giving to the condemned, immediately before his execution, a draught of wine medicated with some powerful opiate. It had been the custom of wealthy ladies in Jerusalem to provide this stupefying potion at their own expense, and they did so quite irrespectively of their sympathy for any individual criminal. It was probably taken freely by the two malefactors, but when they offered it to Jesus he would not take it. The refusal was an act of sublimest heroism. The effect of the draught was to dull the nerves, to cloud the intellect, to provide an anæsthetic against some part at least of the lingering agonies of that dreadful death. But he, whom some modern sceptics have been base enough to accuse of feminine feebleness and cowardly despair, preferred rather "to look Death in the face"—to meet the king of terrors without striving to deaden the force of one agonizing anticipation, or to still the throbbing of one lacerated nerve.

The three crosses were laid on the ground—that of Jesus, which was doubtless taller than the other two, being placed in bitter scorn in the midst. Perhaps the cross-beam was now nailed to the upright, and certainly the title, which had either been borne by Jesus fastened round his neck or carried by one of the soldiers in front of him, was now nailed to the summit of his cross. Then he was stripped naked of all his clothes, and then followed the most awful moment of all. He was laid down upon the implement of torture. His arms were stretched along the cross-beams; and at the centre of the open palms the point of a huge iron nail was placed, which, by the blow of a mallet, was driven home into the wood. Then through either foot separately, or possibly through both together as they were placed one over the other, another huge nail tore its way through the quivering flesh. Whether the sufferer was *also* bound to the cross we do not know; but, to prevent the hands and feet being torn away by the weight of the body, which could not "rest upon nothing but four great wounds," there was, about the centre of the cross, a wooden projection strong enough to support, at least in part, a human body which soon became a weight of agony.

It was probably at this moment of inconceivable horror that the voice of the Son of Man was heard uplifted, not in a scream of natural agony at that fearful torture, but calmly praying in divine compassion for his brutal and pitiless murderers—aye, and for all who in their sinful ignorance crucify him afresh for-ever: "Father, forgive them, for they know not what they do."

And then the accursed tree—with its living human burden hanging upon it in helpless agony, and suffering fresh tortures as every movement irritated the fresh rents in hands and feet —was slowly heaved up by strong arms, and the end of it fixed firmly in a hole dug deep in the ground for that purpose. The feet were but a little raised above the earth. The victim was in full reach of every hand that might choose to strike, in close proximity to every gesture of insult and hatred. He might hang for hours to be abused, outraged, even tortured by the ever-moving multitude who, with that desire to see what is horrible which always characterizes the coarsest hearts, had thronged to gaze upon a sight which should rather have made them weep tears of blood.

And there, in tortures which grew ever more insupportable, ever more maddening as time flowed on, the unhappy victims might linger in a living death so cruelly intolerable that often they were driven to entreat and implore the spectators or the executioners, for dear pity's sake, to put an end to anguish too awful for man to bear—conscious to the last, and often, with tears of abject misery, beseeching from their enemies the price-less boon of death.

For indeed a death by crucifixion seems to include all that pain and death *can* have of horrible and ghastly—dizziness, cramp, thirst, starvation, sleeplessness, traumatic fever, tetanus, publicity of shame, long continuance of torment, horror of an-ticipation, mortification of untended wounds—all intensified just up to the point at which they can be endured at all, but all stopping just short of the point which would give to the sufferer the relief of unconsciousness. The unnatural position made every movement painful; the lacerated veins and crushed tendons throbbed with incessant anguish; the wounds, inflamed by exposure, gradually gangrened; the arteries—especially of the head and stomach — became swollen and oppressed with surcharged blood; and while each variety of misery went on gradually increasing, there was added to them the intolerable pang of a burning and raging thirst; and all these physical complications caused an internal excitement and anxiety which made the prospect of death itself—of death, the awful unknown enemy, at whose approach man usually shudders most—bear the aspect of a delicious and exquisite release.

Such was the death to which Christ was doomed; and though for him it was happily shortened by all that he had previously endured, yet he hung from soon after noon until nearly sunset before "he gave up his soul to death."

When the cross was uplifted the leading Jews, for the first time, prominently noticed the deadly insult in which Pilate had vented his indignation. Before, in their blind rage, they had imagined that the manner of his crucifixion was an insult aimed at *Jesus;* but now that they saw him hanging between the two robbers, on a cross yet loftier, it suddenly flashed upon them that it was a public scorn inflicted upon *them*. For on the white wooden tablet smeared with gypsum, which was to be seen so conspicuously over the head of Jesus on the cross, ran, in black letters, an inscription in the three civilized languages of the ancient world—the three languages of which *one* at least was certain to be known by every single man in that assembled multitude—in the official Latin, in the current Greek, in the vernacular Aramaic—informing all that this Man who was thus enduring a shameful, servile death—this Man thus crucified between two *sicarii* in the sight of the world, was "THE KING OF THE JEWS."

To him who was crucified the poor malice seemed to have in it nothing of derision. Even on his cross he reigned; even there he seemed divinely elevated above the priests who had brought about his death, and the coarse, idle, vulgar multitude who had flocked to feed their greedy eyes upon his sufferings. The malice was quite impotent against One whose spiritual and moral nobleness struck awe into dying malefactors and heathen executioners, even in the lowest abyss of his physical degradation. With the passionate ill-humor of the Roman governor there probably blended a vein of seriousness. While he was delighted to revenge himself on his detested subjects by an act of public insolence, he probably meant, or half meant, to imply that this *was*, in one sense, the King of the Jews—the greatest, the noblest, the truest of his race, whom therefore his race had crucified. The King was not unworthy of his kingdom, but the kingdom of the King. There was something loftier even than royalty in the glazing eyes which never ceased to look with sorrow on the City of Righteousness, which had now become a city of murderers. The Jews felt the intensity of the scorn with which Pilate had treated them. It so completely poisoned their hour of triumph that they sent their chief priests in deputation, begging the governor to alter the obnoxious title. "Write not," they said, "' The King of the Jews,' but that ' He *said*, I am the King of the Jews.'" But Pilate's courage, which had oozed away so rapidly at the name of Cæsar, had now revived. He was glad in any and every way to browbeat and thwart the men whose seditious clamor had forced him in the morning to act against his will. Few men had the power of giving expression to a sovereign contempt more effectually than the Romans. Without deigning any justification of what he had done, Pilate summarily dismissed these solemn hierarchs with the curt and contemptuous reply, "What I have written I have written."

In order to prevent the possibility of any rescue, even at the last moment—since instances had been known of men taken from the cross and restored to life—a quaternion of soldiers with their centurion were left on the ground to guard the cross. The clothes of the victims always fell as perquisites to the men who had to perform so weary and disagreeable an office. Little dreaming how exactly they were fulfilling the mystic intimations of olden Jewish prophecy, they proceeded, therefore, to divide between them the garments of Jesus. The *tallith* they tore into four parts, probably ripping it down the seams; but the *cetoneth*, or undergarment, was formed of one continuous woven texture, and to tear would have been to spoil it; they

therefore contented themselves with letting it become the property of any one of the four to whom it should fall by lot.
When this had been decided, they sat down and watched him
till the end, beguiling the weary lingering hours by eating and
drinking, and gibing, and playing dice.

It was a scene of tumult. The great body of the people
seem to have stood silently at gaze; but some few of them as
they passed by the cross—perhaps some of the many false witnesses and other conspirators of the previous night—mocked at
Jesus with insulting noises and furious taunts, especially bid-
ding him come down from the cross and save himself, since he
could destroy the Temple and build it in three days. And the
chief priests, and scribes, and elders, less awe-struck, less compassionate than the mass of the people, were not ashamed to
disgrace their gray-haired dignity and lofty reputation by adding
their heartless reproaches to those of the evil few. Unrestrained by the noble patience of the sufferer, unsated by the
accomplishment of their wicked vengeance, unmoved by the
sight of helpless anguish and the look of eyes that began to
glaze in death, they congratulated one another under his cross
with scornful insolence: "He saved others, himself he cannot
save;" "Let this Christ, this King of Israel, descend now from
the cross, that we may see and believe." No wonder then that
the ignorant soldiers took their share of mockery with these
shameless and unvenerable hierarchs: no wonder that, at their
mid-day meal, they pledged in mock hilarity the Dying Man,
cruelly holding up toward his burning lips their cups of sour
wine, and echoing the Jewish taunts against the weakness of
the King whose throne was a cross, whose crown was thorns.
Nay, even the poor wretches who were crucified with him caught
the hideous infection; comrades, perhaps, of the respited Barabbas, heirs of the rebellious fury of a Judas the Gaulonite,
trained to recognize no Messiah but a Messiah of the sword,
they reproachfully bade him, if his claims were true, to save
himself and them. So *all* the voices about him rang with blasphemy and spite, and in that long slow agony his dying ear
caught no accent of gratitude, of pity, or of love. Baseness,
falsehood, savagery, stupidity—such were the characteristics of
the world which thrust itself into hideous prominence before

the Saviour's last consciousness, such the muddy and miserable stream that rolled under the cross before his dying eyes.

But amid this chorus of infamy Jesus spoke not. He *could* have spoken. The pains of crucifixion did not confuse the intellect or paralyze the powers of speech. We read of crucified men who, for hours together upon the cross, vented their sorrow, their rage, or their despair in the manner that best accorded with their character; of some who raved and cursed, and spat at their enemies; of others who protested to the last against the iniquity of their sentence; of others who implored compassion with abject entreaties; of one even who, from the cross, as from a tribunal, harangued the multitude of his countrymen, and upbraided them with their wickedness and vice. But, except to bless and to encourage, and to add to the happiness and hope of others, Jesus spoke not. So far as the malice of the passers-by, and of priests and sanhedrists and soldiers, and of these poor robbers who suffered with him, was concerned —as before during the trial so now upon the cross—he maintained unbroken his kingly silence.

But that silence, joined to his patient majesty and the divine holiness and innocence which radiated from him like a halo, was more eloquent than any words. It told earliest on one of the crucified robbers. At first this *bonus latro* of the Apocryphal Gospels seems to have faintly joined in the reproaches uttered by his fellow-sinner; but when those reproaches merged into deeper blasphemy, he spoke out his inmost thought. It is probable that he had met Jesus before, and heard him, and perhaps been one of those thousands who had seen his miracles. There is indeed no authority for the legend which assigns to him the name of Dysmas, or for the beautiful story of his having saved the life of the Virgin and her Child during their flight into Egypt. But on the plains of Gennesareth, perhaps from some robber's cave in the wild ravines of the Valley of the Doves, he may well have approached his presence—he may well have been one of those publicans and sinners who drew near to him for to hear him. And the words of Jesus had found some room in the good ground of his heart; they had not all fallen upon stony places. Even at this hour of shame and death, when he was suffering the just consequence of his past

evil deeds, faith triumphed.   As a flame sometimes leaps up
among dying embers, so amid the white ashes of a sinful life
which lay so thick upon his heart, the flame of love toward his
God and his Saviour was not quite quenched.   Under the hell-
ish outcries which had broken loose around the cross of Jesus
there had lain a deep misgiving.   Half of them seem to have
been instigated by doubt and fear.   Even in the self-congratu-
lations of the priests we catch an undertone of dread.   Suppose that even now some imposing miracle should be wrought!
Suppose that even now that martyr-form should burst indeed
into messianic splendor, and the King, who seemed to be in
the slow misery of death, should suddenly with a great voice
summon his legions of angels, and, springing from his cross
upon the rolling clouds of heaven, come in flaming fire to take
vengeance upon his enemies!   And the air seemed to be full
of signs.   There was a gloom of gathering darkness in the sky,
a thrill and tremor in the solid earth, a haunting presence as of
ghostly visitants who chilled the heart and hovered in awful
witness above that scene.   The dying robber had joined at first
in the half-taunting, half-despairing appeal to a defeat and weakness which contradicted all that he had hoped; but now this
defeat seemed to be greater than victory, and this weakness
more irresistible than strength.   As he looked, the faith in his
heart dawned more and more into the perfect day.   He had
long ceased to utter any reproachful words; he now rebuked
his comrade's blasphemies.   Ought not the suffering innocence
of him who hung between them to shame into silence their just
punishment and flagrant guilt?   And so, turning his head to
Jesus, he uttered the intense appeal, "O Jesus, remember me
when thou comest in thy kingdom."   Then he, who had been
mute amid invectives, spake at once in surpassing answer to
that humble prayer, "Verily, I say to thee, to-day shalt thou be
with me in Paradise."

Though none spoke to comfort Jesus—though deep grief,
and terror, and amazement kept them dumb—yet there were
hearts amid the crowd that beat in sympathy with the awful
sufferer.   At a distance stood a number of women looking on,
and perhaps, even at that dread hour, expecting his immediate
deliverance.   Many of these were women who had ministered

to him in Galilee, and had come from thence in the great band of Galilean pilgrims. Conspicuous among this heart-stricken group were his mother Mary, Mary of Magdala, Mary the wife of Clopas, mother of James and Joses, and Salome the wife of Zebedee. Some of them, as the hours advanced, stole nearer and nearer to the cross, and at length the filming eye of the Saviour fell on his own mother Mary, as, with the sword piercing through and through her heart, she stood with the disciple whom he loved. His mother does not seem to have been much with him during his ministry. It may be that the duties and cares of a humble home rendered it impossible. At any rate, the only occasions on which we hear of her are occasions when she is with his brethren, and is joined with them in endeavoring to influence, apart from his own purposes and authority, his messianic course. But although at the very beginning of his ministry he had gently shown her that the earthly and filial relation was now to be transcended by one far more lofty and divine, and though this end of all her high hopes must have tried her faith with an overwhelming and unspeakable sorrow, yet she was true to him in this supreme hour of his humiliation, and would have done for him all that a mother's sympathy and love can do. Nor had he for a moment forgotten her who had bent over his infant slumbers, and with whom he had shared those thirty years in the cottage at Nazareth. Tenderly and sadly he thought of the future that awaited her during the remaining years of her life on earth, troubled as they must be by the tumults and persecutions of a struggling and nascent faith. After his resurrection her lot was wholly cast among his apostles, and the apostle whom he loved the most, the apostle who was nearest to him in heart and life, seemed the fittest to take care of her. To him, therefore—to John whom he had loved more than his brethren—to John whose head had leaned upon his breast at the Last Supper, he consigned her as a sacred charge. "Woman," he said to her, in fewest words, but in words which breathed the uttermost spirit of tenderness, "behold thy son; ' and then to St. John, "Behold thy mother." He could make no gesture with those pierced hands, but he could bend his head. They listened in speechless emotion, but from that hour—perhaps from that very moment—leading her away from a spectacle which did but torture her soul with unavailing agony, that disciple took her to his own home.

It was now noon, and at the Holy City the sunshine should have been burning over that scene of horror with a power such as it has in the full depth of an English summer-time. But instead of this, the face of the heavens was black, and the noonday sun was "turned into darkness," on "this great and terrible day of the Lord." It could have been no darkness of any natural eclipse, for the Paschal moon was at the full; but it was one of those "signs from heaven" for which, during the ministry of Jesus, the Pharisees had so often clamored in vain. The early Fathers appealed to pagan authorities—the historian Phallus, the chronicler Phlegon—for such a darkness; but we have no means of testing the accuracy of these references, and it is quite possible that the darkness was a local gloom which hung densely over the guilty city and its immediate neighborhood. But whatever it was, it clearly filled the minds of all who beheld it with yet deeper misgiving. The taunts and jeers of the Jewish priests and the heathen soldiers were evidently confined to the earlier hours of the Crucifixion. Its later stages seem to have thrilled alike the guilty and the innocent with emotions of dread and horror. Of the incidents of those last three hours we are told nothing, and that awful obscuration of the noonday sun may well have overawed every heart into an inaction respecting which there was nothing to relate. What Jesus suffered *then* for us men and our salvation we cannot know, for during those three hours he hung upon his cross in silence and darkness; or, if he spoke, there was none there to record his words. But toward the close of that time his anguish culminated, and, emptied to the very uttermost of that glory which he had since the world began, drinking to the very deepest dregs the cup of humiliation and bitterness, enduring not only to have taken upon him the form of a servant, but also to suffer the last infamy which human hatred could impose on servile helplessness, he uttered that mysterious cry, of which the full significance will never be fathomed by man: *Eli, Eli, lama Sabachthani?* ("My God, my God, why hast thou forsaken me?")

In those words, quoting the psalm in which the early Fathers rightly saw a far-off prophecy of the whole passion of Christ, he borrowed from David's utter agony the expression of his own. In that hour he was alone. Sinking from depth to depth of unfathomable suffering, until, at the close approach of a death which—because he was God, and yet had been made man —was more awful to him than it could ever be to any of the sons of men, it seemed as if even his divine humanity could endure no more.

Doubtless the voice of the sufferer—though uttered loudly in that paroxysm of an emotion which, in another, would almost have touched the verge of despair—was yet rendered more uncertain and indistinct from the condition of exhaustion in which he hung; and so, amid the darkness, and confused noise, and dull footsteps of the moving multitude, there were some who did not hear what he had said. They had caught only the first syllable, and said to one another that he had called on the name of Elijah. The readiness with which they seized this false impression is another proof of the wild state of excitement and terror—the involuntary dread of something great and unforeseen and terrible—to which they had been reduced from their former savage insolence. For Elijah, the great prophet of the Old Covenant, was inextricably mingled with all the Jewish expectations of a Messiah, and these expectations were full of wrath. The coming of Elijah would be the coming of a day of fire, in which the sun should be turned into blackness and the moon into blood, and the powers of heaven should be shaken. Already the noonday sun was shrouded in unnatural eclipse; might not some awful form at any moment rend the heavens and come down, touch the mountains and they should smoke? The vague anticipation of conscious guilt was unfulfilled. Not such as yet was to be the method of God's workings. His messages to man for many ages more were not to be in the thunder and earthquake, not in rushing wind or roaring flame, but in the "still small voice" speaking always amid the apparent silences of Time in whispers intelligible to man's heart, but in which there is neither speech nor language, though the voice is heard.

But now the end was very rapidly approaching, and Jesus, who had been hanging for nearly six hours upon the cross, was

suffering from that torment of thirst which is most difficult of
all for the human frame to bear—perhaps the most unmitigated
of the many separate sources of anguish which were combined
in this worst form of death.   No doubt this burning thirst was
aggravated by seeing the Roman soldiers drinking so near the
cross; and happily for mankind, Jesus had never sanctioned the
unnatural affectation of stoic impassibility.   And so he uttered
the one sole word of physical suffering which had been wrung
from him by all the hours in which he had endured the extreme
of all that man can inflict.   He cried aloud, "I thirst."   Probably a few hours before, the cry would have only provoked a
roar of frantic mockery; but now the lookers-on were reduced
by awe to a readier humanity.   Near the cross there lay on the
ground the large earthen vessel containing the *posca*, which
was the ordinary drink of the Roman soldiers.   The mouth of
it was filled with a piece of sponge, which served as a cork.
Instantly some one—we know not whether he was friend or
enemy, or merely one who was there out of idle curiosity—took
out the sponge and dipped it in the posca to give it to Jesus.
But low as was the elevation of the cross, the head of the sufferer, as it rested on the horizontal beam of the accursed tree,
was just beyond the man's reach; and therefore he put the
sponge at the end of a stalk of hyssop—about a foot long—and
held it up to the parched and dying lips.   Even this simple act
of pity, which Jesus did not refuse, seemed to jar upon the
condition of nervous excitement with which some of the multitude were looking on.   "Let be," they said to the man, "let us
see whether Elias is coming to save him."   The man did not
desist from his act of mercy, but when it was done he, too,
seems to have echoed those uneasy words.   But Elias came not,
nor human comforter, nor angel deliverer.   It was the will of
God, it was the will of the Son of God, that he should be "per-
fected through sufferings"; that—for the eternal example of
all his children as long as the world should last—he should
"endure unto the end."

And now the end was come.   Once more, in the words of
the sweet Psalmist of Israel, but adding to them that title of
trustful love which, through him, is permitted to the use of all
mankind, "Father," he said, "into thy hands I commend my

spirit." Then with one more great effort he uttered the last cry—"It is finished." It may be that that great cry ruptured some of the vessels of his heart, for no sooner had it been uttered than he bowed his head upon his breast and yielded his life, "a ransom for many"—a willing sacrifice to his Heavenly Father. "Finished was his holy life; with his life his struggle, with his struggle his work, with his work the redemption, with the redemption the foundation of the new world." At that moment the veil of the Temple was rent in twain from the top to the bottom. An earthquake shook the earth and split the rocks, and as it rolled away from their places the great stones which closed and covered the cavern sepulchres of the Jews, so it seemed to the imaginations of many to have disimprisoned the spirits of the dead, and to have filled the air with ghostly visitants, who after Christ had risen appeared to linger in the Holy City. These circumstances of amazement, joined to all they had observed in the bearing of the Crucified, cowed even the cruel and gay indifference of the Roman soldiers. On the centurion who was in command of them the whole scene had exercised a yet deeper influence. As he stood opposite to the cross and saw the Saviour die, he glorified God and exclaimed, "This Man was in truth righteous"—nay, more, "This Man was a Son of God." Even the multitude, utterly sobered from their furious excitement and frantic rage, began to be weighed down with a guilty consciousness that the scene which they had witnessed had in it something more awful than they could have conceived, and as they returned to Jerusalem they wailed and beat upon their breasts. Well might they do so! This was the last drop in a full cup of wickedness: this was the beginning of the end of their city and name and race.

And in truth that scene was more awful than they, or even we, can know. The secular historian, be he ever so sceptical, cannot fail to see in it the central point of the world's history. Whether he be a believer in Christ or not, he cannot refuse to admit that this new religion grew from the smallest of all seeds to be a mighty tree, so that the birds of the air took refuge in its branches; that it was the little stone cut without hands which dashed into pieces the colossal image of heathen greatness, and grew till it became a great mountain and filled the

earth. Alike to the infidel and to the believer the Crucifixion
is the boundary instant between ancient and modern days.
Morally and physically, no less than spiritually, the faith of
Christ was the *palingenesia* of the world. It came like the
dawn of a new spring to nations "effete with the drunkenness
of crime." The struggle was long and hard, but from the hour
when Christ died began the death-knell to every satanic tyranny and every tolerated abomination. From that hour holiness
became the universal ideal of all who name the name of Christ
as their Lord, and the attainment of that ideal the common
heritage of souls in which his spirit dwells.

The effects, then, of the work of Christ are even to the unbeliever indisputable and historical. It expelled cruelty; it
curbed passion; it branded suicide; it punished and repressed
an execrable infanticide; it drove the shameless impurities of
heathendom into a congenial darkness. There was hardly a
class whose wrongs it did not remedy. It rescued the gladiator; it freed the slave; it protected the captive; it nursed the
sick; it sheltered the orphan; it elevated the woman; it
shrouded as with a halo of sacred innocence the tender years of
the child. In every region of life its ameliorating influence
was felt. It changed pity from a vice into a virtue. It elevated poverty from a curse into a beatitude. It ennobled labor
from a vulgarity into a dignity and a duty. It sanctified marriage from little more than a burdensome convention into little
less than a blessed sacrament. It revealed for the first time
the angelic beauty of a purity of which men had despaired and
of a meekness at which they had utterly scoffed. It created
the very conception of charity, and broadened the limits of its
obligation from the narrow circle of a neighborhood to the wi-
dest horizons of the race. And while it thus evolved the idea of
humanity as a common brotherhood, even where its tidings
were *not* believed — all over the world, wherever its tidings
were believed, it cleansed the life and elevated the soul of each
individual man. And in all lands where it has moulded the
characters of its true believers it has created hearts so pure
and lives so peaceful and homes so sweet that it might seem
as though those angels who had heralded its advent had also
whispered to every depressed and despairing sufferer among the

sons of men: "Though ye have lien among the pots, yet shall ye be as the wings of a dove, that is covered with silver wings, and her feathers like gold."

Others, if they *can* and *will*, may see in such a work as this no divine Providence, they may think it philosophical enlightenment to hold that Christianity and Christendom are adequately accounted for by the idle dreams of a noble self-deceiver and the passionate hallucinations of a recovered demoniac. We persecute them not, we denounce them not, we judge them not; but we say that, unless all life be a hollow, there could have been no such miserable origin to the sole religion of the world which holds the perfect balance between philosophy and popularity, between religion and morals, between meek submissiveness and the pride of freedom, between the ideal and the real, between the inward and the outward, between modest stillness and heroic energy—nay, between the tenderest conservatism and the boldest plans of world-wide reformation. The witness of history to Christ is a witness which has been given with irresistible cogency; and it has been so given to none but him.

But while even the unbeliever must see what the life and death of Jesus have effected in the world, to the believer that life and death are something deeper still; to him they are nothing less than a resurrection from the dead. He sees in the cross of Christ something which far transcends its historical significance. He sees in it the fulfilment of all prophecy as well as the consummation of all history; he sees in it the explanation of the mystery of birth, and the conquest over the mystery of the grave. In that life he finds a perfect example; in that death an infinite redemption. As he contemplates the Incarnation and the Crucifixion, he no longer feels that God is far away, and that this earth is but a disregarded speck in the infinite azure, and he himself but an insignificant atom chance-thrown amid the thousand million living souls of an innumerable race, but he exclaims in faith and hope and love: "Behold, the tabernacle of God is with men; yea, he will be their God, and they shall be his people." "Ye are the temple of the living God; as God hath said, I will dwell in them, and walk in them."

The sun was westering as the darkness rolled away from the completed sacrifice. They who had not thought it a pollution to inaugurate their feast by the murder of their Messiah, were seriously alarmed lest the sanctity of the following day—which began at sunset—should be compromised by the hanging of the corpses on the cross. And horrible to relate, the crucified often lived for many hours—nay, even for two days—in their torture. The Jews therefore begged Pilate that their legs might be broken, and their bodies taken down. This *crurifragium*, as it was called, consisted in striking the legs of the sufferers with a heavy mallet, a violence which seemed always to have hastened, if it did not instantly cause, their death. Nor would the Jews be the only persons who would be anxious to hasten the end by giving the deadly blow. Until life was extinct the soldiers appointed to guard the execution dared not leave the ground. The wish, therefore, was readily granted. The soldiers broke the legs of the two malefactors first, and then, coming to Jesus, found that the great cry had been indeed his last, and that he was dead already. They did not therefore break his legs, and thus unwittingly preserved the symbolism of that Paschal lamb, of which he was the antetype, and of which it had been commanded that "a bone of it shall not be broken." And yet, as he might be only in a syncope—as instances had been known in which men apparently dead had been taken down from the cross and resuscitated—and as the lives of the soldiers would have had to answer for any irregularity, one of them, in order to make death certain, drove the broad head of his *hasta* into his side. The wound, as it was meant to do, pierced the region of the heart, and "forthwith," says St. John, with an emphatic appeal to the truthfulness of his eye-witness—an appeal which would be singularly and impossibly blasphemous if the narrative were the forgery which so much elaborate modern criticism has wholly failed to prove that it is — "forthwith came there out blood and water." Whether the water was due to some abnormal pathological conditions caused by the dreadful complication of the Saviour's sufferings, or whether it rather means that the pericardium had been rent by the spear point, and that those who took down the body observed some drops of its serum mingled with the blood, in either case that lance thrust was sufficient to hush all the heretical assertions that Jesus had only *seemed* to die; and as it assured the soldiers, so should it assure all who have doubted, that he, who on the third day rose again, had in truth been crucified, dead, and buried, and that his soul had passed into the unseen world.

THE RISE AND SPREAD OF CHRISTIANITY

A.D. 33

RENAN   WISE   NEWMAN

It is a favorite view of historians and critical students that Jesus was born at a time when the world seemed especially prepared for his birth. The correspondence between world conditions then and the actual process of Christianity in its rise and early spread appears to conform to evolutionary laws as regarded in the light of modern interpretation.

In its origin Christianity is most intimately connected with Judaism, the parent religion. The known world, however, in the time of Jesus was largely under Roman dominion. This was true of the land where Jesus was born. The Roman Empire was then comparatively at peace, and it was the admonition of St. Paul that the first Christians should maintain that peace. The wide sovereignty of Rome gave the apostles of Christ access to different nations, many of whom had become civilized under Roman influence. But pure monotheism existed only among the Jews. All other nations had a variety of gods and peculiar forms of worship. In most of the pagan religions there were elements of truth and beauty, but they lacked in ethical principles and in moral application to life. Most of their priestcraft was a vulgar imposition upon the ignorance and credulity of the common people. The prevailing philosophies —which, among the more enlightened, took the place of religion—were the Grecian, adopted also by the Romans, and the oriental, with numerous followers in Persia, Syria, Chaldæa, Egypt, and likewise among the Jews. But the philosophers were divided into antagonistic sects. Out of such conditions no practical religion could develop. In the doctrines of Buddhism were to be found the spirit and purpose of a devout and humanely religious people, but the intricate mythology and racial and other iimitations of Buddhism forbade that, although it conquered the half of Asia, it should ever become a universal faith.

The condition of the Jews at this period was little better than that of other peoples. Among the Jews there was a lack of intellectual unity, and their moral ideals had been lowered. Oppressed by Herod, the tributary Roman King—who, although professedly a Jew, copied the open despisers of all religion—they yielded to the influences of Roman luxury and licentiousness which spread over Palestine. Although still conducted by the priests and Levites and under the eye of the Sanhedrim or senate, the Jewish religion had lost much of its earlier character. Like philosophy, it was vexed with contending sects. Strict observance of the Mosaic law and the performance of prescriptive rites and duties were in the main regarded as the sum of religion.

The race of prophets appeared extinct until prophecy was revived in John the Baptist. The successors of the Maccabæan patriots were not animated by their spirit. There was widespread and passionate expectation of a national messiah, but not such a messiah as John proclaimed and Jesus proved to be; rather a powerful warrior and vindicator of Jewish liberty. Galilee, the early home of Jesus, was especially stirred with messianic fervor. In such a condition of the national mind, and at such a stage of the world's empire, it seems natural in the course of spiritual evolution that such a teacher as Jesus—a spiritual messiah—should arise to be the deliverer not of one people only, but of the world itself. Among the Jewish doctors when Jesus was a child was at least one wise and liberal rabbi, Hillel, a Pharisee, the great reformer of his time, and "the most eminent Jew of the generation before the birth of Jesus." At his feet the boy Jesus may have sat and learned lessons of wisdom and liberality. It gives us a reassurance of spiritual continuity to think that the teachings of Hillel may have "helped to inspire the humane and tender counsels of the founder of Christianity."

In grouping the glowing words of Renan, with their fine spiritual interpretations and descriptive eloquence, the judgments of an eminent contemporary Jewish scholar, and Newman's learned yet simple portrayal of the Church as it took form in its early environment, and as it was seen through the media of contemporary governments, customs, and criticisms, it is believed that readers will derive satisfaction, and will be aided in their own inquiries, through this threefold presentation. On so vast a subject, with its momentous implications, no single author, however profound his genius, can do more than contribute a partial essay toward the many-sided truth.

JOSEPH ERNEST RENAN

FROM the moment of the arrest of Jesus, and immediately after his death, it is probable that many of the disciples had already found their way to the northern provinces. At the time of the Resurrection a rumor was spread abroad, according to which it was in Galilee that he would be seen again. Some of the women who had been to the sepulchre came back with the report that the angel had said to them that Jesus had already preceded them into Galilee. Others said that it was Jesus himself who had ordered them to go there. Now and then some people said that they themselves remembered that he had said so during his lifetime.

What is certain is that at the end of a few days, probably after the Paschal Feast of the Passover had been quite over, the disciples believed they had a command to return into their own country, and to it accordingly they returned. Perhaps the visions began to abate at Jerusalem. A species of melancholy seized them. The brief appearances of Jesus were not sufficient to compensate for the enormous void left by his absence. In a melancholy mood they thought of the lake and of the beautiful mountains where they had received a foretaste of the kingdom of God. The women especially wished, at any cost, to return to the country where they had enjoyed so much happiness. It must be observed that the order to depart came especially from them. That odious city weighed them down. They longed to see once more the ground where they had possessed Him whom they loved, well assured in advance of meeting him again there.

The majority of the disciples then departed, full of joy and hope, perhaps in the company of the caravan which took back the pilgrims from the Feast of the Passover. What they hoped to find in Galilee were not only transient visions, but Jesus himself to continue with them, as he had done before his death. An intense expectation filled their souls. Was he going to restore the kingdom of Israel, to found definitely the kingdom of God, and, as was said, "reveal his justice"? Everything was possible. They already called to mind the smiling landscapes where they had enjoyed his presence. Many believed that he had given to them a rendezvous upon a mountain, probably the same to which with them there clung so many sweet recollections. Never, it is certain, had there been a more pleasant journey. All their dreams of happiness were on the point of being realized. They were going to see him once more! And, in fact, they did see him again. Hardly restored to their harmless chimeras, they believed themselves to be in the midst of the gospel-dispensation period. It was now drawing near to the end of April. The ground is then strewn with red anemones, which were probably those "lilies of the fields" from which Jesus delighted to draw his similes. At each step his words were brought to mind, adhering, as it were, to the thousand accidental objects they met by the way. Here was the tree, the flower, the seed, from which he had taken his parables; there was the hill on which he delivered his most touching discourses; here was the little ship from which he taught. It was like the recommencement of a beautiful dream—like a vanished illusion which had reappeared. The enchantment seemed to revive. The sweet Galilean "Kingdom of God" had recovered its sway. The clear atmosphere, the mornings upon the shore or upon the mountain, the nights passed on the lakes watching the nets, all these returned again to them in distinct visions. They saw him everywhere where they had lived with him. Of course it was not the joy of the first enjoyment. Sometimes the lake had to them the appearance of being very solitary. But a great love is satisfied with little. If all of us, while we are alive, could surreptitiously, once a year, and during a moment long enough to exchange but a few words, behold again those loved ones whom we have lost— death would not be death!

Such was the state of mind of this faithful band, in this short period when Christianity seemed to return for a moment to his cradle and bid to him an eternal adieu. The principal disciples, Peter, Thomas, Nathaniel, the sons of Zebedee, met again on the shores of the lake, and henceforth lived together; they had taken up again their former calling of fishermen, at Bethsaida or at Capernaum. The Galilean women were no doubt with them. They had insisted more than the others on that return, which was to them a heartfelt love. This was their last act in the establishment of Christianity. From that moment they disappear. Faithful to their love, their wish was to quit no more the country in which they had tasted their greatest delight. More than five hundred persons were already devoted to the memory of Jesus. In default of the lost master they obeyed the disciples, the most authoritative—Peter— in particular.

The activity of these ardent souls had already turned in another direction. What they believed to have heard from the lips of the dear risen One was the order to go forth and preach, and to convert the world. But where should they commence? Naturally, at Jerusalem. The return to Jerusalem was then resolved upon by those who at that time had the direction of the sect. As these journeys were ordinarily made by caravan at the time of the feasts, we now suppose, with all manner of

likelihood, that the return in question took place at the Feast
of Tabernacles at the close of the year 33, or the Paschal Feast
of the year 34. Galilee was thus abandoned by Christianity,
and abandoned forever. The little Church which remained
there continued, no doubt, to exist; but we hear it no more
spoken of. It was probably broken up, like all the rest, by the
frightful disaster which then overtook the country during the
war of Vespasian; the wreck of the dispersed community
sought refuge beyond Jordan. After the war it was not Christianity which was brought back into Galilee; it was Judaism.

Galilee thus counted but an hour in the history of Christianity; but it was the sacred hour, *par excellence;* it gave to
the new religion that which has made it endure—its poetry, its
penetrating charms. "The Gospel," after the manner of the
synoptics, was a Galilean work. But "the Gospel" thus extended has been the principal cause of the success of Christianity, and continues to be the surest guarantee of its future.
It is probable that a fraction of the little school which surrounded Jesus in his last days remained at Jerusalem.

It is about this period that we can place the vision of James,
mentioned by St. Paul. James was the brother, or at least a
relation, of Jesus. We do not find that he had accompanied
Jesus on his last sojourn to Jerusalem. He probably went
there with the apostles, when the latter quitted Galilee.

It is very remarkable that the family of Jesus, some of
whose members during his life had been incredulous and hostile to his mission, constituted now a part of the Church, and
held in it a very exalted position. One is led to suppose that
the reconciliation took place during the sojourn of the apostles
in Galilee. The celebrity which had attached itself to the
name of their relative, those who believed in him, and were
assured of having seen him after he had arisen, served to make
an impression on their minds. From the time of the definite
establishment of the apostles at Jerusalem, we find with them
Mary, the mother of Jesus, and the brothers of Jesus. In
what concerns Mary, it appears that John, thinking in this to
obey a recommendation of the Master, had adopted and taken
her to his own home. He perhaps took her back to Jerusalem.
This woman, whose personal history and character have re-

mained veiled in obscurity, assumed hence great importance. The words that the evangelist put into the mouth of some unknown woman, "Blessed is the womb that bare thee, and the paps which thou hast sucked," began to be verified. It is probable that Mary survived her son a few years. As for the brothers of Jesus, their history is wrapped in obscurity. Jesus had several brothers and sisters. It seemed probable, however, that in the class of persons which were called "Brothers of the Lord" there were included relations in the second degree. The question is only of moment so far as it concerns James, whom we see playing a great part in the first thirty years of Christianity.

The apostles henceforth separated no more, except to make temporary journeys. Jerusalem became their head-quarters; they seemed to be afraid to disperse, while certain acts served to reveal in them the prepossession of being opposed to return again into Galilee, which latter had dissolved its little society. An express order of Jesus is supposed to have interdicted their quitting Jerusalem, before, at least, the great manifestations which were to take place. People's thoughts were turned with great force toward a promise which it was supposed Jesus had made. During his lifetime Jesus, it was said, had often spoken of the Holy Spirit, which was understood to mean a personification of divine wisdom. He had promised his disciples that the Spirit would nerve them in the combats that they would have to engage in, would be their inspirer in difficulties, and their advocate if they had to speak in public. Sometimes it was supposed that Jesus suddenly presented himself in the midst of his disciples assembled, and breathed on them out of his own mouth a current of vivifying air. At other times the disappearance of Jesus was regarded as a premonition of the coming of the Spirit. Many people established an intimate connection between this descent and the restoration of the kingdom of Israel.

The affection that the disciples had the one for the other, while Jesus was alive, was thus enhanced tenfold after his death. They formed a very small and very retired society, and lived exclusively by themselves. At Jerusalem they numbered about one hundred and twenty. Their piety was active, and, as yet, completely restrained by the forms of Jewish piety. The Temple was then the chief place of devotion. They worked, no doubt, for a living; but at that time manual labor in Jewish society engaged very few. Everyone had a trade, but that trade by no means hindered a man from being educated and well-bred.

The dominant idea in the Christian community, at the moment at which we are now arrived, was the coming of the Holy Spirit. People were believed to receive it in the form of a mysterious breath, which passed over the assembly. Every inward consolation, every bold movement, every flush of enthusiasm, every feeling of lively and pleasant gayety, which was experienced without knowing whence it came, was the work of the Spirit. These simple consciences referred, as usual, to some exterior cause the exquisite sentiments which were being created in them. When all were assembled, and when they awaited in silence inspiration from on high, a murmur, any noise whatever, was believed to be the coming of the Spirit. In the early times, it was the apparitions of Jesus which were produced in this manner. Now the turn of ideas had changed. It was the divine breath which passed over the little Church, and filled it with a celestial effluvium. These beliefs were strengthened by notions drawn from the Old Testament. The prophetic spirit is represented in the Hebrew books as a breathing which penetrates man and inspires him. In the beautiful vision of Elijah, God passes by in the form of a gentle wind, which produces a slight rustling noise.

Among all these "descents of the Spirit," which appear to have been frequent enough, there was one which left a profound impression on the nascent Church. One day, when the brethren were assembled, a thunder-storm burst forth. A violent wind threw open the windows: the heavens were on fire. Thunder-storms, in these countries, are accompanied by prodigious sheets of lightning; the atmosphere is, as it were, everywhere furrowed with ridges of flame. Whether the electric fluid had penetrated the room itself or whether a dazzling flash of lightning had suddenly illuminated the faces of all, everyone was convinced that the Spirit had entered, and that it had alighted on the head of each in the form of tongues of fire.

The idea that the Spirit had alighted on them in the form of jets of flame, resembling tongues of fire, gave rise to a series of singular ideas, which took a foremost place in the thought of the period.

The tongues of fire appeared a striking symbol. People were convinced that God desired to signify in this manner that he poured out upon the apostles his most precious gifts of eloquence and of inspiration. But they did not stop there. Jerusalem was, like the majority of the large cities of the East, a city in which many languages were spoken. The diversity of tongues was one of the difficulties which one found there in the way of propagating a universal form of faith. One of the things, moreover, which alarmed the apostles, at the commencement of a ministry destined to embrace the world, was the number of languages which were spoken there: they were asking themselves incessantly how they could learn so many tongues. "The gift of tongues" became thus a marvellous privilege. It was believed that the preaching of the Gospel would clear away the obstacle which was created by the diversity of idioms. There was in this a liberal idea; they meant to imply that the Gospel should have no language of its own; that it should be translatable into every tongue; and that the translation should be of the same value as the original.

The custom of living together, holding the same faith, and indulging the same expectation, necessarily produced many common habits. All lived in common, having but one heart and one mind. No one possessed anything which was his own. On becoming a disciple of Jesus, one sold one's goods and made a gift of the proceeds to the society. The chiefs of the society then distributed the common possessions to each, according to his needs. They lived in the same quarter. They took their meals together, and continued to attach to them the mystic sense that Jesus had prescribed. They passed long hours in prayers. Their prayers were sometimes improvised aloud, but more often meditated in silence. The concord was perfect; no dogmatic quarrels, no disputes in regard to precedence. The tender recollection of Jesus effaced all dissensions. Joy, lively and deep-seated, was in every heart. Their morals were austere, but pervaded by a soft and tender sentiment.

They assembled in houses to pray and to devote themselves to ecstatic exercises. The recollection of these two or three first years remained and seemed to them like a terrestrial paradise, which Christianity will pursue henceforth in all its dreams and to which it will vainly endeavor to return. Such an organization could only be applicable to a very small church.

The apostles chosen by Jesus, and who were supposed to have received from him a special mandate to announce to the world the kingdom of God, had, in the little community, an incontestable superiority. One of the first cares, as soon as they saw the sect settle quietly down at Jerusalem, was to fill the vacancy that Judas of Kerioth had left in its ranks. The opinion that the latter had betrayed his master, and had been the cause of his death, became more and more general. The legend was mixed up with him, and every day one heard of some new circumstance which enhanced the black-heartedness of his deed. In order to replace him, it was resolved to have recourse to a vote of some sort. The sole condition was that the candidate should be chosen from the groups of the oldest disciples, who had been witnesses of the whole series of events, from the time of the baptism of John. This reduced considerably the number of those eligible. Two only were found in the ranks, Joseph Bar-Saba, who bore the name of Justus, and Matthias. The lot fell upon Matthias, who was accounted as one of the Twelve. But this was the sole instance of such a replacing.

The body of Twelve lived, generally, permanently at Jerusalem. Till about the year 60 the apostles did not leave the holy city except upon temporary missions. This explains the obscurity in which the majority of the members of the central council remained. Very few of them had a *rôle*. This council was a kind of sacred college or senate, destined only to represent tradition and a spirit of conservatism. It finished by being relieved of every active function, so that its members had nothing to do but to preach and pray; but as yet the brilliant feats of preaching had not fallen to their lot. Their names were hardly known outside Jerusalem, and about the year 70 or 80 the lists which were given of these chosen Twelve agreed only in the principal names.

The "Brothers of the Lord" appear often by the side of the "apostles," although they were distinct from them. Their authority, however, was equal to that of the apostles. Here two groups constituted, in the nascent Church, a sort of aristocracy founded solely on the more or less intimate relations that their members had had with the Master. These were the men whom Paul denominated "the pillars" of the Church at Jerusalem. For the rest, we see that no distinctions in the ecclesiastical hierarchy yet existed. The title was nothing; the personal authority was everything. The principle of ecclesiastical celibacy was already established, but it required time to bring all these germs to their complete development. Peter and Philip were married and had sons and daughters.

The term used to designate the assembly of the faithful was the Hebrew *Kahal*, which was rendered by the essentially democratic word *Ecclesia*, which is the convocation of the people in the ancient Grecian cities, the summons to the Pnyx or the *Agora*. Commencing with the second or the third century before Jesus Christ, the words of the Athenian democracy became a sort of common law in Hellenic language; many of these terms, on account of their having been used in the Greek confraternities, entered into the Christian vocabulary. It was, in reality, the popular life, which, restrained for centuries, resumed its power under forms altogether different. The primitive Church was, in its way, a little democracy.

The power which was ascribed to the Church assembled and to its chiefs was enormous. The Church conferred every mission, and was guided solely in its choice by the signs given by the Spirit. Its authority went as far as decreeing death. It is recorded that at the voice of Peter several delinquents had fallen back and expired immediately. St. Paul, a little later, was not afraid, in excommunicating a fornicator, "to deliver him to Satan for the destruction of the flesh, that the spirit may be saved in the day of the Lord Jesus." Excommunication was held to be equivalent to a sentence of death The apostles were believed to be invested with supernatural powers. In pronouncing such condemnations, they thought that their anathemas could not fail but be effectual. The terrible impression which their excommunications produced, and the hatred manifested by the brethren against all the members thus cut off, were sufficient, in fact, in many cases, to bring about death, or at least to compel the culprit to expatriate himself. Accounts like those of the death of Ananias and Sapphira did not excite any scruple. The idea of the civil power was so foreign to all that world placed without the pale of the Roman law, people were so persuaded that the Church was a complete society, sufficient in itself, that no person saw, in a miracle leading to death or the mutilation of an individual, an outrage punishable by the civil law. Enthusiasm and faith covered all, excused everything. But the frightful danger which these theocratic maxims laid up in store for the future is readily perceived. The Church is armed with a sword; excommunication is a sentence of death. There was henceforth in the world a power outside that of the State, which disposed of the life of citizens.

Peter had among the apostles a certain precedence, derived directly from his zeal and his activity. In these first years he was hardly ever separate from John, son of Zebedee. They went almost always together, and their amity was doubtless the corner-stone of the new faith. James, the brother of the Lord, almost equalled them in authority, at least among a fraction of the Church.

It is needless to remark that this little group of simple people had no speculative theology. Jesus wisely kept himself far removed from all metaphysics. He had only one dogma, his own divine Sonship and the divinity of his mission. The whole symbol of the primitive Church might be embraced in one line: "Jesus is the Messiah, the Son of God." This belief rested upon a peremptory argument—the fact of the resurrection, of which the disciples claimed to be witnesses. To attest the resurrection of Jesus was the task which all considered as being specially imposed upon them. It was, however, very soon put forth that the Master had predicted this event. Different sayings of his were recalled, which were represented as having not been well understood, and in which was seen, on second thoughts, an announcement of the Resurrection. The belief in the near glorious manifestation of Jesus was universal. The secret word which the brethren used among themselves, in order to be recognized and confirmed, was *maran-atha*, "the Lord is at hand."

Jesus, with his exquisite tact in religious matters, had instituted no new ritual. The new sect had not yet any special ceremonies. The practices of piety were Jewish. The assemblies had, in a strict sense, nothing liturgic. They were the meetings of confraternities, at which prayers were offered up, devoted themselves to *glossolaly* or prophecy, and the reading of correspondence. There was nothing yet of sacerdotalism. There was no priest (*cohen*); the *presbyter* was the "elder," nothing more. The only priest was Jesus: in another sense, all the faithful were priests. Fasting was considered a very meritorious practice. Baptism was the token of admission to the sect. The rite was the same as administered by John, but it was administered in the name of Jesus. Baptism was, however, considered an insufficient initiation. It had to be followed by the gifts of the Holy Spirit, which were effected by means of a prayer, offered up by the apostles, upon the head of the new convert, accompanied by the imposition of hands.

This imposition of hands, already so familiar to Jesus, was the sacramental act *par excellence*. It conferred inspiration, universal illumination, the power to produce prodigies, prophesying, and the speaking of languages. It was what was called the Baptism of the Spirit. It was supposed to recall a saying of Jesus: "John baptized you with water; but as for you, you shall be baptized by the Spirit." Gradually all these ideas became amalgamated, and baptism was conferred "in the name of the Father and of the Son and of the Holy Ghost." But it is not probable that this formula, in the early days in which we now are, was yet employed. We see the simplicity of this primitive Christian worship. Neither Jesus nor the apostles had invented it. Certain Jewish sects had adopted, before them, these grave and solemn ceremonies, which appeared to have come in part from Chaldæa, where they are still practised with special liturgies by the Sabeans or Mendaites. The religion of Persia embraced also many rites of the same description.

The beliefs in popular medicine, which constituted a part of the force of Jesus, were continued in his disciples. The power of healing was one of the marvellous gifts conferred by the Spirit. The first Christians, like almost all the Jews of the time, looked upon diseases as the punishment of a transgression, or the work of a malignant demon. The apostles passed, just as Jesus did, for powerful exorcists. People imagined that the anointings of oil administered by the apostles, with imposition of hands and invocation of the name of Jesus, were all-powerful to wash away the sins which were the cause of disease, and to heal the afflicted one. Oil has always been in the East the medicine *par excellence*. For the rest, the simple imposition of the hands of the apostles was reputed to have the same effect. This imposition was made by immediate contact. Nor is it impossible that, in certain cases, the heat of the hands, being communicated suddenly to the head, insured to the sick person a little relief.

The sect being young and not numerous, the question of deaths was not taken into account until later on. The effect caused by the first demises which took place in the ranks of the brethren was strange. People were troubled by the manner of the deaths. It was asked whether they were less favored than those who were reserved to see with their eyes the advent of the Son of Man? They came generally to consider the interval between death and the resurrection as a kind of blank in the consciousness of the defunct. At the time of which we speak, belief in the resurrection almost alone prevailed. The funeral rite was undoubtedly the Jewish rite. No importance was attached to it; no inscription indicated the name of the dead. The great resurrection was near; the bodies of the faithful had only to make in the rock a very short sojourn. It did not require much persuasion to put people in accord on the question as to whether the resurrection was to be universal, that is to say, whether it would embrace the good and the bad, or whether it would apply to the elect only. One of the most remarkable phenomena of the new religion was the reappearance of prophecy. For a long time people had spoken but little of prophets in Israel. That particular species of inspiration seemed to revive in the little sect. The primitive Church had several prophets and prophetesses analogous to those of the Old Testament. The psalmists also reappeared. The model of our Christian psalms is without doubt given in the canticles which Luke loved to disseminate in his gospel, and which were copied from the canticles of the Old Testament. These psalms and prophecies are, as regards form, destitute of originality, but an admirable spirit of gentleness and of piety animates and pervades them. It is like a faint echo of the last productions of the sacred lyre of Israel. The Book of Psalms was in a measure the calyx from which the Christian bee sucked its first juice. The Pentateuch, on the contrary, was, as it would seem, little read and little studied; there was substituted for it allegories after the manner of the Jewish *midraschim* in which all the historic sense of the books was suppressed.

The music which was sung to the new hymns was probably that species of sobbing, without distinct notes, which is still the music of the Greek Church, of the Maronites, and in general of the Christians of the East. It is less a musical modulation than a manner of forcing the voice and of emitting by the nose a sort of moaning in which all the inflections follow each other with rapidity. That odd melopœia was executed standing, with the eyes fixed, the eyebrows crumpled, the brow knit, and with an appearance of effort. The word *amen*, in particular, was given out in a quivering, trembling voice. That word played a great part in the liturgy. In imitation of the Jews, the new adherents employed it to mark the assent of the multitude to the words of the prophet or the precentor. People, perhaps, already attributed to it some secret virtues and pronounced it with a certain emphasis. We do not know whether that primitive ecclesiastical song was accompanied by instruments. As to the inward chant, by which the faithful "made melody in their hearts," and which was but the overflowing of those tender, ardent, pensive souls, it was doubtless executed like the *catilenes* of the Lollards of the Middle Ages, in medium voice. In general, it was joyousness which was poured out in these hymns.

Till now the Church of Jerusalem presents itself to the outside world as a little Galilean colony. The friends whom Jesus had made at Jerusalem and in its environs, such as Lazarus, Martha, Mary of Bethany, Joseph of Arimathea, and Nicodemus, had disappeared from the scene. The Galilean group, who pressed around the Twelve, alone remained compact and active. The proselytism of the faithful was chiefly carried on by means of struggling conversions, in which the fervor of their souls was communicated to their neighbors. Their preachings under the porticoes of Solomon were addressed to circles not at all numerous. But the effect of this was only the more profound. Their discourses consisted principally of quotations from the Old Testament, by which it was sought to prove that Jesus was the Messiah.

The real preaching was the private conversations of these good and sincere men; it was the reflection, always noticeable in their discourses, of the words of Jesus; it was, above all, their piety, their gentleness. The attraction of communistic life carried with it also a great deal of force. Their houses were a sort of hospitals, in which all the poor and the forsaken found asylum and succor.

One of the first to affiliate himself with the rising society was a Cypriote, named Joseph Hallevi, or the Levite. Like the others, he sold his land and carried the price of it to the feet of the Twelve. He was an intelligent man, with a devotion proof against everything, and a fluent speaker. The apostles attached him closely to themselves and called him *Barnaba*, that is to say, "the son of prophecy" or of "preaching." He was accounted, in fact, of the number of the prophets, that is to say, of the inspired preachers. Later on we shall see him play a capital part. Next to St. Paul, he was the most active missionary of the first century. A certain Mnason, his countryman, was converted about the same time. Cyprus possessed many Jews. Barnabas and Mnason were undoubtedly Jewish by race. The intimate and prolonged relations of Barnabas with the Church at Jerusalem induces the belief that Syro-Chaldaic was familiar to him.

A conquest, almost as important as that of Barnabas, was that of one John, who bore the Roman surname of Marcus. He was a cousin of Barnabas, and was circumcised. His mother, Mary, enjoyed an easy competency; she was likewise converted, and her dwelling was more than once made the rendezvous of the apostles. These two conversions appear to have been the work of Peter.

The first flame was thus spread with great rapidity. The men, the most celebrated of the apostolic century, were almost all gained over to the cause in two or three years, by a sort of simultaneous attraction. It was a second Christian generation, similar to that which had been formed five or six years previously, upon the shores of Lake Tiberias. This second generation had not seen Jesus, and could not equal the first in authority. But it was destined to surpass it in activity and in its love for distant missions. One of the best known among the new converts was Stephen, who, before his conversion, appears to have been only a simple proselyte. He was a man full of ardor and of passion. His faith was of the most fervent, and he was considered to be favored with all the gifts of the Spirit. Philip, who, like Stephen, was a zealous deacon and evangelist, attached himself to the community about the same time. He was often confounded with his namesake, the apostle. Finally, there were converted at this epoch, Andronicus and Junia, probably husband and wife, who, like Aquila and Priscilla, later on, were the model of an apostolic couple, devoted to all the duties of missionary work. They were of the blood of Israel, and were in the closest relations with the apostles.

The new converts, when touched by grace, were all Jews by religion, but they belonged to two very different classes of Jews. The one class was the Hebrews; that is to say, the Jews of Palestine, speaking Hebrew or rather Armenian, reading the Bible in the Hebrew text; the other class was "Hellenists," that is to say, Jews speaking Greek, and reading the Bible in Greek. These last were further subdivided into two classes, the one being of Jewish blood, the other being proselytes, that is to say, people of non-Israelitish origin, allied in divers degrees to Judaism. These Hellenists, who almost all came from Syria, Asia Minor, Egypt, or Cyrene, lived at Jerusalem in distinct quarters. They had their separate synagogues, and formed thus little communities apart. Jerusalem contained a great number of these special synagogues. It was in these that the words of Jesus found the soil prepared to receive it and to make it fructify.

The primitive nucleus of the Church at Jerusalem had been

composed wholly and exclusively of Hebrews; the Aramaic dialect, which was the language of Jesus, was alone known and employed there. But we see that from the second or third year after the death of Jesus, Greek was introduced into the little community, where it soon became dominant. In consequence of their daily relations with the new brethren, Peter, John, James, Jude, and in general the Galilean disciples acquired the Greek with much more facility than if they had already known something of it. The Palestinian dialect came to be abandoned from the day in which people dreamed of a widespread propaganda. A provincial *patois*, which was rarely written, and which was not spoken beyond Syria, was as little adapted as could be to such an object. Greek, on the contrary, was necessarily imposed on Christianity. It was at the time the universal language, at least for the eastern basin of the Mediterranean. It was, in particular, the language of the Jews who were dispersed over the Roman Empire.

The conversions to Christianity became soon much more numerous among the "Hellenists" than among the "Hebrews." The old Jews at Jerusalem were but little drawn toward a sect of provincials, moderately advanced in the single science that a Pharisee appreciated—the science of the law. The position of the little Church in regard to Judaism was, as with Jesus himself, rather equivocal. But every religious or political party carries in itself a force that dominates it, and obliges it, despite itself, to revolve in its own orbit. The first Christians, whatever their apparent respect for Judaism was, were in reality only Jews by birth or by exterior customs. The true spirit of the sect came from another source. That which grew out of official Judaism was the *Talmud;* but Christianity has no affinity with the Talmudic school. This is why Christianity found special favor among the parties the least Jewish belonging to Judaism. The rigid orthodoxists took to it but little; it was the newcomers, people scarcely catechized, who had not been to any of the great schools, free from routine, and not initiated into the holy tongue, which lent an ear to the apostles and the disciples.

This family of simple and united brethren drew associates from every quarter. In return for that which these brought, they obtained an assured future, the society of a congenial brotherhood, and precious hopes. The general custom, before entering the sect, was for each one to convert his fortune into specie. These fortunes ordinarily consisted of small rural, semi-barren properties, and difficult of cultivation. It had one advantage, especially for unmarried people: it enabled them to exchange these plots of land against funds sunk in an assurance society, with a view to the Kingdom of God. Even some married people came to the fore in that arrangement; and precautions were taken to insure that the associates brought all that they really possessed, and did not retain anything outside the common fund. Indeed, seeing that each one received out of the latter a share, not in proportion to what one put in, but in proportion to one's needs, every reservation of property was actually a theft made upon the community. The Christian communism had religion for a basis, while modern socialism has nothing of the kind.

Under such a social constitution, the administrative difficulties were necessarily very numerous, whatever might be the degree of fraternal feeling which prevailed. Between two factions of a community, whose language was not the same, misapprehensions were inevitable. It was difficult for well-descended Jews not to entertain some contempt for their coreligionists who were less noble. In fact, it was not long before murmurs began to be heard. The "Hellenists," who each day became more numerous, complained because their widows were not so well treated at the distributions as those of the "Hebrews." Till now, the apostles had presided over the affairs of the treasury. But in face of these protestations they felt the necessity of delegating to others this part of their powers. They proposed to the community to confide these administrative cares to seven experienced and considerate men. The proposition was accepted. The seven chosen were Stephanas, or Stephen, Philip, Prochorus, Nicanor, Timon, Parmenas, and Nicholas. Stephen was the most important of the seven, and, in a sense, their chief.

To the administrators thus designated were given the Syriac name of *Schammaschin*. They were also sometimes called "the Seven," to distinguish them from "the Twelve." Such, then, was the origin of the diaconate, which is found to be the most ancient ecclesiastical function, the most ancient of sacred orders. Later, all the organized churches, in imitation of that of Jerusalem, had deacons. The growth of such an institution was marvellous. It placed the claims of the poor on an equality with religious services. It was a proclamation of the truth that social problems are the first which should occupy the attention of mankind. It was the foundation of political economy in the religious sense. The deacons were the first preachers of Christianity. As organizers, financiers, and administrators, they filled a yet more important part. These practical men, in constant contact with the poor, the sick, the women, went everywhere, observed everything, exhorted, and were most efficacious in converting people. They accomplished more than the apostles, who remained on their seats of honor at Jerusalem. They were the founders of Christianity, in respect of that which it possessed which was most solid and enduring.

At an early period women were admitted to this office. They were designated, as in our day, by the name of "sisters." At first widows were selected; later, virgins were preferred. The tact which guided the primitive Church in all this was admirable. The grand idea of consecrating by a sort of religious character and of subjecting to a regular discipline the women who were not in the bonds of marriage, is wholly Christian. The term "widow" became synonymous with religious person, consecrated to God, and, by consequence, a "deaconess." In those countries where the wife, at the age of twenty-four, is already faded, where there is no middle state between the infant and the old woman, it was a kind of new life, which was created for that portion of the human species the most capable of devotion. These women, constantly going to and fro, were admirable missionaries of the new religion.

The bishop and the priest, as we now know them, did not yet exist. Still, the pastoral ministry, that intimate familiarity of souls, not bound by ties of blood, had already been established. This latter has ever been the special gift of Jesus, and a kind of heritage from him. Jesus had often said that to everyone he was more than a father and a mother, and that in order to follow him it was necessary to forsake those the most dear to us.   Christianity placed some things above family; it instituted brotherhood and spiritual marriage.   The ancient form of marriage, which placed the wife unreservedly in the power of the husband, was pure slavery.   The moral liberty of the woman began when the Church gave to her in Jesus a guide and a confidant, who should advise and console her, listen always to her, and on occasion counsel resistance on her part. Woman needs to be governed, and is happy in so being; but it is necessary that she should love him who governs her.   This is what neither ancient societies nor Judaism nor Islamism have been able to do.   Woman has never had, up to the present time, a religious conscience, a moral individuality, an opinion of her own, except in Christianity.

It was now about the year 36.   Tiberius, at Caprea, has little idea of the enemy to the empire which is growing up. In two or three years the sect had made surprising progress. It numbered several thousand of the faithful.   It was already easy to foresee that its conquests would be effected chiefly among the Hellenists and proselytes.   The Galilean group which had listened to the Master, though preserving always its precedence, seemed as if swamped by the floods of new-comers speaking Greek.   One could already perceive that the principal parts were to be played by the latter.   At the time at which we are arrived no pagan, that is to say, no man without some anterior connection with Judaism, had entered into the Church.   Proselytes, however, performed very important functions in it.   The circle *de provenance* of the disciples had likewise largely extended; it is no longer a simple little college of Palestineans; we can count in it people from Cyprus, Antioch, and Cyrene, and from almost all the points of the eastern coasts of the Mediterranean, where Jewish colonies had been established.   Egypt alone was wanting in the primitive Church, and for a long time continued to be so.

It was inevitable that the preachings of the new sect, although delivered with so much reserve, should revive the animosities which had accumulated against its Founder, and eventually brought about his death.   The Sadducee family of Hanan, who had caused the death of Jesus, was still reigning. Joseph Caiaphas occupied, up to 36, the sovereign pontificate, the effective power of which he gave over to his father-in-law Hanan, and to his relatives, John and Alexander. These arrogant and pitiless men viewed with impatience a troop of good and holy people, without official title, winning the favor of the multitude. Once or twice Peter, John, and the principal members of the apostolic college were put in prison and condemned to flagellation. This was the chastisement inflicted on heretics. The authorization of the Romans was not necessary in order to apply it. As we might indeed suppose, these brutalities only served to inflame the ardor of the apostles. They came forth from the Sanhedrim, where they had just undergone flagellation, rejoicing that they were counted worthy to suffer shame for Him whom they loved. Eternal puerility of penal repressions applied to things of the soul! They were regarded, no doubt, as men of order, as models of prudence and wisdom; these blunderers, who seriously believed in the year 36 to gain the upper hand of Christianity by means of a few strokes of a whip!

These outrages proceeded chiefly from the Sadducees, that is to say, from the upper clergy, who crowded the Temple and derived from it immense profits. We do not find that the Pharisees exhibited toward the sect the animosity they displayed to Jesus. The new believers were strict and pious people, somewhat resembling in their manner of life the Pharisees themselves. The rage which the latter manifested against the Founder arose from the superiority of Jesus — a superiority which he was at no pains to dissimulate. His delicate railleries, his wit, his charm, his contempt for hypocrites, had kindled a ferocious hatred. The apostles, on the contrary, were devoid of wit; they never employed irony. The Pharisees were at times favorable to them; many Pharisees had even become Christians. The terrible anathemas of Jesus against Pharisaism had not yet been written, and the accounts of the words of the Master were neither general nor uniform. These first Christians were, besides, people so inoffensive that many persons of the Jewish aristocracy, who did not exactly form part of the sect, were well disposed toward them. Nicodemus and Joseph of Arimathea, who had known Jesus, remained no doubt with the Church in the bonds of brotherhood.

The most celebrated Jewish doctor of the age, Rabbi Gamaliel the elder, grandson of Hillel, a man of broad and very tolerant ideas, spoke, it is said, in the Sanhedrim in favor of permitting gospel preaching. The author of the Acts credits him with some excellent reasoning, which ought to be the rule of conduct of governments on all occasions when they find themselves confronted with novelties of an intellectual or moral order. "If this work is frivolous," said he, "leave it alone—it will fall of itself; if it is serious, how dare you resist the work of God? In any case, you will not succeed in stopping it." Gamaliel's words were hardly listened to. Liberal minds in the midst of opposing fanaticisms have no chance of succeeding.

A terrible commotion was produced by the deacon Stephen. His preaching had, as it would appear, great success. Multitudes flocked around him, and these gatherings resulted in acrimonious quarrels. It was chiefly Hellenists, or proselytes, *habitués* of the synagogue, called *Libertini*, people of Cyrene, of Alexandria, of Cilicia, of Ephesus, who took an active part in these disputes. Stephen passionately maintained that Jesus was the Messiah, that the priests had committed a crime in putting him to death, that the Jews were rebels, sons of rebels, people who rejected evidence. The authorities resolved to despatch this audacious preacher. Several witnesses were suborned to seize upon some words in his discourses against Moses. Naturally they found that for which they sought. Stephen was arrested and led into the presence of the Sanhedrim. The sentence with which they reproached him was almost identical with the one which led to the condemnation of Jesus. They accused him of saying that Jesus of Nazareth would destroy the Temple and change the traditions attributed to Moses. It is quite possible, indeed, that Stephen had used such language. A Christian of that epoch could not have had the idea of speaking directly against the Law, inasmuch as all still observed it; as for traditions, however, Stephen might combat them as Jesus had himself done; nevertheless, these traditions were foolishly ascribed by the orthodox to Moses, and people attributed to them a value equal to that of the written Law.

Stephen defended himself by expounding the Christian

thesis, with a wealth of citations from the written Law, from the Psalms, from the Prophets, and wound up by reproaching the members of the Sanhedrim with the murder of Jesus. "Ye stiff-necked and uncircumcised in heart," said he to them, "you will then ever resist the Holy Ghost as your fathers also have done. Which of the prophets have not your fathers prosecuted? They have slain those who announced the coming of the Just One, whom you have betrayed, and of whom you have been the murderers. This law that you have received from the mouth of angels you have not kept." At these words a scream of rage interrupted him. Stephen, his excitement increasing more and more, fell into one of those transports of enthusiasm which were called the inspiration of the Holy Spirit. His eyes were fixed on high; he witnessed the glory of God, and Jesus by the side of his Father, and cried out, "Behold, I see the heavens opened, and the Son of Man sitting on the right hand of God." The whole assembly stopped their ears and threw themselves upon him, gnashing their teeth. He was dragged outside the city and stoned. The witnesses, who, according to the law, had to cast the first stones, divested themselves of their garments and laid them at the feet of a young fanatic named Saul, or Paul, who was thinking with secret joy of the renown he was acquiring in participating in the death of a blasphemer.

In that epoch the persecutors of Christianity were not Romans; they were orthodox Jews. The Romans preserved in the midst of this fanaticism a principle of tolerance and of reason. If we can reproach the imperial authority with anything it is with being too lenient, and with not having cut short with a stroke the civil consequences of a sanguinary law which visited with death religious derelictions. But as yet the Roman domination was not so complete as it became later.

As Stephen's death may have taken place at any time during the years 36, 37, 38, we cannot, therefore, affirm whether Caiaphas ought to be held responsible for it. Caiaphas was deposed by Lucius Vitellius, in the year 36, shortly after the time of Pilate; but the change was inconsiderable. He had for a successor his brother-in-law, Jonathan, son of Hanan. The latter, in turn, was succeeded by his brother Theophilus, son of Hanan, who continued the pontificate in the house of Hanan till the year 42. Hanan was still alive, and, possessed of the real power, maintained in his family the principles of pride, severity, hatred against innovators, which were, so to speak, hereditary.

The death of Stephen produced a great impression. The proselytes solemnized his funeral with tears and groanings. The separation of the new sectaries from Judaism was not yet absolute. The proselytes and the Hellenists, less strict in regard to orthodoxy than the pure Jews, considered that they ought to render public homage to a man who respected their constitution, and whose peculiar beliefs did not put him without the pale of the law. Thus began the era of Christian martyrs.

The murder of Stephen was not an isolated event. Taking advantage of the weakness of the Roman functionaries, the Jews brought to bear upon the Church a real persecution. It seems that the vexations pressed chiefly on the Hellenists and the proselytes, whose free behavior exasperated the orthodox. The Church of Jerusalem, though already strongly organized, was compelled to disperse. The apostles, according to a principle which seems to have seized strong hold of their minds, did not quit the city. It was probably so, too, with the whole purely Jewish group, those who were denominated the "Hebrews." But the great community with its common table, its diaconal services, its varied exercises, ceased from that time, and was never reformed upon its first model. It had endured for three or four years. It was for nascent Christianity an unequalled good fortune that its first attempts at association, essentially communistic, were so soon broken up. Essays of this kind engender such shocking abuses that communistic establishments are condemned to crumble away in a very short time or to ignore very soon the principle upon which they are founded.

Thanks to the persecution of the year 37, the cenobitic Church of Jerusalem was saved from the test of time. It was nipped in the bud before interior difficulties had undermined it. It remained like a splendid dream, the memory of which animated in their life of trial all those who had formed part of it, like an ideal to which Christianity incessantly aspires with-out ever succeeding in reaching its goal.

The leading part in the persecution we have just related belonged to that young Saul, whom we have above found abet-ting, as far as in him lay, the murder of Stephen. This hot-headed youth, furnished with a permission from the priests, entered houses suspected of harboring Christians, laid violent hold on men and women, and dragged them to prison or before the tribunals. Saul boasted that there was no one of his gen-eration so zealous as himself for the traditions. True it is that often the gentleness and the resignation of his victims aston-ished him; he experienced a kind of remorse; he fancied he heard these pious women, whom, hoping for the Kingdom of God, he had cast into prison, saying during the night, in a sweet voice, "Why persecutest thou us?" The blood of Ste-phen, which had almost smothered him, sometimes troubled his vision. Many things that he had heard said of Jesus went to his heart. This superhuman being, in his ethereal life, whence he sometimes emerged, revealing himself in brief appa-ritions, haunted him like a spectre. But Saul shrunk with horror from such thoughts; he confirmed himself with a sort of frenzy in the faith of his traditions, and meditated new cruel-ties against those who attacked him. His name had become a terror to the faithful; they dreaded at his hands the most atro-cious outrages and the most sanguinary treacheries.

The persecution of the year 37 had for its result, as is always the case, the spread of the doctrine which it was wished to arrest. Till now the Christian preaching had not extended far beyond Jerusalem; no mission had been undertaken; en-closed within its exalted but narrow communion, the mother Church had spread no halos around herself nor formed any branches. The dispersion of the little circle scattered the good seed to the four winds of heaven. The members of the Church of Jerusalem, driven violently from their quarters, spread them-selves over every part of Judea and Samaria, and preached everywhere the Kingdom of God. The deacons, in particular, freed from their administrative functions by the destruction of the community, became excellent evangelists.

The scene of the first missions, which was soon to embrace

the whole basin of the Mediterranean, was the region about Jerusalem, within a radius of two or three days' journey Philip the Deacon was the hero of this first holy expedition. He evangelized Samaria most successfully. Peter and John, after confirming the Church of Sebaste, departed again for Jerusalem, evangelizing on their way the villages of the country of Samaria. Philip the Deacon continued his evangelizing journeys, directing his steps toward the south, into the ancient country of the Philistines.

Azote and the Gaza route were the limits of the first evangelical preachings toward the south. Beyond were the desert and the nomadic life upon which Christianity has never taken much hold. From Azote Philip the Deacon turned toward the north and evangelized all the coast as far as Cæsarea, where he settled and founded an important church. Cæsarea was a new city and the most considerable of Judea. It was in a kind of way the port of Christianity, the point by which the Church of Jerusalem communicated with all the Mediterranean.

Many other missions, the history of which is unknown to us, were conducted simultaneously with that of Philip. The very rapidity with which this first preaching was done was the reason of its success. In the year 38, five years after the death of Jesus, and probably one year after the death of Stephen, all this side of Jordan had heard the glad tidings from the mouths of missionaries hailing from Jerusalem. Galilee, on its part, guarded the holy seed and probably scattered it around her, although we know of no missions issuing from that quarter. Perhaps the city of Damascus, from the period at which we now are, had also some Christians, who received the faith from Galilean preachers.

The year 38 is marked in the history of the nascent Church by a much more important conquest. During that year we may safely place the conversion of that Saul whom we witnessed participating in the stoning of Stephen, and as a principal agent in the persecution of 37, but who now, by a mysterious act of grace, becomes the most ardent of the disciples of Jesus.

From the year 38 to the year 44 no persecution seems to have been directed against the Church. The faithful were, no doubt, far more prudent than before the death of Stephen, and avoided speaking in public. Perhaps, too, the troubles of the Jews who, during all the second part of the reign of Caligula, were at variance with that prince, contributed to favor the nascent sect.

This period of peace was fruitful in interior developments. The nascent Church was divided into three provinces, Judea, Samaria, Galilee, to which Damascus was no doubt attached. The primacy of Jerusalem was uncontested. The Church of this city, which had been dispersed after the death of Stephen, was quickly reconstituted. The apostles had never quitted the city. The brothers of the Lord continued to reside there and to wield a great authority.

Peter undertook frequent apostolical journeys in the environs of Jerusalem. He had always a great reputation as a thaumaturgist. At Lydda in particular he was reputed to have cured a paralytic named Æneas, a miracle which is said to have led to numerous conversions in the plain of Saron. From Lydda he repaired to Joppa, a city which appears to have been a centre for Christianity. Peter made a long sojourn at Joppa, at the house of a tanner named Simon, who dwelt near the sea. The organization of works of charity was soon actively entered upon.

The germ of those associations of women, which are one of the glories of Christianity, existed in the first churches of Judea. At Jaffa commenced those societies of veiled women, clothed in linen, who were destined to continue through centuries the tradition of charitable secrets. Tabitha was the mother of a family which will have no end as long as there are miseries to be relieved and feminine instincts to be gratified.

The Church of Jerusalem was still exclusively composed of Jews and of proselytes. The Holy Ghost being shed upon the uncircumcised before baptism, appeared an extraordinary fact. It is probable that there existed thenceforward a party opposed in principle to the admission of Gentiles, and that all did not accept the explanations of Peter. The author of the Acts would have us believe that the approbation was unanimous. But in a few years we shall see the question revived with much greater intensity. This matter of the good centurion was, perhaps, like that of the Ethiopian eunuch, accepted as an exceptional case, justified by a revelation and an express order from God. Still the matter was far from being settled. This was the first controversy which had taken place in the bosom of the Church; the paradise of interior peace had lasted for six or seven years.

About the year 40 the great question upon which depended all the future of Christianity appears thus to have been propounded. Peter and Philip took a very just view of what was the true solution, and baptized pagans.

The new faith was spread from place to place with marvellous rapidity. The members of the Church of Jerusalem, who had been dispersed immediately after the death of Stephen, pushing their conquests along the coast of Phœnicia, reached Cyprus and Antioch. They were at first guided by the sole principle of preaching the Gospel to the Jews only.

Antioch, "the metropolis of the East," the third city of the world, was the centre of this Christian movement in Northern Syria. It was a city with a population of more than five hundred thousand souls, and the residence of the imperial legate of Syria. Suddenly advanced to a high degree of splendor by the Seleucidæ, it reaped great benefit from the Roman occupation. Antioch, from its foundation, had been wholly a Grecian city. The Macedonians of Antigone and Seleucus had brought with them into that country of the Lower Orontes their most lively recollections, their worship, and the names of their country. The Grecian mythology was there adopted as it were in a second home; they pretended to show in the country a crowd of "holy places" forming part of this mythology. The city was full of the worship of Apollo and of the nymphs. The degradation of the people was awful. The peculiarity of these centres of moral putrefaction is to reduce all the race of mankind to the same level. The depravity of certain Levantine cities, which are dominated by the spirit of intrigue and delivered up entirely to low cunning, can scarcely give us an idea of the degree of corruption reached by the human race at Antioch. It was an inconceivable medley of mountebanks, quacks, buffoons, magicians, miracle-mongers, sorcerers, false priests; a city of races, games, dances, processions, *fêtes*, revels, of unbridled luxury, of all the follies of the East, of the most unhealthy superstitions, and of the fanaticism of the orgy. The city was very literary, but literary only in the literature of rhetoricians. The beauty of works of art and the infinite charm of nature prevented this moral degradation from sinking entirely into hideousness and vulgarity.

The Church of Antioch owed its foundation to some be-lievers originally from Cyprus and Cyrene, who had already been much engaged in preaching. Up to this time they had only addressed themselves to the Jews. But in a city where pure Jews—Jews who were proselytes, "people fearing God" —or half-Jewish pagans and pure pagans, lived together, exclu-sive preaching restricted to a group of houses became impossi-ble. That feeling of religious aristocracy on which the Jews of Jerusalem so much prided themselves did not exist in those large cities, where civilization was altogether of the profane sort, where the scope was greater, and where prejudices were less firmly rooted. The Cypriot and Cyrenian missionaries were then constrained to depart from their rule. They preached to the Jews and to the Greeks indifferently.

The success of the Christian preaching was great. A young, innovating, and ardent Church, full of the future, be-cause it was composed of the most diverse elements, was quickly founded. All the gifts of the Holy Spirit were there poured out, and it was easy to perceive that this new Church, emancipated from the strict Mosaism which erected an in-superable barrier around Jerusalem, would become the second cradle of Christianity. Assuredly, Jerusalem must remain for-ever the capital of the Christian world; nevertheless, the point of departure of the Church of the Gentiles, the primordial focus of Christian missions, was, in truth, Antioch. It was there that for the first time a Christian church was established, freed from the bonds of Judaism; it was there that the great propa-ganda of the apostolic age was established; it was there that St. Paul assumed a definite character. Antioch marks the sec-ond halting-place of the progress of Christianity, and, in respect of Christian nobility, neither Rome nor Alexandria nor Con-stantinople can be at all compared with it.

The foundation of Christianity, from this point of view, is the greatest work that the men of the people have ever achieved.

Very quickly, without doubt, men and women of the high Roman nobility joined themselves to the Church. At the end of the first century, Flavius Clemens and Flavia Domitilla show us Christianity penetrating almost into the palace of the Cæsars.

ISAAC M. WISE

In the rabbinical literature several successes of the apostles are noticed, especially at Capernaum and Capersamia. One of them is most remarkable, viz., the conversion of Rabbi Eliezer ben Hyrcan by the apostle James. This rabbi, the *Talmud* narrates, was actually arrested by Roman officers, and, in obedience to the edict against Christianity, was accused of the crime of being a Christian, which he did not deny, although he repented it.

The most important success, however, which the apostles could boast was the conversion of Paul. The man whose colossal genius and gigantic energies grasped the pillars upon which the superstructure of Græco-Roman paganism rested, bent and broke them like rotten staves, till with a thundering noise down came the ancient fabric, with its gods, altars, temples, priests, and priestesses, depositing *débris* that took centuries to remove and remodel; the man whose hands were against all, and against whom were all hands; who defied the philosophy of the philosophers, the power of the priests, and the religions of the world; who was all alone all in all—this man was Paul of Tarsus, the great apostle to the Gentiles, with an original gospel of his own. He kindled a fire in the very heart of the Roman Empire, under the eyes of the authorities of Rome and of Jerusalem, which in a few centuries consumed ancient heathenism from the Tigris to the Tiber, and from the Tiber to the Thames. With a skilful hand he threw the sparks upon the accumulated combustibles of error, corruption, and slavery, and ancient society exploded, to make room and furnish the material for a new civilization. The conversion of this man was the apostles' great success. If it had not been for him the nascent Church, like other Jewish sects, would have perished in the catastrophe of Jerusalem, because the apostles did not possess that vigor and energy to resist the violent shock. In Paul, however, the spirit of John and of Jesus resurrected with double vigor, and he became the actual founder of the Christianity of history.

Few and far apart are the brilliant stars in the horizon of history. Strike out a hundred names and their influence upon the fate of man, and you have no history.

Those brilliant stars, however, did not always make history from their own wealth, from the original resources of their minds. Ideas which tens of thousands have held, without an attempt to carry them into effect, and others have unsuccessfully attempted to realize, in the right time and under favorable circumstances are seized upon by an executive genius, and a new epoch in history is opened. The numerous minor spirits which contributed to the sum total of the creative idea disappear in the brilliancy of the one star which remains visible in history. The world is a machine shop. Each artificer makes the part of a machine. One master mind combines the parts, and he is known as the master machinist.

Paul was one of those master machinists, one of those brilliant stars in the horizon of history. In him the spirit of Jesus resurrected as eminently and vigorously as John had resurrected in Jesus. He was the author of Gentile Christianity. He conceived the idea of carrying into effect what all the prophets, all pious Israelites of all ages, hoped and expected—the denationalization of the Hebrew ideas, and their promulgation in the form of universal religion among the Gentiles; to conciliate and unite the human family under the great banner inscribed with the motto of "One God and one code of morals to all." All Jews of all ages hoped and expected that the kingdom of heaven should be extended to all nations and tongues; but Paul went forth TO DO it; this is his particular greatness.

The circumstances, of course, favored his enterprise. Græco-Roman paganism was undermined. The gods stood in disrepute, and the augurs smiled. The state religion was an organized hypocrisy. The learned believed nothing; the vulgar almost everything, if it was but preposterously absurd enough. The progress of Grecian philosophy and the inroads of Judaism in the Roman world were so considerable that royal families had embraced Judaism, and the emperor Tiberius had found it necessary to drive the Jews, together with the Egyptian priests, from Rome, because their religion had its admirers in the very palace of the Cæsars, as well as among priests, nobles, and plebeians. All the devout Gentiles whom Paul met on his journeys were Judaized Greeks or Syrians; for the Pharisees traversed land and sea to make one proselyte. Therefore, when Paul preached in Asia Minor, Cicero and Cato *had* spoken in Rome; Seneca and Epictetus gave utterance to sentiments as nearly like those of Paul and other Jews as are the two eyes of the same head.

Again, on the other hand, Epicurism in its worst sequences, sensualism in its most outrageous form, the despotism and brutality of the Cæsars and their favorites, had so undermined the moral sentiments and religious feelings of the masses that scepticism, fraught with shocking vices and unnatural crimes, coupled with contemptible hypocrisy and ridiculous superstition, demoralized the masses and brought truth itself into ill-repute. To add to all this there came the steady decline of the Jewish state, the growing demonstration of fast-approaching ruin, and, in consequence thereof, the growth of superstition among the Hebrews, among whom a class of mystics sprang up, who professed to know what God and his angels do, speak, and think in the secret cabinet of heaven, where the throne of the Almighty stands, splendidly and minutely described by those mystics who supposed that they received superior knowledge by special impressions from on high, without study or research on their part; and expected to see the status of social and political affairs suddenly changed by miraculous interpositions of the Deity, without human exertion and coöperation. This state of affairs was highly favorable to Paul's stupendous enterprise.

But who was Paul himself? Notwithstanding all the attempts of the author of the Acts to mystify him into as mythical a character as the Gospels made of Jesus, Paul is an open book in history. We have his genuine epistles, in which he gives considerable account of himself and his exploits. We have one portion of the Acts in which, contrary to the rest of that book, the author narrates in the first person plural, "we," which appears to be taken from the notes of one of Paul's companions—Luke, Timothy, Silas, or any other. Then we have the *Talmud*, with its numerous anecdotes about *Acher*, as the rabbis called Paul, which are of inestimable value to the historian. These sources enable us to form a conception of the man. A few remarks on his life will be found interesting.

Paul is not a proper name. It signifies "the little one." The author of the Acts states that his name was Saul. But, it appears, he knew no more about it than we do, and changed the P of Paul into an S, to make of it the Hebrew name Saul. In his epistles he invariably calls himself Paul, and not Saul. So the author of the "we" portion of the Acts always calls him Paul. Passing under an assumed name, the rabbis called him *Acher*, "another," *i.e.*, one who passes under another or assumed name. They maintain that his name was Elisha ben Abujah. But this name must be fictitious, because it is a direct and express reference to Paul's theology. It signifies "the saving deity, son of the father god," and Paul was the author of the "Son of God" doctrine. The fact is, he was known to the world under his assumed name only.

Nothing is known of his youth, except a few spurious anecdotes recorded in the *Talmud*. When quite young he studied the law and some Grecian literature at the feet of Gamaliel in Jerusalem, among the thousand students who listened to the wisdom of that master. He states that he was a very zealous Pharisee, who persecuted the Christians. But all of a sudden he embraced the cause of the persecuted, and became one of its most zealous apostles. We can easily imagine the nature of that persecution, although the Stephen story, like the Damascus story and the vision on the way, as narrated in the Acts, is spurious, because Paul never alludes to it, and the Jews of Jerusalem had no jurisdiction in Damascus over anybody. But what caused his remarkable transition from one extreme to the other? First a Pharisee, with law and nothing but law, and then the author of the epistles, which reject and abrogate the entire law. Transitions of this nature require time, and are wrought by violent agencies only.

A number of stories narrated in the *Talmud*, together with those of the Acts, point to the fact that the youthful Paul, with his vivid imagination, witnessed many an act of barbarous violence and outrageous injustice. Occurrences of this nature were not rare under the military despotism of Rome in Judea. The soil was saturated with innocent blood. The world was governed by the sword, and Rome groaned under the unnatural crimes of her Cæsars. There was universal depravity among the governing class, and endless misery among the governed. The rabbis give us to understand that this state of affairs misled Paul into the belief that there was no justice in heaven or earth, no hope for Israel, no reward and no punishment, that the balance of justice was destroyed. It is quite natural that under such circumstances such a scepticism should overpower young and sensitive reasoners.

King Saul, in a state of despair, receiving no reply from the prophets, none from the Urim and Thumim, deeply fallen as he was, went in disguise to the Witch of Endor. Goethe's Faust, in imitation thereof, receiving no answer to his questions addressed to heaven and eternity, no answer through his knowledge of nature's laws and nature's forces, no answer from the philosophy of his century and the theology of his priests, throws himself into the embrace of Mephistopheles. That is human nature. Exactly the same thing was done in the days of Paul, and exactly the same thing he himself did. There was the indescribable misery of the age, and there were the knowledge and theories of that overburdened century, and no answer, no reply to the questions addressed to heaven and eternity; and they went to the fountains of mysticism and secret knowledge to quench the thirst of the soul. There sprung up the visionary Gnostics among the Gentiles, and the Cabalistic Mystics among the Jews. History notices the same rotation continually — idealism, sensualism, scepticism, and finally mysticism.

The mystic art among the Hebrews then was of two different kinds, either to attract an evil spirit or to be transported alive into paradise or heaven. An evil spirit was attracted by fasting and remaining for days and nights alone in burial-grounds, till the brain was maddened and infatuated, when the artificial demoniac prophesied and performed sundry miracles. The transportation to heaven or paradise was more difficult. The candidate for a tour into heaven would retire to some isolated spot, fast until the brain was maddened with delirium and the nerves excited to second sight by the loss of sleep. Then, in that state of trance, he would sit down on the ground, draw up his knees, bend down his head between them, and murmur magic spells, until, through the reversed circulation of the blood, the maddened brain, and the unstrung nerves, he would imagine that he saw the heaven opening to his inspection, palace after palace thrown widely open to his gaze, hosts of angels passing within view, until finally he imagined himself entirely removed from the earth, transported aloft into those diamond palaces on high, or, as Paul calls it, "caught up into paradise," where he heard "unspeakable words, which it is not possible for a man to utter," and the throne of God, with all the seraphim and cherubim, archangels and angels, became visible and their conversation intelligible to the enraptured and transported mystic, in a fit of hallucination, when the bewildered imagination sees objectively its own subjective phantasma, and hears from without, in supposed articulate sounds, its own silent thoughts. It requires no great stretch of the imagination to form a correct idea of the mystic eccentricities to which this awful practice must have led those who frequently indulged in it. Rabbinical mystics, like modern trance-speakers, gave vivid descriptions of the interior splendor and grand sceneries of heaven and of the conversations of angels. One of those descriptions is preserved in *Pirke Rabbi Eliezer*, and others in various fragments of the *Talmud*.

Among those particularly noticed in the *Talmud* as having been in heaven or paradise there is also Acher, or Paul, who states so himself in his Second Epistle to the Corinthians (xii.). That passage gave rise to the story of Jesus appearing in person to Paul, just as the rabbinical mystics claimed to have had frequent intercourse with the prophet Elijah, who had been transported alive to heaven.

So Paul passed the transition from the law school of the Pharisees to the new school of mystics. In this state of trance he discovered that central figure of the Cabalistic speculation, the *Metathron*, the co-regent of the Almighty; or, as he otherwise was called, the *Synadelphos*, the *confrère* of the Deity, or Suriel, the "Prince of the Countenance," whom the Cabalists imagined to be the chief marshal or chief scribe in heaven; who was once on earth, as Enoch or as Elijah, and was advanced to that high position in heaven.

It is the Demiurge, the highest magistrate in heaven, whom the gnostic Valentine calls a godlike angel, and of whom the rabbis said, "His name is like unto the name of his Master."

This central figure, blended with the messianic speculations of that age, with the doctrines of Peter and the nascent Church, combined in Paul's mind to one mystic conception of the "Son of God," intelligible to pagan ears. So he went forth and proclaimed Jesus of Nazareth the Son of God. In substance, the expression is about the same as Metathron and Synadelphos, and the office which Paul ascribed to Jesus is precisely of the same nature with that which the Cabalists ascribed to the angel who was the *Saar Haolom*, the prince or ruler of this world, who stands before God, or also sits before him, as Paul's Jesus stands before God or sits at his right hand. It is precisely the same in both systems, the names only are changed; so that it is difficult to decide whether Paul was or the rabbis were the authors of the metathronic speculations, especially as these two angels only have Greek names, while all others are Hebrew or Chaldæan, and later Cabalists frequently put down Joshua or Jesus in the place of Metathron.

Those who believe that Acher's dualism of the Deity was the Persian *Ormuzd* and *Ahriman*, hence a good and an evil principle, and that Metathron never was an evil demon, are as decidedly mistaken as those who believe that Paul had more than one God. Paul's Son of God and Acher's Metathron are the same central figure before the throne of God, and the two authors are identical.

In that world of secret thoughts Paul discovered the harmonization of discordant speculations and the remedy for all existing evils. "The world must be regenerated by a new religion," was his great ideal. The ancient religions and the philosophies have produced the corruption which rages universally. They must be swept away. Society must be reconstructed on a new basis, and this basis is in the theology and ethics of Israel, separated and liberated from their climatical and national limitations, their peculiar Jewish garb. There was no hope left of saving the Jewish nationality and political organization from the hands of omnipotent Rome, which swallowed and neutralized kingdoms and nations with wonderful ease; nor was there any particular necessity for it if society at large was reconstructed on the new basis.   The object of Jesus was to reconstruct the kingdom of heaven *in Israel*, and he was crucified.   All Israel had the same object in view, and stood at the brink of dissolution.   If the basis and principles of the kingdom of heaven became the postulate of society at large, Jesus is resurrected in the world, and Israel is saved, was Paul's main idea.

The Pharisean rabbis hoped that this would come to pass at some future day, when, they maintained, all sacrifices and all laws would be abolished, and all the nations of the earth would be one family, with one God and one moral law.   Paul seized upon the idea, and added to it the simple dogma of Peter, "The Messiah has come."   That hoped-for future is now.   God's promise to Abraham, "And there shall be blessed by thee, and by thy seed, all the families of the earth," is to be fulfilled at once.   So he came forth from his mystical paradise an apostle of Jesus and a new redeemer of Israel.   He argued exactly as the Pharisean doctors did who maintained that the Messiah would come when all mankind should be guilty or all righteous.   In the estimation of Paul, at that particular time all mankind was corrupt and demoralized, and so that was the time for the Messiah to make his appearance.

He went to work at once.   He began to preach his new Christianity at Damascus about the year 51, and found out that the world was not prepared for his ideas.   He had a narrow escape at Damascus, where the governor and soldiers pursued him.   Like the spies at Jericho, he was let down in a basket over the city walls and made his escape.   So *he* narrates the story.   The author of the Acts, true to his hostility to the Jews, of course brings them in as the persecutors.   But Paul, in general, never speaks otherwise than with the highest regard and love of his kinsmen and his brothers according to the flesh.

The failure at Damascus did not discourage Paul.   It only convinced him that he was too young—he could not at that time have been much over twenty-one years; that he was not sufficiently prepared for the great enterprise; that it was not such an easy task to throw down the superannuated heathenism and to reorganize society on a new basis. He retired into Arabia and remained there nearly three years, to perfect a plan of operation. Nearly three years he spent in silent contemplation, to discover the proper means, to take the right hold upon the heathen world, and to unfurl a new banner of heaven upon this wicked earth. In 53 or 54 we meet him again at Antioch, with his new and original gospel—the gospel for the Gentiles —prepared for his mission and ready to embark in the great enterprise, to wage active war upon all existing systems of religion and philosophy, and to replace all of them by Paul's gospel. He had been in Jerusalem fifteen days, had conversed with Peter and nobody else, but he repeatedly tells us that he had taken advice of none, consulted none, was appointed by nobody, and learned nothing of anybody. The gospel was his gospel, and he was an apostle by the appointment of God Almighty himself, who had revealed his Son to him. In Antioch he established the first congregation of Jews and Gentiles, and called them Christians. So Paul was the actual author of Christianity among the Gentiles.

What was Paul's gospel? Paul, setting out on his journeys with the great idea of converting heathens, was obliged to paganize the Gospel. The heathens knew nothing of the Jewish Messiah, and he gave him the name popularly known among them—he called him the Son of God, which was a common name in mythology. The Son of God and Mary was a term as popular among heathens as it was foreign to the Jews, among whom Jesus was to remain the Messiah, only that he became also the Metathron. This explained to Jewish mystics the possibility of the second advent, and gave a metaphysical foundation to the resurrection doctrine. The kingdom of heaven, or the theocracy, was another unintelligible idea to the heathen. Israel's laws and form of government were as odious and decried among the pagans as the hostility to that people was fierce and implacable. Paul made thereof a theological kingdom of heaven, when all the dead shall resurrect in spiritual bodies, and the living shall be changed accordingly, together with this earth and all that is thereon; and declared all the laws of Israel abrogated, so that only the spirit thereof, the precepts and not the laws, should be obligatory in the new state of society.

The sins and wickedness of the world are forgiven to all who believe in the Son, and whose flesh is crucified with him, to resurrect with him in purity; for he died a vicarious atonement for all. He was the last sacrifice, to blot out the sins of all who have faith in him.

The Crucified One did not resurrect merely in the spirit, of which the heathens could not form a satisfactory conception, because the immortality of the soul was by no means a general belief among them, and their gods were no spirits; he resurrected in his very body, and was caught up to heaven, to sit or stand there at God's right hand, to come down again in proper time. "Here, then, is your tangible proof of immortality," he said to the heathens. "Like the Crucified One, all of you will resurrect from the dead, or be changed on the day of judgment." This was plain language to heathens, who knew that but lately Cæsar had been caught up to heaven as Romulus was before him, and asked no questions as to how a human body can rise in the atmosphere and become incorruptible; none as to what means above or below, up or down, as to where God is and where he is not, where his right hand, where before and where behind him; or as to whether the world is full of his glory. No such questions were asked, and there was the ocular demonstration of immortality, tangible and intelligible to the grossest intellect.

The Jewish nationality and the Jewish law are at their end, and the world is the heir to that covenant and to the blessing of God by Abraham and his seed. With the new covenant the old one ceases. It has fulfilled its destiny. It was a state of preparation for this period of universal salvation to all who have love, hope, and faith. With Adam and the flesh came the sin, law, and death; with Jesus the flesh ceases, hence no more sin, law, or death.

These are the main features of Paul's gospel: The Son of God, the theological kingdom of heaven, the vicarious atonement, the bodily resurrection of the Crucified One, the abrogation of the law, and the beginning of the new covenant. He was the first man to utter these doctrines; with him Christianity begins, and he named it.

But Paul knew well that doctrines alone would be insufficient to rouse the heathen world from its demoralized state, its dreary and stupid dreams; and he resorted to the most terrible and most shocking of all messages. He came to the heathens with the terror-striking proclamation, "The end is nigh!" The whole earth, with all the creatures thereon; the whole human family, with all its wickedness, all its atrocious crimes, will be destroyed in one moment. All of you, men, women, and children, with all your vices and crimes, will be suddenly summoned before the Eternal and All-just; you have to go, all of you, and appear before the omniscient God. The end is nigh, the destruction of the human family is certain and right before you. It will come soon. It may come any day, at any moment.

Now Paul's gospel came in. Here is your choice. There are death and damnation; here are life and happiness everlasting. God has sent his Son in advance of the approaching catastrophe to warn you, and he is appointed now to conduct the end of all flesh. Cling to him and be saved, or believe not and be condemned forever. So he came to the heathens. This was his gospel. How did he succeed? We will explain after a brief pause.

All passages in the Gospels and the Acts which have reference to the above Christology, to the end of things or against it—in which the synoptics most fatally contradict one another—are the products of writers long after Paul, when the attempts to reconcile Jewish and Gentile Christianity were made. For with Paul begins the new form of Christianity and the struggle with the representatives of the old form. Within ten years he traversed the land from Antioch to Athens, in three different journeys, and established his bishopric, the first Christian congregations among the Gentiles. He organized them fully, with deacons and deaconesses, preachers and prophets; and he was their bishop, their oracle, their revelation, and their demigod. He let his converts believe that they could do wonderful things, in healing the sick, driving out demons, prophesying and speaking with strange tongues, because it served his purposes, although he did none of these things. He gave them the Holy Ghost, *i.e.*, he regenerated their feelings and pacified their stormy passions, suppressed their brutal lusts, and elevated their aspirations to higher ideals. He did not feel that sovereign contempt for money which the Master did whom he glorified; for he, like the other apostles, took his pay, and argued with the Corinthians, like a good Pharisean lawyer, that bishops and preachers must be paid—an argument well understood by the dignitaries of the Church to this day.

Wonderful, indeed, is the progress which Paul made among the Gentiles in ten years. Like a pillar of fire, he traversed the deserts of heathenism; like a second Elijah, he battled against the priests and prophets of Baal, and conjured down the fire from heaven to his assistance. Within ten years he laid the foundation of a new civilization, of the reorganization of society on the new basis. He did not live to see it realized, but he saw the new system take root and promise golden fruit. Wonderful, we maintain, was his success; for he was not only opposed by the entire heathen world, and by the orthodox Jews, although he proclaimed their God and their doctrines, their religion and their hopes, but was also most strenuously opposed by the apostles and the nascent congregation in Jerusalem, whose Master he glorified and whose cause he made the cause of the world. The dissensions between Paul and the apostles were of a very serious character, and there was ample cause for them.

In the first place, he took it upon himself to be an apostle, and they had their college of Twelve, to which none could be added, especially not Paul, who had never seen Jesus of Nazareth. He maintained that God had appointed him, God had revealed his Son and his Gospel to him; but the apostles did not believe it, and never acknowledged him as an apostle. At the end of his journeys, Peter, James, and John, three out of Twelve, acknowledged him as an apostle to the Gentiles, but not to the Jews. The rest never did, which, of course, was a great trouble and drawback to Paul among his own converts.

In the second place, they could never forgive him for the idea of going to the Gentiles. Peter, who had become a pious

Essene and considered it unlawful to go to the house or into the company of a Gentile; James, who dreaded the idea of eating of the bread of the Gentile, and made a hypocrite in this point of Peter at Antioch—and they were the heads of the Church—could not forgive Paul's innovation in going to the Gentiles. Paul was sensible enough to silence them by begging money for them, and to appoint the Sunday for collections to be made for the saints of Jerusalem. But it was too much for them that Paul went to the Gentiles.

In the third place, he changed their whole religion into a new sort of mythology. He made of Jesus a Son of God, of which they had no knowledge. He preached vicarious atonement, bodily resurrection, the end of the old covenant and the beginning of a new, the end of all flesh, the last judgment—all of which was foreign to them; not one word of all that had their Master told them, and they knew only what he did tell them. They naturally looked upon him as an unscrupulous innovator. They had not experience and forethought enough to understand that Paul's success among the heathens depended on that means. They were pious men who prayed much, believed seriously, and had no knowledge of the world as it was.

In the fourth place, they could not possibly give their consent to Paul's abrogation of the whole law, knowing, as they did, how their Master respected every tittle, every iota of the law; that he had come to fulfil the law, and to reëstablish the theocracy; how could they possibly think of the idea of abolishing Sabbath and holidays, circumcision and ablutions, all and everything, to be guided by the phantom of hope, love, and faith, against which James argues in his epistle with all the energy of his soul? Those inexperienced saints did not know that the Pharisean doctors held similar theories, and that Paul could not possibly hope to meet with any success among the Gentiles if he had come to them with the laws of the Jews. They were Roman citizens, who contemned the laws of the barbarians. Had Paul come with the word Judaism on his lips, he would have surely failed. Had he come to enforce a foreign law, he would have been laughed at as a madman. They did not know that Paul cared not for an hundred and one laws, as long as the essence and substance could be saved and preserved; that he held that laws are local, the spirit is universal; that laws are limitations, the spirit is free and the property of all men of all ages and climes; that he was determined to drop everything which could retard his progress.

In the fifth place, and this was the worst, they could not forgive him for preaching the theological kingdom of heaven. A kingdom of Israel—a throne of David, a Davidian prince, a Zion and a Jerusalem in heaven, and slavery, misery, and oppression on earth—was so new and foreign to them, so contrary to what they had heard from their Master, that they could not accept it. What should become of Peter's Messiah, of the hopes and promises connected with the second advent, if all at once the whole scheme is transported from earth to heaven? It was too much disappointment, they could not endure it. Those men did not understand that Paul had carefully to avoid every conflict with the Roman authorities. He was too prudent to be crucified. They could not comprehend that his great object was not to remove the evil at once; he intended to sow the seed, to bring forth the plant; to give to the heathens correct notions of God, duty, responsibility, purity, holiness, morality, justice, humanity, and freedom, which in proper time should necessarily break the chains, revolutionize the sentiments, and elevate the views, hopes, aspirations, and designs of the nations.

They could not comprehend that their Messiah and kingdom of heaven, together with his terrible message of the end of all flesh and the last judgment day, were means, and nothing but means, to captivate and reform the heathen. His Son of God was crucified and resurrected from the dead to forewarn all of the approaching end of all flesh; to show that in a little while all the dead should resurrect and the living should be changed to spiritual beings. He had been given all power by the Almighty to conduct the catastrophe of the world, and would be present at the last judgment day. But after all that is over, the earth and man changed to a new state of spiritual life, then the Son of God returns the kingdom to the Father, and God will be again all in all. So the Son of God was a general superintendent, the demiurge for the time being, a doctrine of which the apostles had no knowledge, and to which they could not give their consent. He could not get them to understand that these were the means for the conversion of the Gentiles, and that he had quite another gospel for the enlightened portion of the community. They could not see that among heathens used to apotheosis, man-worship, and plastic gods, ideas, to become effective, must put on concrete and tangible bodies.

They could not imagine that the sensuality and corruption of the age required heroic and terror-striking means to rouse and to move the masses; and so the dissensions and troubles between Paul and the nascent Church increased with the success of Paul among the Gentiles. His epistles, one and all, are polemics, not against heathenism or against Judaism, but against his colleagues in Jerusalem, whom, together with their doctrines, he treats in a most reckless manner. They could not write to counterbalance Paul—in fact, there were no writers of any note among them. Therefore, only one side of the polemics, that of Paul, is fully represented in the New Testament; and the side of the Jewish Christians remained mostly matter of tradition.

Messengers were sent to follow Paul to undo his gospel and preach that of the apostles; to introduce the law and circumcision among the Gentile Christians. Those messengers in many cases succeeded, notwithstanding the thundering epistles of Paul. So his influence was weakened and his progress retarded among the Gentiles till finally, after ten years of hard work, he concluded upon going to Jerusalem and, if possible, effecting a compromise with the apostolic congregation. It was a dangerous time for him to go to Jerusalem, for just then the fanatic high-priest, Ananias, had convened a court of his willing tools, tried James, the brother of Jesus, and, finding him guilty, of what God only knows, had him and some of his associates executed —a bloody deed, which cost him his office, on account of the loud and emphatic protestations of the Jews before Agrippa II and the Roman governor. Therefore, Paul was cautioned by prophets and friends not to go to Jerusalem.

But he was not the man to be frightened by dangers; he was the very type of boldness and courage. He went to Jerusalem to effect a conciliation with the Church. A synod met in the house of James the apostle, who had succeeded the former James as head of the Church, and Paul was told to do that against which his conscience, his honor, his manhood must have revolted: he was required to play the hypocrite in Jerusalem, in order to pacify the brethren who were angry at him. The thousands of Jews, they said, who were zealous for the law, and were informed how Paul taught the people to forsake Moses, to give up circumcision and the ancient customs, hearing of his presence in Jerusalem, "the multitude must needs come together," which points to the Jewish Christians faithful to the law. Therefore they advised him to go through the mockery of a purification at the Temple, "to be at charges," as they called it, with some who had vowed a vow, and make the prescribed sacrifices after the purification.

Poor man! After so much labor, such ardent toils, such numerous perils, dangers, anxieties, trials, reverses, and triumphs, after ten long years of such work and such dangers, he is not safe in Jerusalem among his own kinsmen and among those whose Master he glorified, whose doctrines he taught, and whose interests he protected. How small must he have appeared to himself when walking up the Temple Mount in the company of the four men, whose expenses he paid, to be purified with them: "And all may know that those things, whereof they were informed concerning thee, are nothing; but that thou thyself also walkest orderly and keepest the law." The man who had defied a world, to submit to the humbling dictation of his colleagues, who were children in comparison with him—this is mortifying to the utmost. This is the time of which it is said in the *Talmud* that Paul or Acher narrated, that on passing behind the *sanctum sanctorum* he heard the *Bath-kol* or Holy Ghost exclaim: "Return, all ye froward children; all return, except Paul, who has known me and rebelled against me." Paul never forgot, never forgave, this humiliation. It estranged his feelings altogether from his colleagues in Jerusalem, and he embraced the first best opportunity to rid himself entirely of his Jewish associations.

The opportunity soon offered. While near the Temple some Jews from Asia Minor recognized him. A disturbance ensued. He was arrested and locked up in the castle by the

Roman commander. Here the author of the Acts brings in a terrible tumult—speeches, trials, a Jewish mob, with a noble Roman stepping in in time to wind up dramatically—not one word of which is historical. Paul, standing accused as the ringleader of the new sect who expected the second advent of the Messiah, could only appear dangerous to the zealous and vigilant Roman authorities. Nothing else was necessary to put his life in jeopardy. In the night he made up his mind to appeal to Cæsar, because he was a Roman citizen. Therefore he was sent to Cæsarea, to the governor, under the protection of soldiers. Not a sound was heard in his favor among the Jewish Christians. Not an angel appeared. Not a solitary miracle was wrought; none dreamed a dream; nobody had a vision; the Holy Ghost was as silent as the grave; none of all the Christians in Palestine showed his face, when Paul, loaded with chains, was transported from Jerusalem to Cæsarea. This silence speaks volumes. They did not care much about the innovator. Therefore Paul's epistles from his prison in Cæsarea are thunder-bolts against the law, circumcision, and his colleagues in Jerusalem. It is the offended man, the wounded lion, who retaliates in his anger.

In Cæsarea another mock trial is described by the author of the Acts. There can be little doubt that Ananias, the Sadducean high-priest who had slain James, thirsted also after the blood of Paul. But it is certainly not true that Felix was governor of Judea when Ananias was high-priest. Felix and Festus had been removed from their offices before Ananias was made high-priest, as the authentic sources of history show. If tried at Cæsarea at all—which is doubtful, because Paul had appealed to Cæsar—he was tried before Albinus. His speeches recorded in the Acts contain sentences of Paul, but many more additions from the author of the Acts.

It matters little, however, whether Paul was tried before Albinus or Felix, or whether there was a trial at all. He had appealed to Cæsar, in order to estrange himself from his colleagues in Jerusalem and to come before his converts as an expatriated man, although Agrippa himself had said, "This man might have been set at liberty had he not appealed unto Cæsar."

Fortunately he was detained in Cæsarea, when Nero in Rome put to death the Christians in his own gardens with exquisite cruelty, and added mockery and derision to their sufferings. Had he been brought to Rome *then*, no angels could have saved his life, and no power could have protected him for two years. He came to Rome in the year 65, when the cruelty of Nero's proceedings against the Christians filled every breast with compassion, and humanity relented in favor of the Christians. Then it was possible for Paul to have a hearing in Rome, where he lived in a hired house for two years.

Neither Paul nor Peter was ever bishop of Rome, nor was either of them beheaded in Rome or anywhere else. All the legends and myths concerning them are void of truth. We know that Paul, who was then about thirty-five years old, wrote from Rome epistles in defence of his gospel and against his colleagues in Jerusalem, in the same spirit as those from Cæsarea. We know, furthermore, that he went from Rome to Illyricum, where he preached his gospel. We know that he returned to Asia, and wrote the quintessence of his gospel in his epistle to the Romans. We know that many passages in his epistles were written after the destruction of Jerusalem, when Paul was about forty years old, and his principal activity commenced still later, in opposition to Rabbi Akiba and his colleagues. We know from the *Talmud* that he married and left daughters. We know also numerous stories of Acher or Paul and his disciple, Rabbi Mair.

Long after the death of the apostles the Christianity of Paul and the Messiahism of Peter were Platonized by the Alexandrian eclectics in a semi-gnostic manner, which gave birth to the fourth gospel, according to John, and the two epistles of John the Elder, not the apostle, about A.D. 160, of which the Synoptics have no idea. They had only the Christianity of Paul and of Peter before them. An original Peter gospel, Paul's epistles, and the different traditions of the various congregations were their sources, which they attempted to blend into one system. All the gospel writers lived in the second century; were not acquainted with the particulars of the story; had an imperfect knowledge of the Jews, their laws and doctrines; wrote in favor of the Romans, whom they wished to convert, and against the Jews, whom they could not convert.

The third century inherited four distinct systems of Christianity: that of Jesus with the pure theocracy, that of Peter with the Messiah and his second advent, that of Paul with the Son of God and the approaching end of all flesh, and that of John with the Logos and the self-aggrandizing demi-god or man-god on earth. The difficulties and dissensions arising from the attempts at uniting all these contradictory systems in one, ended with the Council of Nice, in the beginning of the fourth century, and the establishment of an orthodox creed, the excommunication of the Jewish Christians, and the establishment of the Church as a state institution. Then the sword and the pyre established doctrines.

On comparison you will find that Jesus became the Saviour of the Gentiles by the exertion of Paul; that the means which Peter and Paul adopted for momentary purposes have been turned into main dogmas; that the religion which Jesus taught and believed is partly laid aside, and the rest is unimportant in Christology, but he himself has been adopted in place of his religion; and that the entire New Testament has no knowledge of the Trinity and the orthodox creed. On comparison you will discover that, if any of our modern congregations are Christian, the apostolic congregation of Jerusalem was heretic. If the pope is a Christian, Paul was not. If the orthodox creed tells what one must believe in order to be a Christian, then Jesus of Nazareth was a Jew. If the religion and the theocracy which Jesus preached are to become the universal religion, all dogmas must fall, and God alone be all in all. Man must become his own priest, prince, and prophet. Justice must govern the nations, love must construe the law, virtue and righteousness must lead to satisfaction and happiness, and man's consciousness of God, immortality, morals, and moral responsibility must be his catechism, his guiding star, his protecting angel in life and death. No dogmas; truth, in the name of God!

I see it, although it is not now; I behold it, although it is not nigh. A star will arise from Jacob in whose soft brilliancy will shine forth all the great and redeeming truth. Freedom and humanity, justice and love in the name of God, are the right religion; to strive for them is divine worship, to love them is holiness.

This was the object of Paul. The means to accomplish that object were the necessities of the age to convert that generation. He could not dream of the idea that the means would obscure the object, that the servant would occupy the master's seat. His was a fearless, powerful, and unyielding character, terribly in earnest to break down the ancient world and create a new one, and his success, though incomplete, was wonderful. Men like Jesus and Paul, whose great aim was to benefit and to elevate human nature, however widely we may differ from them, deserve the student's laborious research, the philanthropist's most profound admiration, the monuments which the human mind rears to their memory. Great works are the testimony of their authors, and great minds are the diadem and honor, the ornament and pride of human nature. The God Jesus and the supernatural Paul appear small in the focus of reason. The patriotic and enthusiastic Jesus and the brave, bold, wise, and mighty Paul are grand types of humanity among those hundred stars in the horizon of history which have made the history of the human family.

JOHN HENRY NEWMAN

The *prima-facie* view of early Christianity, in the eyes of witnesses external to it, is presented to us in the brief but vivid descriptions given by Tacitus, Suetonius, and Pliny, the only heathen writers who distinctly mention it for the first hundred and fifty years.

Tacitus is led to speak of the religion, on occasion of the conflagration of Rome, which was popularly imputed to Nero. "To put an end to the report," he says, "he laid the guilt on others, and visited them with the most exquisite punishment, those, namely, who, held in abhorrence for their crimes (*per flagitia invisos*), were popularly called Christians. The author of that profession (*nominis*) was Christ, who, in the reign of Tiberius, was capitally punished by the procurator, Pontius Pilate. The deadly superstition (*exitiabilis superstitio*), though checked for a while, broke out afresh; and that, not only throughout Judea, the original seat of the evil, but through the city also, whither all things atrocious or shocking (*atrocia aut pudenda*) flow together from every quarter and thrive. At first, certain were seized who avowed it; then, on their report, a vast multitude were convicted not so much of firing the city, as of hatred of mankind (*odio humani generis*)." After describing their tortures, he continues: "In consequence, though they were guilty, and deserved most signal punishment, they began to be pitied, as if destroyed not for any public object, but from the barbarity of one man."

Suetonius relates the same transactions thus: "Capital punishments were inflicted on the Christians, a class of men of a new and magical superstition (*superstitionis novæ et maleficæ*)." What gives additional character to this statement is its context, for it occurs as one out of various police or sanctuary or domestic regulations, which Nero made, such as "controlling private expenses, forbidding taverns to serve meat, repressing the contests of theatrical parties, and securing the integrity of wills."

When Pliny was governor of Pontus, he wrote his celebrated letter to the emperor Trajan, to ask advice how he was to deal with the Christians, whom he found there in great numbers. One of his points of hesitation was whether the very profession of Christianity was not by itself sufficient to justify punishment; "whether the name itself should be visited, though clear of flagitious acts (*flagitia*), or only when connected with them." He says he had ordered for execution such as persevered in their profession after repeated warnings, "as not doubting, whatever it was they professed, that at any rate contumacy and inflexible obstinacy ought to be punished." He required them to invoke the gods, to sacrifice wine and frankincense to the images of the Emperor, and to blaspheme Christ; "to which," he adds, "it is said no real Christian can be compelled." Renegades informed him that "the sum total of their offence or fault was meeting before light on an appointed day, and saying with one another a form of words (*carmen*) to Christ, as if to a god, and binding themselves by oath (not to the commission of any wickedness, but) against the commission of theft, robbery, adultery, breach of trust, denial of deposits; that, after this they were accustomed to separate, and then to meet again for a meal, but eaten all together and harmless; however, that they had even left this off after his edicts enforcing the imperial prohibition of *hetæriæ* or associations." He proceeded to put two women to the torture, but "discovered nothing beyond a bad and excessive superstition" (*superstitionem pravam et immodicam*), "the contagion" of which, he continues, "had spread through villages and country, till the temples were emptied of worshippers."

In these testimonies, which will form a natural and convenient text for what is to follow, we have various characteristics brought before us of the religion to which they relate. It was a superstition, as all three writers agree; a bad and excessive superstition, according to Pliny; a magical superstition, according to Suetonius; a deadly superstition, according to Tacitus. Next, it was embodied in a society, and, moreover, a secret and unlawful society or *hetæria ;* and it was a proselytizing society; and its very name was connected with "flagitious," "atrocious," and "shocking" acts.

Now these few points, which are not all which might be set down, contain in themselves a distinct and significant description of Christianity; but they have far greater meaning when illustrated by the history of the times, the testimony of later writers, and the acts of the Roman government toward its professors. It is impossible to mistake the judgment passed on the religion by these three writers, and still more clearly by other writers and imperial functionaries. They evidently associated Christianity with the oriental superstitions, whether propagated by individuals or embodied in a rite, which were in that day traversing the empire, and which in the event acted so remarkable a part in breaking up the national forms of worship, and so in preparing the way for Christianity. This, then, is the broad view which the educated heathen took of Christianity; and, if it had been very unlike those rites and curious arts in external appearance, they would not have confused it with them.

Changes in society are by a providential appointment commonly preceded and facilitated by the setting in of a certain current in men's thoughts and feelings in that direction toward which a change is to be made. And, as lighter substances whirl about before the tempest and presage it, so words and deeds, ominous but not effective of the coming revolution, are circulated beforehand through the multitude or pass across the field of events. This was specially the case with Christianity, as became its high dignity; it came heralded and attended by a crowd of shadows, shadows of itself, impotent and monstrous as shadows are, but not at first sight distinguishable from it by common spectators. Before the mission of the apostles a movement, of which there had been earlier parallels, had begun in Egypt, Syria, and the neighboring countries, tending to the propagation of new and peculiar forms of worship throughout the empire. Prophecies were afloat that some new order of things was coming in from the East, which increased the existing unsettlement of the popular mind; pretenders made attempts to satisfy its wants, and old traditions of the truth, embodied for ages in local or in national religions, gave to these attempts a doctrinal and ritual shape, which became an additional point of resemblance to that truth which was soon visibly to appear.

The distinctive character of the rites in question lay in their appealing to the gloomy rather than to the cheerful and hopeful feelings, and in their influencing the mind through fear. The notions of guilt and expiation, of evil and good to come, and of dealings with the invisible world, were in some shape or other preëminent in them, and formed a striking contrast to the classical polytheism, which was gay and graceful, as was natural in a civilized age. The new rites, on the other hand, were secret; their doctrine was mysterious; their profession was a discipline, beginning in a formal initiation, manifested in an association, and exercised in privation and pain. They were from the nature of the case proselytizing societies, for they were rising into power; nor were they local, but vagrant, restless, intrusive, and encroaching. Their pretensions to supernatural knowledge brought them into easy connection with magic and astrology, which are as attractive to the wealthy and luxurious as the more vulgar superstitions to the populace.

The Christian, being at first accounted a kind of Jew, was

even on that score included in whatever odium, and whatever bad associations, attended on the Jewish name. But in a little time his independence of the rejected people was clearly understood, as even the persecutions show; and he stood upon his own ground. Still his character did not change in the eyes of the world; for favor or for reproach, he was still associated with the votaries of secret and magical rites. The emperor Hadrian, noted as he is for his inquisitive temper, and a partaker in so many mysteries, still believed that the Christians of Egypt allowed themselves in the worship of Serapis. They are brought into connection with the magic of Egypt in the history of what is commonly called the Thundering legion, so far as this, that the rain which relieved the Emperor's army in the field, and which the Church ascribed to the prayers of the Christian soldiers, is by Dio Cassius attributed to an Egyptian magician, who obtained it by invoking Mercury and other spirits. This war had been the occasion of one of the first recognitions which the State had conceded to the oriental rites, though statesmen and emperors, as private men, had long taken part in them. The emperor Marcus had been urged by his fears of the Marcomanni to resort to these foreign introductions, and is said to have employed Magi and Chaldæans in averting an unsuccessful issue of the war.

It is observable that, in the growing countenance which was extended to these rites in the third century, Christianity came in for a share. The chapel of Alexander Severus contained statues of Abraham, Orpheus, Apollonius, Pythagoras, and our Lord. Here indeed, as in the case of Zenobia's Judaism, an eclectic philosophy aided the comprehension of religions. But, immediately before Alexander, Heliogabalus, who was no philosopher, while he formally seated his Syrian idol in the Palatine, while he observed the mysteries of Cybele and Adonis, and celebrated his magic rites with human victims, intended also, according to Lampridius, to unite with his horrible superstition "the Jewish and Samaritan religions and the Christian rite, that so the priesthood of Heliogabalus might comprise the mystery of every worship." Hence, more or less, the stories which occur in ecclesiastical history of the conversion or goodwill of the emperors to the Christian faith, of Hadrian, Mammæa, and others, besides Heliogabalus and Alexander. Such stories might often mean little more than that they favored it among other forms of oriental superstition.

What has been said is sufficient to bring before the mind an historical fact, which indeed does not need evidence. Upon the established religions of Europe the East had renewed her encroachments, and was pouring forth a family of rites which in various ways attracted the attention of the luxurious, the political, the ignorant, the restless, and the remorseful. Armenian, Chaldee, Egyptian, Jew, Syrian, Phrygian, as the case might be, was the designation of the new hierophant; and magic, superstition, barbarism, jugglery, were the names given to his rite by the world. In this company appeared Christianity. When then three well-informed writers call Christianity a superstition and a magical superstition, they were not using words at random, or the language of abuse, but they were describing it in distinct and recognized terms as cognate to those gloomy, secret, odious, disreputable religions which were making so much disturbance up and down the empire.

The Gnostic family suitably traces its origin to a mixed race, which had commenced its national history by associating orientalism with revelation. After the captivity of the ten tribes Samaria was colonized by "men from Babylon and Cushan, and from Ava, and from Hamath, and from Sepharvaim," who were instructed at their own instance in "the manner of the God of the land," by one of the priests of the Church of Jeroboam. The consequence was that "they feared the Lord and served their own gods." Of this country was Simon, the reputed patriarch of the Gnostics; and he is introduced in the Acts of the Apostles as professing those magical powers which were so principal a characteristic of the oriental mysteries. His heresy, though broken into a multitude of sects, was poured over the world with a catholicity not inferior in its day to that of Christianity. St. Peter, who fell in with him originally in Samaria, seems to have encountered him again at Rome. At Rome St. Polycarp met Marcion of Pontus, whose followers spread through Italy, Egypt, Syria, Arabia, and Persia.

"When [the reader of Christian history] comes to the second century," says Dr. Burton, "he finds that Gnosticism,

under some form or other, was professed in every part of the
then civilized world. He finds it divided into schools, as nu-
merously and as zealously attended as any which Greece or Asia
could boast in their happiest days. He meets with names to-
tally unknown to him before, which excited as much sensation
as those of Aristotle or Plato. He hears of volumes having
been written in support of this new philosophy, not one of
which has survived to our own day." Many of the founders of
these sects had been Christians. Others were of Jewish parent-
age; others were more or less connected in fact with the pagan
rites to which their own bore so great a resemblance.

Whatever might be the history of these sects, and though
it may be a question whether they can be properly called "superstitions," and though many of them numbered educated
men among their teachers and followers, they closely resem-
bled—at least in ritual and profession—the vagrant pagan mysteries which have been above described. Their very name of
"Gnostic" implied the possession of a secret, which was to
be communicated to their disciples. Ceremonial observances
were the preparation, and symbolical rites the instrument, of
initiation. Tatian and Montanus, the representatives of very
distinct schools, agreed in making asceticism a rule of life.

Such were the Gnostics; and to external and prejudiced
spectators, whether philosophers, as Celsus and Porphyry, or
the multitude, they wore an appearance sufficiently like the
Church to be mistaken for her in the latter part of the ante-
Nicene period, as she was confused with the pagan mysteries in
the earlier.

Let us proceed in our contemplation of this reflection, as it
may be called, of primitive Christianity in the mirror of the
world. All three writers, Tacitus, Suetonius, and Pliny, call it
a "superstition"; this is no accidental imputation, but is repeated by a variety of subsequent writers and speakers. The
charge of Thyestean banquets scarcely lasts a hundred years;
but, while pagan witnesses are to be found, the Church is accused of superstition. Now what is meant by the word thus
attached by a *consensus* of heathen authorities to Christianity?
At least it cannot mean a religion in which a man might think
what he pleased, and was set free from all yokes, whether of

ignorance, fear, authority, or priestcraft. When heathen writers call the oriental rites superstitions, they evidently use the word in its modern sense. It cannot surely be doubted that they apply it in the same sense to Christianity. But Plutarch explains for us the word at length in his treatise which bears the name: "Of all kinds of fear," he says, "superstition is the most fatal to action and resource. He does not fear the sea who does not sail, nor war who does not serve, nor robbers who keeps at home, nor the sycophant who is poor, nor the envious if he is a private man, nor an earthquake if he lives in Gaul, nor thunder if he lives in Æthiopia; but he who fears the gods fears everything—earth, seas, air, sky, darkness, light, noises, silence, sleep. Slaves sleep and forget their masters; of the fettered doth sleep lighten the chain; inflamed wounds, ulcers cruel and agonizing, are not felt by the sleeping. Superstition alone has come to no terms with sleep; but in the very sleep of her victims, as though they were in the realms of the impious, she raises horrible spectres and monstrous phantoms and various pains, and whirls the miserable soul about and persecutes it. They rise, and, instead of making light of what is unreal, they fall into the hands of quacks and conjurers, who say, ' Call the crone to expiate, bathe in the sea, and sit all day on the ground.' "

Here we have a vivid picture of Plutarch's idea of the essence of superstition; it was the imagination of the existence of an unseen ever-present Master; the bondage of a rule of life, of a continual responsibility; obligation to attend to little things, the impossibility of escaping from duty, the inability to choose or change one's religion, an interference with the enjoyment of life, a melancholy view of the world, sense of sin, horror at guilt, apprehension of punishment, dread, self-abasement, depression, anxiety, and endeavor to be at peace with heaven, and error and absurdity in the methods chosen for the purpose. Such, too, had been the idea of the Epicurean Velleius, when he shrunk with horror from the "*sempiternus dominus*" and "*curiosus Deus*" of the Stoics. Such, surely, was the meaning of Tacitus, Suetonius, and Pliny. And hence, of course, the frequent reproach cast on Christians as credulous, weak-minded, and poor-spirited. The heathen objectors in Minucius

and Lactantius speak of their "old-woman's tales." Celsus
accuses them of "assenting at random and without reason,"
saying, "Do not inquire, but believe." "They lay it down,"
he says elsewhere: "Let no educated man approach, no man of
wisdom, no man of sense; but if a man be unlearned, weak in
intellect, an infant, let him come with confidence. Confessing
that these are worthy of their God, they evidently desire, as
they are able, to convert none but fools, and vulgar, and stupid,
and slavish, women and boys." They "take in the simple and
lead him where they will." They address themselves to
"youths, house-servants, and the weak in intellect." They
"hurry away from the educated, as not fit subjects of their imposition, and inveigle the rustic." "Thou," says the heathen
magistrate to the martyr Fructuosus, "who as a teacher dost
disseminate a new fable, that fickle girls may desert the groves
and abandon Jupiter, condemn, if thou art wise, the anile
creed."

Hence the epithets of itinerant, mountebank, conjurer, cheat,
sophist, and sorcerer, heaped upon the teachers of Christianity; sometimes to account for the report or apparent truth
of their miracles, sometimes to explain their success. Our
Lord was said to have learned his miraculous power in Egypt;
"wizard, mediciner, cheat, rogue, conjurer," were the epithets
applied to him by the opponents of Eusebius; they "worship
that crucified sophist," says Lucian; "Paul, who surpasses all
the conjurers and impostors who ever lived," is Julian's account
of the apostle. "You have sent through the whole world,"
says St. Justin to Trypho, "to preach that a certain atheistic
and lawless sect has sprung from one Jesus, a Galilean cheat."
"We know," says Lucian, speaking of Chaldæans and magicians, "the Syrian from Palestine, who is the sophist in these
matters, how many lunatics, with eyes distorted and mouth in
foam, he raises and sends away restored, ridding them from the
evil at a great price." "If any conjurer came to them, a man
of skill and knowing how to manage matters," says the same
writer, "he made money in no time, with a broad grin at the
simple fellows." The officer who had custody of St. Perpetua
feared her escape from prison "by magical incantations."
When St. Tiburtius had walked barefoot on hot coals, his judge

cried out that Christ had taught him magic. St. Anastasia was thrown into prison as a mediciner; the populace called out against St. Agnes, "Away with the witch," *Tolle magam, tolle maleficam.* When St. Bonosus and St. Maximilian bore the burning pitch without shrinking, Jews and Gentiles cried out, "*Isti magi et malefici.*" "What new delusion," says the heathen magistrate concerning St. Romanus, "has brought in these sophists to deny the worship of the gods? How doth this chief sorcerer mock us, skilled by his Thessalian charm (*carmine*) to laugh at punishment!"

It explains the phenomenon, which has created so much surprise to certain moderns—that a grave, well-informed historian like Tacitus should apply to Christians what sounds like abuse. Yet what is the difficulty, supposing that Christians were considered *mathematici* and *magi,* and these were the secret intriguers against established government, the allies of desperate politicians, the enemies of the established religion, the disseminators of lying rumors, the perpetrators of poisonings and other crimes? "Read this," says Paley, after quoting some of the most beautiful and subduing passages of St. Paul, "read this, and then think of *exitiabilis superstitio*"*;* and he goes on to express a wish "in contending with heathen authorities, to produce our books against theirs," as if it were a matter of books.

Public men care very little for books; the finest sentiments, the most luminous philosophy, the deepest theology, inspiration itself, moves them but little; they look at facts, and care only for facts. The question was, What was the worth, what the tendency of the Christian body in the State? What Christians said, what they thought, was little to the purpose. They might exhort to peaceableness and passive obedience as strongly as words could speak; but what did they *do,* what was their political position? This is what statesmen thought of then, as they do now. What had men of the world to do with abstract proofs or first principles? A statesman measures parties and sects and writers by their bearing upon *him ;* and he has a practised eye in this sort of judgment, and is not likely to be mistaken. "'What is Truth?' said jesting Pilate." Apologies, however eloquent or true, availed nothing with the Ro-

man magistrate against the sure instinct which taught him to
dread Christianity. It was a dangerous enemy to any power
not built upon itself; he felt it, and the event justified his apprehension.

We must not forget the well-known character of the Roman
State in its dealings with its subjects. It had had from the
first an extreme jealousy of secret societies; it was prepared to
grant a large toleration and a broad comprehension, but, as is
the case with modern governments, it wished to have jurisdiction and the ultimate authority in every movement of the body
politic and social, and its civil institutions were based, or essentially depended, on its religion. Accordingly, every innovation
upon the established paganism, except it was allowed by the
law, was rigidly repressed. Hence the professors of low superstitions, of mysteries, of magic, of astrology, were the outlaws
of society, and were in a condition analogous, if the comparison
may be allowed, to smugglers or poachers among ourselves, or
perhaps to burglars and highwaymen; for the Romans had ever
burnt the sorcerer and banished his consulters for life. It was
an ancient custom. And at mysteries they looked with especial
suspicion, because, since the established religion did not include
them in its provisions, they really did supply what may be called
a demand of the age.

We know what opposition had been made in Rome even to
the philosophy of Greece; much greater would be the aversion
of constitutional statesmen and lawyers to the ritual of barbarians. Religion was the Roman point of honor. "Spaniards
might rival them in numbers," says Cicero, "Gauls in bodily
strength, Carthaginians in address, Greeks in the arts, Italians
and Latins in native talent, but the Romans surpassed all nations in piety and devotion." It was one of their laws, "Let
no one have gods by himself, nor worship in private new gods
nor adventitious, unless added on public authority." Mæcenas
in *Dio* advises Augustus to honor the gods according to the
national custom, because the contempt of the country's deities
leads to civil insubordination, reception of foreign laws, con-
spiracies, and secret meetings. "Suffer no one," he adds, "to
deny the gods or to practise sorcery." The civilian Julius
Paulus lays it down as one of the leading principles of Roman

law, that those who introduce new or untried religions should be degraded, and if in the lower orders put to death. In like manner, it is enacted in one of Constantine's laws that the haruspices should not exercise their art in private; and there is a law of Valentinian's against nocturnal sacrifices or magic. It is more immediately to our purpose that Trajan had been so earnest in his resistance to *hetæriæ* or secret societies, that, when a fire had laid waste Nicomedia, and Pliny proposed to him to incorporate a body of a hundred and fifty firemen in consequence, he was afraid of the precedent and forbade it.

What has been said will suggest another point of view in which the oriental rites were obnoxious to the government— namely, as being vagrant and proselytizing religions. If it tolerated foreign superstitions, this would be on the ground that districts or countries within its jurisdiction held them; to proselytize to a rite hitherto unknown, to form a new party, and to propagate it through the empire — a religion not local, but catholic—was an offence against both order and reason. The State desired peace everywhere, and no change; "considering," according to Lactantius, "that they were rightly and deservedly punished who execrated the public religion handed down to them by their ancestors."

It is impossible, surely, to deny that, in assembling for religious purposes, the Christians were breaking a solemn law, a vital principle of the Roman constitution; and this is the light in which their conduct was regarded by the historians and philosophers of the empire. This was a very strong act on the part of the disciples of the great apostle, who had enjoined obedience to the powers that be. Time after time they resisted the authority of the magistrate; and this is a phenomenon inexplicable on the theory of private judgment or of the voluntary principle. The justification of such disobedience lies simply in the necessity of obeying the higher authority of some divine law; but if Christianity were in its essence only private and personal, as so many now think, there was no necessity of their meeting together at all. If, on the other hand, in assembling for worship and holy communion, they were fulfilling an indispensable observance, Christianity has imposed a social law on the world, and formally enters the field of politics. Gibbon says that, in consequence of Pliny's edict, "the prudence of the Christians suspended their *agapæ;* but it was *impossible* for them to omit the exercise of public worship." We can draw no other conclusion.

At the end of three hundred years a more remarkable violation of law seems to have been admitted by the Christian body. It shall be given in the words of Dr. Burton; he has been speaking of Maximin's edict, which provided for the restitution of any of their lands or buildings which had been alienated from them. "It is plain," he says, "from the terms of this edict, that the Christians had for some time been in possession of property. It speaks of houses and lands which did not belong to individuals, but to the whole body. Their possession of such property could hardly have escaped the notice of the government; but it seems to have been held in direct violation of a law of Diocletian, which prohibited corporate bodies or associations which were not legally recognized, from acquiring property. The Christians were certainly not a body recognized by law at the beginning of the reign of Diocletian, and it might almost be thought that this enactment was specially directed against them. But, like other laws which are founded upon tyranny, and are at variance with the first principles of justice, it is probable that this law about corporate property was evaded. We must suppose that the Christians had purchased lands and houses before the law was passed; and their disregard of the prohibition may be taken as another proof that their religion had now taken so firm a footing that the executors of the laws were obliged to connive at their being broken by so numerous a body."

No wonder that the magistrate who presided at the martyrdom of St. Romanus calls them in Prudentius "a rebel people"; that Galerius speaks of them as "a nefarious conspiracy"; the heathen in Minucius, as "men of a desperate faction"; that others make them guilty of sacrilege and treason, and call them by those other titles which, more closely resembling the language of Tacitus, have been noticed above. Hence the violent accusations against them as the destructors of the empire, the authors of physical evils, and the cause of the anger of the gods.

"Men cry out," says Tertullian, "that the State is beset, that the Christians are in their fields, in their forts, in their islands. They mourn as for a loss that every sex, condition, and now even rank is going over to this sect. And yet they do not by this very means advance their minds to the idea of some good therein hidden; they allow not themselves to conjecture more rightly, they choose not to examine more closely. The generality run upon a hatred of this name, with eyes so closed that in bearing favorable testimony to anyone they mingle with it the reproach of the name. ' A good man Caius Seius, only he is a Christian.' So another, ' I marvel that that wise man Lucius Titius hath suddenly become a Christian.' No one reflecteth whether Caius be not therefore good and Lucius wise because a Christian, or therefore a Christian because wise and good. They praise that which they know, they revile that which they know not. Virtue is not in such account as hatred of the Christians. Now, then, if the hatred be of the name, what guilt is there in names? What charge against words? Unless it be that any word which is a name have either a barbarous or ill-omened, or a scurrilous or an immodest sound. If the Tiber cometh up to the walls, if the Nile cometh not up to the fields, if the heaven hath stood still, if the earth hath been moved, if there be any famine, if any pestilence, ' The Christians to the lions' is forthwith the word."

"Men of a desperate, lawless, reckless faction," says the heathen Cæcilius, in the passage above referred to, "who collect together out of the lowest rabble the thoughtless portion, and credulous women seduced by the weakness of their sex, and form a mob of impure conspirators, of whom nocturnal assemblies and solemn fastings and unnatural food, no sacred rite but pollution, is the bond. A tribe lurking and light-hating, dumb for the public, talkative in corners, they despise our temples as if graves, spit at our gods, deride our religious forms; pitiable themselves, they pity, forsooth, our priests; half-naked themselves, they despise our honors and purple; monstrous folly and incredible impudence! . . . Day after day their abandoned morals wind their serpentine course; over the whole world are those most hideous rites of an impious association growing into shape; . . . they recognize each other by marks and signs, and love each other almost before they recognize; promiscuous lust is their religion. Thus does their vain and mad superstition glory in crimes. . . . The writer who tells the story of a criminal capitally punished, and of the gibbet (*ligna feralia*) of the cross being their observance (*ceremonias*), assigns to them thereby an altar in keeping with the abandoned and wicked, that they may worship (*colant*) what they merit. . . . Why their mighty effort to hide and shroud whatever it is they worship (*colunt*), since things honest ever like the open day, and crimes are secret? Why have they no altars, no temples, no images known to us, never speak abroad, never assemble freely, were it not that what they worship and suppress is subject either of punishment or of shame?

"What monstrous, what portentous notions do they fabricate! that that God of theirs, whom they can neither show nor see, should be inquiring diligently into the characters, the acts —nay, the words and secret thoughts of all men; running to and fro, forsooth, and present everywhere, troublesome, restless—nay, impudently curious they would have him; that is, if he is close at every deed, interferes in all places, while he can neither attend to each as being distracted through the whole, nor suffice for the whole as being engaged about each. Think, too, of their threatening fire, meditating destruction to the whole earth—nay, the world itself with its stars! . . . Nor content with this mad opinion, they add and append their old wives' tales about a new birth after death, ashes and cinders, and by some strange confidence believe each other's lies.

"Poor creatures! consider what hangs over you after death, while you are still alive. Lo, the greater part of you, the better, as you say, are in want, cold, toil, hunger, and your God suffers it; but I omit common trials. Lo, threats are offered to you, punishments, torments; crosses to be undergone now, not worshipped (*adorandæ*); fires, too, which ye predict and fear; where is that God who can recover, but cannot preserve your life? The answer of Socrates, when he was asked about heavenly matters, is well known: ' What is above us does not concern us.' My opinion also is, that points which are doubtful, as are the points in question, must be left; nor, when so many and such great men are in controversy on the subject, must judgment be rashly and audaciously given on either side, lest the consequence be either anile superstition or the overthrow of all religion."

Such was Christianity in the eyes of those who witnessed its rise and propagation—one of a number of wild and barbarous rites which were pouring in upon the empire from the ancient realms of superstition, and the mother of a progeny of sects which were faithful to the original they had derived from Egypt or Syria; a religion unworthy of an educated person, as appealing, not to the intellect, but to the fears and weaknesses of human nature, and consisting, not in the rational and cheerful enjoyment, but in a morose rejection of the gifts of Providence; a horrible religion, as inflicting or enjoining cruel sufferings, and monstrous and loathsome in its very indulgence of the passions; a religion leading by reaction to infidelity; a religion of magic, and of the vulgar arts, real and pretended, with which magic was accompanied; a secret religion which dared not face the day; an itinerant, busy, proselytizing religion, forming an extended confederacy against the State, resisting its authority and breaking its laws. There may be some exceptions to this general impression, such as Pliny's discovery of the innocent and virtuous rule of life adopted by the Christians of Pontus; but this only proves that Christianity was not in fact the infamous religion which the heathen thought it; it did not reverse their general belief to that effect.

Now it must be granted that, in some respects, this view of Christianity depended on the times, and would alter with their alteration. When there was no persecution, martyrs could not be obstinate; and when the Church was raised aloft in high places, it was no longer in caves. Still, I believe, it continued substantially the same in the judgment of the world external to it while there was an external world to judge of it. "They thought it enough," says Julian in the fourth century, of our Lord and his apostles, "to deceive women, servants, and slaves, and by their means wives and husbands." "A human fabrication," says he elsewhere, "put together by wickedness, having nothing divine in it, but making a perverted use of the fable-loving, childish, irrational part of the soul, and offering a set of wonders to create belief."

"Miserable men," he says elsewhere, "you refuse to worship the ancile, yet you worship the wood of the cross, and sign it on your foreheads, and fix it on your doors. Shall one for this hate the intelligent among you, or pity the less understanding, who in following you have gone to such an excess of perdition as to leave the everlasting gods and go over to a dead Jew?" He speaks of their adding other dead men to him who died so long ago. "You have filled all places with sepulchres and monuments, though it is nowhere told you in your religion to haunt the tombs and to attend upon them." Elsewhere he speaks of their "leaving the gods for corpses and relics." On the other hand, he attributes the growth of Christianity to its humanity toward strangers, care in burying the dead, and pretended religiousness of life. In another place he speaks of their care of the poor.

Libanius, Julian's preceptor in rhetoric, delivers the same testimony, as far as it goes. He addressed his *Oration for the Temples* to a Christian emperor, and would in consequence be guarded in his language; however it runs in one direction. He speaks of "those black-habited men," meaning the monks, "who eat more than elephants, and by the number of their potations trouble those who send them drink in their chantings, and conceal this by paleness artificially acquired." They "are in good condition out of the misfortunes of others, while they pretend to serve God by hunger." Those whom they attack "are like bees, they like drones." I do not quote this passage to prove that there were monks in Libanius' days, which no one doubts, but to show his impression of Christianity, as far as his works betray it.

Numantian in the same century describes in verse his voyage from Rome to Gaul: one book of the poem is extant; he falls in with Christianity on two of the islands which lie in his course. He thus describes them as found on one of these: "The island is in a squalid state, being full of light-haters. They call themselves monks, because they wish to live alone without witness. They dread the gifts, from fearing the reverses, of fortune." He meets on the other island a Christian, whom he had known, of good family and fortune, and happy in his marriage, who "impelled by the Furies had left men and gods, and, credulous exile, was living in base concealment. Is not this herd," he continues, " worse than Circean poison? then bodies were changed, now minds."

In the *Philopatris*, which is the work of an author of the fourth century, Critias is introduced pale and wild. His friend asks him if he has seen Cerberus or Hecate; and he answers that he has heard a rigmarole from certain " thrice-cursed sophists "; which he thinks would drive him mad if he heard it again, and was nearly sending him headlong over some cliff as it was. He retires for relief with his inquirer to a pleasant place, shadowed by planes, where swallows and nightingales are singing, and a quiet brook is purling. Triephon, his friend, expresses a fear lest he has heard some incantation, and is led by the course of the dialogue, before his friend tells his tale, to give some account of Christianity, being himself a Christian. After speaking of the creation, as described by Moses, he falls at once upon that doctrine of a particular providence which is so distasteful to Plutarch, Velleius in Cicero, and Cæcilius, and generally to unbelievers. "He is in heaven," he says, "looking at just and unjust, and causing actions to be entered in books; and he will recompense all on a day which he has appointed." Critias objects that he cannot make this consistent with the received doctrine about the Fates, "even though he has perhaps been carried aloft with his master, and initiated in unspeakable mysteries." He also asks if the deeds of the Scythians are written in heaven for if so there must be many scribes there.

Such was the language of paganism after Christianity had for fifty years been exposed to the public gaze; after it had been before the world for fifty more, St. Augustine had still to defend it against the charge of being the cause of the calamities of the empire. And for the charge of magic, when the Arian bishops were in formal disputations with the Catholic, before Gungebald, Burgundian king of France, at the end of the fifth century, we find still that they charged the Catholics with being "*præstigiatores*," and worshipping a number of gods; and when the Catholics proposed that the King should repair to the shrine of St. Justus, where both parties might ask him concerning their respective faiths, the Arians cried out that "they would not seek enchantments like Saul, for Scripture was enough for them, which was more powerful than all bewitchments." This was said, not against strangers of whom they knew nothing, as Ethelbert might be suspicious of St. Augustine and his brother missionaries, but against a body of men who lived among them.

I do not think it can be doubted then that, had Tacitus, Suetonius, and Pliny, Celsus, Porphyry, and the other opponents of Christianity lived in the fourth century, their evidence concerning Christianity would be very much the same as it has come down to us from the centuries before it. In either case, a man of the world and a philosopher would have been disgusted at the gloom and sadness of its profession, its mysteriousness, its claim of miracles, the want of good sense imputable to its rule of life, and the unsettlement and discord it was introducing into the social and political world.

On the whole then I conclude as follows: If there is a form of Christianity now in the world which is accused of gross superstition, of borrowing its rites and customs from the heathen, and of ascribing to forms and ceremonies an occult virtue; a religion which is considered to burden and enslave the mind by its requisitions, to address itself to the weak-minded and ignorant, to be supported by sophistry and imposture, and to contradict reason and exalt mere irrational faith; a religion which impresses on the serious mind very distressing views of the guilt and consequences of sin, sets upon the minute acts of the day, one by one, their definite value for praise or blame, and thus casts a grave shadow over the future; a religion which holds up to admiration the surrender of wealth, and disables serious persons from enjoying it if they would; a religion, the doctrines of which, be they good or bad, are to the generality of men unknown; which is considered to bear on its very surface signs of folly and falsehood so distinct that a glance suffices to judge of it, and that careful examination is preposterous; which is felt to be so simply bad that it may be calumniated at hazard and at pleasure, it being nothing but absurdity to stand upon the accurate distribution of its guilt among its particular acts, or painfully to determine how far this or that story concerning it is literally true, or what has to be allowed in candor, or what is improbable, or what cuts two ways, or what is not proved, or what may be plausibly defended; a religion such that men look at a convert to it with a feeling which no other denomination raises except Judaism, socialism, or Mormonism—namely, with curiosity, suspicion, fear, disgust, as the case may be, as if something strange had befallen him, as if he had had an initiation into a mystery, and had come into communion with dreadful influences, as if he were now one of a confederacy which claimed him, absorbed him, stripped him of his personality, reduced him to a mere organ or instrument of a whole; a religion which men hate as proselytizing, anti-social, revolutionary, as dividing families, separating chief friends, corrupting the maxims of government, making a mock at law, dissolving the empire, the enemy of human nature, and a "conspirator against its rights and privileges"; a religion which they consider the champion and instrument of darkness, and a pollution calling down upon the land the anger of heaven; a religion which they associate with intrigue and conspiracy, which they speak about in whispers, which they detect by anticipation in whatever goes wrong, and to which they impute whatever is unaccountable; a religion, the very name of which they cast out as evil, and use simply as a bad epithet, and which from the impulse of self-preservation they would persecute if they could —if there be such a religion now in the world, it is not unlike Christianity as that same world viewed it when first it came forth from its divine Author.

BURNING OF ROME UNDER NERO

A.D. 64

SIENKIEWICZ

TACITUS

Nero when a youth was placed under charge of the philosopher Seneca, who carefully attended to his education. During Nero's nonage he was persevering in his studies and made great progress in Greek. By a subterfuge of his mother's he was proclaimed emperor in the place of Britannicus, the real heir to the throne. In the early part of his reign public affairs were wisely conducted, but the private life of Nero was given up to vice and profligacy. His love for Poppæa led him into the crime of matricide, for she, wishing to share the imperial throne, and knowing it was impossible while his mother, Agrippina, lived, induced him to authorize her assassination. Strange that Seneca and Burrhus should have approved of this, yet Tacitus admits that such was the case. In the eighth year of his reign Nero divorced his wife, Octavia, and married Poppæa.

Nero was an accomplished musician and sang verses composed by himself. He eagerly sought the plaudits of the multitude by reciting his compositions in public. Historians are divided in opinion as to whether Nero was the cause of the burning of Rome. During the conflagration, to court popularity he ordered temporary shelters to be provided for the houseless; yet the people did not acclaim this deed, as it was reported that Nero, at "the very time Rome was in flames," sang the destruction of Troy in his private theatre, likening the present disaster to that ancient catastrophe. In order to divert the masses from what they believed the true origin of the fire, Nero charged it upon the Christians, many hundreds of whom were sacrificed to his fury. He was the last of the Cæsars, and died by his own hand amid universal execrations, in June, A.D. 68, four years after the destruction of Rome.

HENRYK SIENKIEWICZ

THE fire began at the Circus Maximus, in that section which touches the Palatine and Cælian hill; it rushed on with inconceivable rapidity and fastened upon the whole centre of Rome. Since the time of Brennus never had the city witnessed such an awful catastrophe.

A freedman of Cæsar's, Phaon by name, ran panting into Nero's presence, shrieking: "Rome is in flames! the conflagration is great."

All Cæsar's guests arose from their recumbent attitude. "Ye gods! I shall see a burning city; now can I finish the *Troyade*," exclaimed Nero, placing his lute aside. "If I go at once, can I view the fire?"

"My lord, the whole city is as a sea of flame; the smoke is suffocatingly heavy and is destroying the people. The inhabitants faint away or rashly cast themselves into the fire, maddened with terror. All Rome perishes." And Nero raised his hands and cried, "Woe, woe to thee, thou sacred city of Priam!"

Fires were frequent enough in Rome; during these conflagrations violence and robbery were rampant, particularly so in those sections of the city inhabited by needy half-barbarian peoples, a folk comprising rabble from every part of the world. The fear of servile rebellion was like a nightmare, which had stifled Rome for many years. It was believed that hundreds of thousands of those people were thinking of the times of Spartacus, and merely waiting for a favorable moment to seize arms against their oppressors and Rome. Now the moment had come! Perhaps war and slaughter were raging in the city together with fire.

It was possible even that the prætorians had hurled themselves on the city and were slaughtering at command of Cæsar. And that moment the hair rose on Vinicius' head from terror. He recalled all the conversations about burning cities which for some time had been repeated at Cæsar's court with wonderful persistence; well he recalled Cæsar's complaints that he was forced to describe a burning city without having seen an actual fire; his contemptuous answer to Tigellinus, who offered to burn Antium or an artificial wooden city; finally, his complaints against Rome, and the pestilential alleys of the Subura.

Yes; truly Cæsar has commanded the burning of the city! Only he could give such a command, as Tigellinus alone could accomplish it. But if Rome is burning at command of Cæsar, who can be sure that the population will not be slaughtered at his command? The monster is capable of just such a deed.

Conflagration, a servile revolt, and slaughter! What a horrible chaos, what a letting loose of destructive elements and horrid, universal frenzy!

The night had paled long since, the dawn had passed into light, and on all the nearer summits golden, rosy gleams were shining, which might come either from burning Rome or the rising daylight. Vinicius ran to the hill, the summit was reached, and then a terrible sight struck his eyes.

All the lower region was covered with smoke, forming, as it were, one gigantic cloud lying close to the earth. In this cloud towns, aqueducts, villas, trees, disappeared; but farther beyond this gray, ghastly plain the city was burning on the hills. The conflagration had not the form of a pillar of fire, as happens when a single building is burning, even when of the greatest size. That was a long belt, rather, shaped like the belt of dawn. Above this belt rose a wave of smoke, in places entirely black, in places looking rose-colored, in places like blood, in places turning in on itself, in some places inflated, in others squeezed and squirming, like a serpent which is unwinding and extending.

That monstrous wave seemed at times to cover even the belt of fire, which became then as narrow as a ribbon; but later this ribbon illuminated the smoke from beneath, changing its lower rolls into waves of flame. The two extended from one side of the sky to the other, hiding its lower part, as at times a stretch of forest hides the horizon. The Sabine hills were not visible in the least.

It seemed at the first glance of the eye that not only the city was burning, but the whole world, and that no living being could save itself from that ocean of flame and smoke. The wind blew with increasing strength from the region of the fire, bringing the smell of burnt things and of smoke, which began to hide even nearer objects. Clear daylight had come, and the sun lighted up the summits surrounding the Alban Lake.

But the bright golden rays of the morning appeared reddish and sickly through the haze. Vinicius, while descending toward Albanum, entered smoke which was denser, less and less transparent. The town itself was buried in it thoroughly. The alarmed citizens had moved out to the street. It was a

terror to think of what might be in Rome, when it was difficult to breathe in Albanum.

He met increasing numbers of people, who had deserted
the city and were going to the Alban hills; they had escaped
the fire and wished to go beyond the line of smoke. Before
he had reached Ustrinum he had to slacken his pace because
of the throng. Besides pedestrians with bundles on their backs
he met horses with packs, mules and vehicles laden with effects,
and finally litters in which slaves were bearing the wealthier
citizens. The town of Ustrinum was so thronged with fugitives
from Rome that it was difficult to push through the crowd. On
the market square, under temple porticos, and on the streets
were swarms of fugitives.

Here and there people were erecting tents under which
whole families were to find shelter. Others settled down under
the naked sky, shouting, calling on the gods, or cursing the
Fates. In the general terror it was difficult to inquire about
anything. New crowds of men, women, and children arrived
from the direction of Rome every moment; these increased
the disorder and outcry. Some, gone astray in the throng,
sought desperately those whom they had lost; others fought
for a camping place.

Half-crazy shepherds from the Campania crowded to the
town to hear news, or find profit in plunder made easy by the
uproar. Here and there crowds of slaves of every nationality
and gladiators fell to robbing houses and villas in the town,
and to fighting with the soldiers who appeared in defence of the
citizens.

Junius, a friend of Vinicius, said, after a moment's hesitation, in a low voice: "I know that thou wilt not betray me,
so I will tell thee that this is no common fire. People were not
permitted to save the Circus. When houses began to burn in
every direction, I myself heard thousands of voices exclaiming,
'Death to those who save!' Certain people ran through the
city and hurled burning torches into buildings.

"On the other hand, people are revolting and crying that
the city is burning at command. I can say nothing more.
Woe to the city, woe to us all and to me! The tongue of man
cannot tell what is happening there. People are perishing in

flames or slaying one another in the throng.   This is the end of
Rome!"

Vinicius, nearing the walls, found it easier to reach Rome
than penetrate to the middle of the city.   It was difficult to
push along the Appian Way, because of the throng of people.
Houses, cemeteries, fields, gardens, and temples, lying on both
sides of it, were turned into camping places.   In the temple of
Mars, which stood near the Porta Appia, the crowd had thrown
down the doors, so as to find a refuge within during night hours.
In the cemeteries the larger monuments were seized, and battles
fought in defence of them, which were carried to bloodshed.
Ustrinum with its disorder gave barely a slight foretaste of that
which was happening beneath the walls of the capital.

All regard for the dignity of law, for family ties, for difference of position, had ceased.   Gladiators drunk with wine seized
in the Emporium, gathered in crowds and ran with wild shouts
through the neighboring squares, trampling, scattering, and
robbing the people.   A multitude of barbarian slaves, exposed
for sale in the city, escaped from the booths.   For them the
burning and ruin of Rome were at once the end of slavery and
the hour of revenge; so that when the permanent inhabitants,
who had lost all they owned in the fire, stretched their hands
to the gods in despair, calling for rescue, these slaves with
howls of delight scattered the crowds, dragged clothing from
people's backs, and bore away the younger women.   They
were joined by other slaves serving in the city from of old,
wretches who had nothing on their bodies save woollen girdles
around their hips, dreadful figures from the alleys, who were
hardly ever seen on the streets in the daytime, and whose existence in Rome it was difficult to suspect.

Men of this wild and unrestrained crowd—Asiatics, Africans, Greeks, Thracians, Germans, Britons—howling in every
language of the earth, raged, thinking that the hour had come
in which they were free to reward themselves for years of misery and suffering.   In the midst of that surging throng of humanity, in the glitter of day and of fire, shone the helmets of
prætorians, under whose protection the more peaceable population had taken refuge, and who in hand-to-hand battle had to
meet the raging multitude in many places.   Vinicius had seen

captured cities, but never had his eyes beheld a spectacle in which despair, tears, pain, groans, wild delight, madness, rage, and license were mingled together in such immeasurable chaos. Above this heaving, mad human multitude roared the fire, surging up to the hill-tops of the greatest city on earth, sending into the whirling throng its fiery breath, and covering it with smoke, through which it was impossible to see the blue sky.

The young tribune with supreme effort, and exposing his life every moment, forced his way at last to the Appian Gate; but there he saw that he could not reach the city through the division of the Porta Capena, not merely because of the throng, but also because of the terrible heat from which the whole atmosphere was quivering inside the gate. Besides, the bridge at the Porta Trigenia, opposite the temple of the Bona Dea, did not exist yet, hence those who wished to go beyond the Tiber had to pass through to the Pons Sublicius—that is, to pass around the Aventine through a part of the city covered now with one sea of flame. That was an impossibility. Vinicius understood that he must return toward Ustrinum, turn from the Appian Way, cross the river below the city, and go to the Via Portuensis, which led straight to the Trans-Tiber.

That was not easy because of the increasing disorder on the Appian Way. At the fountain of Mercury, however, he saw a centurion who was known to him. This man, at the head of a few tens of soldiers, was defending the precinct of the temple; he commanded him to follow. Recognizing a tribune and an Augustian, the centurion did not dare to disobey the order.

He and his men were followed by curses and a shower of stones; but to these he gave no heed, caring only to reach freer spaces at the earliest. Still he advanced with the greatest effort. People who had encamped would not move, and heaped loud curses on Cæsar and the prætorians. The throng assumed in places a threatening aspect. Thousands of voices accused Nero of burning the city. He and Poppæa were threatened with death. Shouts of "Buffoon, actor, matricide!" were heard round about. Some shouted to drag him to the Tiber; others that Rome had shown patience enough. It was clear that were a leader found these threats could be changed into open rebellion which might break out any moment.

Meanwhile the rage and despair of the crowd turned against the prætorians, who for another reason could not make their way out of the crowd: the road was blocked by piles of goods, borne from the fire previously, boxes, barrels of provisions, furniture the most costly, vessels, infants' cradles, beds, carts, hand-packs. Here and there they fought hand-to-hand; but the prætorians conquered the weaponless multitude easily. After they had ridden with difficulty across the Viæ Latina, Numitia, Ardea, Lavinia, and Ostia, and passed around villas, gardens, cemeteries, and temples, Vinicius reached at last a village called Vicus Alexandri, beyond which he crossed the Tiber. There was more open space at this spot and less smoke. From fugitives, of whom there was no lack even there, he learned that only certain alleys of the Trans-Tiber were burning, but that surely nothing could resist the fury of the conflagration, since people were spreading the fire purposely, and permitted no one to quench it, declaring that they acted at command.

The young tribune had not the least doubt then that Cæsar had given command to burn Rome; and the vengeance which people demanded seemed to him just and proper. What more could Mithradates or any of Rome's most inveterate enemies have done? The measure had been exceeded; his madness had grown to be too enormous, and the existence of people too difficult because of him. All believed that Nero's hour had struck, that those ruins into which the city was falling should and must overwhelm the monstrous buffoon together with all those crimes of his. Should a man be found of courage sufficient to stand at the head of the despairing people, that might happen in a few hours. Here vengeful and daring thoughts began to fly through his head. But if he should do that?

The family of Vinicius, which till recent times counted a whole series of consuls, was known throughout Rome. The crowds needed only a name. Once, when four hundred slaves of the prefect Pedanius Secundus were sentenced, Rome reached the verge of rebellion and civil war. What would happen to-day in view of a dreadful calamity surpassing almost everything which Rome had undergone in the course of eight centuries? Whoever calls the *quirites* to arms, thought Vinicius, will overthrow Nero undoubtedly, and clothe himself in purple.

The Trans-Tiber was full of smoke, and crowds of fugitives made it more difficult to reach the interior of the place, since people, having more time there, had saved greater quantities of goods. The main street itself was in many parts filled completely, and around the Naumachia Augusta great heaps were piled up. Narrow alleys, in which smoke had collected more densely, were simply impassable. The inhabitants were fleeing in thousands. On the way Vinicius saw wonderful sights. More than once two rivers of people, flowing in opposite directions, met in a narrow passage, stopped each other, men fought hand-to-hand, struck and trampled one another. Families lost one another in the uproar; mothers called on their children despairingly. The young tribune's hair stood on end at thought of what must happen nearer the fire.

Amid shouts and howls it was difficult to inquire about anything or understand what was said. At times new columns of smoke from beyond the river rolled toward them, smoke black and so heavy that it moved near the ground, hiding houses, people, and every object, just as night does. The fervor of a July day, increased by the heat of the burning parts of the city, became unendurable. Smoke pained the eyes; breath failed in men's breasts. Even the inhabitants who, hoping that the fire would not cross the river, had remained in their houses so far, began to leave them, and the throng increased hourly. The prætorians accompanying Vinicius were in the rear. In the crush some one wounded his horse with a hammer; the beast threw up its bloody head, reared, and refused obedience. The crowd recognized in Vinicius an Augustian by his rich tunic, and at once cries were raised round about, "Death to Nero and his incendiaries!" This was a moment of terrible danger; hundreds of hands were stretched toward Vinicius; but his frightened horse bore him away, trampling people as he went, and the next moment a new wave of black smoke rolled in and filled the street with darkness. Vinicius, seeing that he could not ride past, sprang to the earth and rushed forward on foot, slipping along walls, and at times waiting till the fleeing multitude passed him. He said to himself in spirit that these were vain efforts.

At times he stopped and rubbed his eyes. Tearing off the edge of his tunic, he covered his nose and mouth with it and ran on. As he approached the river the heat increased terribly. Vinicius, knowing that the fire had begun at the Circus Maximus, thought at first that that heat came from its cinders and from the Forum Boarium and the Velabrum, which, situated near by, must be also in flames. But the heat was growing unendurable. One old man on crutches and fleeing, the last whom Vinicius noticed, cried: "Go not near the bridge of Cestius! The whole island is on fire!" It was, indeed, impossible to be deceived any longer. At the turn toward the Vicus Judæorum the young tribune saw flames amid clouds of smoke. Not only the island was burning, but the Trans-Tiber and the other end of the street on which he ran.

The thunder of the flames was more terrible than the roar of wild beasts, and the hour had come now in which he must think of his own safety, for the river of fire was flowing nearer and nearer from the direction of the island, and rolls of smoke covered the alley almost completely. The taper which he carried was quenched from the current of air. Vinicius rushed to the street, and ran at full speed toward the Via Portuensis, whence he had come; the fire seemed to pursue him with burning breath, now surrounding him with fresh clouds of smoke, now covering him with sparks, which fell on his hair, neck, and clothing. The tunic began to smoulder on him in places; he cared not, but ran forward lest he might be stifled from smoke. He had the taste of soot and burning in his mouth; his throat and lungs were as if on fire. The blood rushed to his head, and at moments all things, even the smoke itself, seemed red to him.

Then he thought: "This is living fire! Better throw myself upon the ground and quickly perish." The running tortured him more and more. His head, neck, and shoulders were streaming with sweat, which scalded like boiling water.

But he ran on as if drunk, staggering from one side of the street to the other. Meanwhile something changed in that monstrous conflagration which had embraced the giant city. Everything which till then had only glimmered, burst forth visibly into one sea of flame; the wind had ceased to bring smoke. That smoke which had collected in the streets was borne away by a mad whirl of heated air. That whirl drove with it millions of sparks, so that Vinicius was running in a fiery cloud, as it were. But he was able to see before him all the better, and in a moment, almost when he was ready to fall, he saw the end of the street. That sight gave him fresh strength. Passing the corner, he found himself in a street which led to the Via Portuensis and the Codetan Field. The sparks ceased to drive him. He understood that if he could run to the Via Portuensis he was safe, even were he to faint on it.

At the end of the street he saw again a cloud, as it seemed, which stopped the exit. "If that is smoke," thought he, "I cannot pass." He ran with the remnant of his strength. On the way he threw off his tunic, which, on fire from the sparks, was burning him like the shirt of Nessus, having only a *capitium* around his head and before his mouth. When he had run farther, he saw that what he had taken for smoke was dust, from which rose a multitude of cries and voices.

"The rabble are plundering houses," thought Vinicius. But he ran toward the voices. In any case people were there; they might assist him. In this hope he shouted for aid with all his might before he reached them. But this was his last effort. It grew redder still in his eyes, breath failed his lungs, strength failed his bones; he fell.

They heard him, however, or rather saw him. Two men ran with gourds full of water. Vinicius, who had fallen from exhaustion, but had not lost consciousness, seized a gourd with both hands and emptied one-half of it.

"Thanks," said he; "place me on my feet; I can walk on alone."

The other laborer poured water on his head; the two not only placed him on his feet, but raised him from the ground and carried him to the others, who surrounded him and asked if he had suffered seriously. This tenderness astonished Vinicius.

"People, who are ye?" asked he.

"We are breaking down houses, so that the fire may not reach the Via Portuensis," answered one of the laborers.

"Ye came to my aid when I had fallen. Thanks to you."

"We are not permitted to refuse aid," answered a number of voices.

Vinicius, who from early morning had seen brutal crowds slaying and robbing, looked with more attention on the faces around him and said:

"May Christ reward you."

"Praise to his name!" exclaimed a whole chorus of voices.

It was evening, but one could see as in daylight, for the conflagration had increased. It seemed that not single parts of the city were burning, but the whole city through the length and the breadth of it. The sky was red as far as the eye could see it, and that night in the world was a red night.

The light from the burning city filled the sky as far as human eye could reach. The moon rose large and full from behind the mountains, and, inflamed at once by the glare, took on the color of heated brass. It seemed to look with amazement on the world-ruling city which was perishing. In the rose-colored abysses of heaven rose-colored stars were glittering; but in distinction from usual nights the earth was brighter than the heavens. Rome, like a giant pile, illuminated the whole Campania.

In the bloody light were seen distant mountains, towns, villas, temples, monuments, and the aqueducts stretching toward the city from all the adjacent hills; on the aqueducts were swarms of people who had gathered there for safety or to gaze at the burning. Meanwhile the dreadful element was embracing new divisions of the city. It was impossible to doubt that criminal hands were spreading the fire, since new conflagrations were breaking out all the time in places remote from the principal fire.

From the heights on which Rome was founded the flames flowed like waves of the sea into the valleys densely occupied by houses—houses of five and six stories, full of shops, booths, movable wooden amphitheatres, built to accommodate various spectacles; and finally storehouses of wood, olives, grain, nuts, pine cones, the kernels of which nourished the more needy population, and clothing, which through Cæsar's favor was distributed from time to time among the rabble huddled into

narrow alleys. In those places the fire, finding abundance of in-
flammable materials, became almost a series of explosions, and
took possession of whole streets with unheard-of rapidity.
People encamping outside the city or standing on the aqueducts knew from the color of the flame what was burning. The
furious power of the wind carried forth from the fiery gulf
thousands and millions of burning shells of walnuts and al-
monds, which, shooting suddenly into the sky, like countless
flocks of bright butterflies, burst with a crackling, or, driven
by the wind, fell in other parts of the city, on aqueducts and
fields beyond Rome.

All thought of rescue seemed out of place; confusion increased every moment, for on one side the population of the
city was fleeing through every gate to places outside; on the
other the fire had lured in thousands of people from the neighborhood, such as dwellers in small towns, peasants, and half-
wild shepherds of the Campania brought in by hope of plunder.
The shout, "Rome is perishing!" did not leave the lips of the
crowd; the ruin of the city seemed at that time to end every
rule and loosen all bonds which hitherto had joined people in
a single integrity. The mob, in which slaves were more numerous, cared nothing for the lordship of Rome. Destruction
of the city could only free them; hence here and there they
assumed a threatening attitude.

Violence and robbery were extending. It seemed that only
the spectacle of the perishing city arrested attention, and restrained for the moment an outburst of slaughter, which would
begin as soon as the city was turned into ruins. Hundreds of
thousands of slaves, forgetting that Rome, besides temples and
walls, possessed some tens of legions in all parts of the world,
appeared merely waiting for a watchword and a leader. People
began to mention the name of Spartacus; but Spartacus was
not alive. Meanwhile citizens assembled and armed themselves each with what he could. The most monstrous reports
were current at all the gates. Some declared that Vulcan,
commanded by Jupiter, was destroying the city with fire from
beneath the earth; others that Vesta was taking vengeance for
Rubria. People with these convictions did not care to save
anything, but, besieging the temples, implored mercy of the

gods. It was repeated most generally, however, that Cæsar had given command to burn Rome, so as to free himself from odors which rose from the Subura, and build a new city under the name of Neronia. Rage seized the populace at thought of this; and if, as Vinicius believed, a leader had taken advantage of that outburst of hatred, Nero's hour would have struck whole years before it did.

It was said also that Cæsar had gone mad, that he would command prætorians and gladiators to fall upon the people and make a general slaughter. Others swore by the gods that wild beasts had been let out of all the *vivaria* at Bronzebeard's command. Men had seen on the streets lions with burning manes, and mad elephants and bisons, trampling down people in crowds. There was even some truth in this; for in certain places elephants, at sight of the approaching fire, had burst the vivaria, and, gaining their freedom, rushed away from the fire in wild fright, destroying everything before them like a tempest. Public report estimated at tens of thousands the number of persons who had perished in the conflagration. In truth a great number had perished. There were people who, losing all their property, or those dearest their hearts, threw themselves willingly into the flames from despair. Others were suffocated by smoke. In the middle of the city, between the Capitol on one side, and the Quirinal, the Viminal, and the Esquiline on the other, as also between the Palatine and the Cælian hill, where the streets were most densely occupied, the fire began in so many places at once that whole crowds of people, while fleeing in one direction, struck unexpectedly on a new wall of fire in front of them, and died a dreadful death in a deluge of flame.

In terror, in distraction and bewilderment, people knew not where to flee. The streets were obstructed with goods and in many narrow places were simply closed. Those who took refuge in those markets and squares of the city where the Flavian Amphitheatre stood afterward, near the temple of the Earth, near the Portico of Silvia, and higher up, at the temples of Juno and Lucinia, between the Clivus Virbius and the old Esquiline gate, perished from heat, surrounded by a sea of fire. In places not reached by the flames were found afterward

hundreds of bodies burned to a crisp, though here and there
unfortunates tore up flat stones and half buried themselves in
defence against the heat. Hardly a family inhabiting the
centre of the city survived in full; hence along the walls, at the
gates, on all roads were heard howls of despairing women, calling on the dear names of those who had perished in the throng
or the fire.

And so, while some were imploring the gods, others blas-
phemed them because of this awful catastrophe. Old men
were seen coming from the temple of Jupiter Liberator,
stretching forth their hands and crying, "If thou be a liberator, save thy altars and the city!" But despair turned mainly
against the old Roman gods, who, in the minds of the populace,
were bound to watch over the city more carefully than others.
They had proved themselves powerless; hence were insulted.
On the other hand, it happened on the Via Asinaria that when
a company of Egyptian priests appeared conducting a statue of
Isis, which they had saved from the temple near the Porta Cæ-
limontana, a crowd of people rushed among the priests, attached
themselves to the chariot, which they drew to the Appian
gate, and seizing the statue placed it in the temple of Mars,
overwhelming the priests of that deity who dared to resist
them.

In other places people invoked Serapis, Baal, or Jehovah,
whose adherents, swarming out of the alleys in the neighborhood of the Subura and the Trans-Tiber, filled with shouts and
uproar the fields near the walls. In their cries were heard tones
as if of triumph; when, therefore, some of the citizens joined
the chorus and glorified "the Lord of the World," others, in-
dignant at this glad shouting, strove to repress it by violence.
Here and there hymns were heard, sung by men in the bloom of
life, by old men, by women and children—hymns wonderful and
solemn, whose meaning they understood not, but in which
were repeated from moment to moment the words "Behold the
Judge cometh in the day of wrath and disaster." Thus this
deluge of restless and sleepless people encircled the burning
city, like a tempest-driven sea. But neither despair nor blasphemy nor hymn helped in any way.

The destruction seemed as irresistible, perfect, and pitiless

as Predestination itself.   Around Pompey's Amphitheatre
stores of hemp caught fire, and ropes used in circuses, arenas,
and every kind of machine at the games, and with them the
adjoining buildings containing barrels of pitch with which ropes
were smeared.   In a few hours all that part of the city beyond
which lay the Campus Martius was so lighted by bright yellow
flames that for a time it seemed to the spectators, only half conscious from terror, that in the general ruin the order of night
and day had been lost, and that they were looking at sunshine.
But later a monstrous bloody gleam extinguished all other col-
ors of flame.   From the sea of fire shot up to the heated sky
gigantic fountains, and pillars of flame spreading at their summits into fiery branches and feathers; then the wind bore them
away, turned them into golden threads, into hair, into sparks,
and swept them on over the Campania toward the Alban hills.
The night became brighter; the air itself seemed penetrated,
not only with light, but with flame.   The Tiber flowed on as
living fire.   The hapless city was turned into one pandemonium.
The conflagration seized more and more space, took hills by
storm, flooded level places, drowned valleys, raged, roared, and
thundered.

The city burned on.   The Circus Maximus had fallen in
ruins.   Entire streets and alleys in parts which began to burn
first were falling in turn.   After every fall pillars of flame rose
for a time to the very sky.   The wind had changed, and blew
now with mighty force from the sea, bearing toward the Cælian,
the Esquiline, and the Viminal rivers of flame, brands, and cinders.   Still the authorities provided for rescue.   At command
of Tigellinus, who had hastened from Antium the third day
before, houses on the Esquiline were torn down so that the
fire, reaching empty spaces, died of itself.   That was, however,
undertaken solely to save a remnant of the city; to save that
which was burning was not to be thought of.   There was need
also to guard against further results of the ruin.   Incalculable
wealth had perished in Rome; all the property of its citizens
had vanished; hundreds of thousands of people were wandering
in utter want outside the walls.   Hunger had begun to pinch
this throng the second day, for the immense stores of provisions
in the city had burned with it.   In the universal disorder and

in the destruction of authority no one had thought of furnishing new supplies.   Only after the arrival of Tigellinus were proper orders sent to Ostia; but meanwhile the people had grown more threatening.

Besides flour, as much baked bread as possible was brought at his command, not only from Ostia, but from all towns and neighboring villages.   When the first instalment came at night to the Emporium, the people broke the chief gate toward the Aventine, seized all supplies in the twinkle of an eye, and caused terrible disturbance.   In the light of the conflagration they fought for loaves, and trampled many of them into the earth. Flour from torn bags whitened like snow the whole space from the granary to the arches of Drusus and Germanicus.   The uproar continued till soldiers seized the building and dispersed the crowd with arrows and missiles.

Never since the invasion by the Gauls under Brennus had Rome beheld such disaster.   People in despair compared the two conflagrations.   But in the time of Brennus the Capitol re-mained.   Now the Capitol was encircled by a dreadful wreath of flame.   The marbles, it is true, were not blazing; but at night, when the wind swept the flames aside for a moment, rows of columns in the lofty sanctuary of Jove were visible, red as glowing coals.   In the days of Brennus, moreover, Rome had a disciplined integral people, attached to the city and its altars; but now crowds of a many-tongued populace roamed nomad-like around the walls of burning Rome, people composed for the greater part of slaves and freedmen, excited, disorderly, and ready, under the pressure of want, to turn against authority and the city.

But the very immensity of the fire which terrified every heart disarmed the crowd in a certain measure.   After fire might come famine and disease; and to complete the misfortune the terrible heat of July had appeared.   It was impossible to breathe air inflamed both by fire and the sun.   Night brought no relief; on the contrary, it presented a hell.   During daylight an awful and ominous spectacle met the eye.   In the centre a giant city on heights was turned into a roaring volcano; round about as far as the Alban hills was one boundless camp, formed of sheds, tents, huts, vehicles, bales, packs, stands, fires, and all covered with smoke and dust, lighted by sun rays reddened by passing through smoke—everything filled with roars, shouts, threats, hatred, and terror, a monstrous swarm of men, women, and children. Mingled with *quirites* were Greeks, shaggy men from the North with blue eyes, Africans, and Asiatics; among citizens were slaves, freedmen, gladiators, merchants, mechanics, servants, and soldiers—a real sea of people, flowing around the island of fire.

Various reports moved this sea as wind does a real one. These reports were favorable and unfavorable. People told of immense supplies of wheat and clothing to be brought to the Emporium and distributed gratis. It was said, too, that provinces in Asia and Africa would be stripped of their wealth at Cæsar's command, and the treasures thus gained be given to the inhabitants of Rome, so that each man might build his own dwelling.

But it was noised about also that water in the aqueducts had been poisoned; that Nero intended to annihilate the city, destroy the inhabitants to the last person, then move to Greece or to Egypt, and rule the world from a new place. Each report ran with lightning speed, and each found belief among the rabble, causing outbursts of hope, anger, terror, or rage. Finally a kind of fever mastered those nomadic thousands. The belief of Christians that the end of the world by fire was at hand spread even among adherents of the gods and extended daily. People fell into torpor or madness. In clouds lighted by the burning, gods were seen gazing down on the ruin; hands were stretched toward those gods then to implore pity or send them curses.

Meanwhile soldiers, aided by a certain number of inhabitants, continued to tear down houses on the Esquiline and the Cælian, as also in the Trans-Tiber; these divisions were saved therefore in considerable part. But in the city itself were destroyed incalculable treasures accumulated through centuries of conquest—priceless works of art, splendid temples, the most precious monuments of Rome's past and Rome's glory. They foresaw that of all Rome there would remain barely a few parts on the edges, and that hundreds of thousands of people would be without a roof. Some spread reports that the soldiers were tearing down houses, not to stop the fire, but to prevent any part of the city from being saved. Tigellinus sent courier after courier to Antium, imploring Cæsar in each letter to come and calm the despairing people with his presence. But Nero moved only when fire had seized the *domus transitoria* and he hurried so as not to miss the moment in which the conflagration should be at its highest.

Meanwhile fire had reached the Via Nomentana, but turned from it at once with a change of wind toward the Via Lata and the Tiber. It surrounded the Capitol, spread along the Forum Boarium, destroyed everything which it had spared before, and approached the Palatine a second time.

Tigellinus, assembling all the prætorian forces, despatched courier after courier to Cæsar with an announcement that he would lose nothing of the grandeur of the spectacle, for the fire had increased.

But Nero, who was on the road, wished to come at night, so as to sate himself all the better with a view of the perishing capital. Therefore he halted, in the neighborhood of Aqua Albana, and, summoning to his tent the tragedian Aliturus, decided with his aid on posture, look, and expression; learned fitting gestures, disputing with the actor stubbornly whether at the words, "O sacred city, which seemed more enduring than Ida," he was to raise both hands, or, holding in one the *forminga*, drop it by his side, and raise only the other. This question seemed to him then more important than all others. Starting at last about nightfall, he took counsel of Petronius also whether to the lines describing the catastrophe he might add a few magnificent blasphemies against the gods, and whether, considered from the standpoint of art, they would not have rushed spontaneously from the mouth of a man in such a position, a man who was losing his birthplace.

At length he approached the walls about midnight with his numerous court, composed of whole detachments of nobles, senators, knights, freedmen, slaves, women, and children. Sixteen thousand prætorians, arranged in line of battle along the road, guarded the peace and safety of his entrance, and held the excited populace at a proper distance. The people cursed, shouted, and hissed on seeing the retinue, but dared not attack

it. In many places, however, applause was given by the rabble, which, owning nothing, had lost nothing in the fire, and
which hoped for a more bountiful distribution than usual of
wheat, olives, clothing, and money. Finally, shouts, hissing,
and applause were drowned in the blare of horns and trumpets,
which Tigellinus had caused to be sounded.

Nero, on arriving at the Ostian gate, halted, and said:
"Houseless ruler of a houseless people, where shall I lay my
unfortunate head for the night?"

After he had passed the Clivus Delphini, he ascended the
Appian aqueduct on steps prepared purposely. After him followed the Augustians and a choir of singers, bearing *citharæ*,
lutes, and other musical instruments.

And all held the breath in their breasts, waiting to learn if
he would say some great words, which for their own safety
they ought to remember. But he stood solemn, silent, in a
purple mantle and a wreath of golden laurels, gazing at the
raging might of the flames.

When Terpnos gave him a golden lute, he raised his eyes
to the sky, filled with the conflagration, as if he were waiting
for inspiration. The people pointed at him from afar as he
stood in the bloody gleam. In the distance fiery serpents were
hissing. The ancient and most sacred edifices were in flames;
the temple of Hercules, reared by Evander, was burning; the
temple of Jupiter Stator was burning, the temple of Luna, built
by Servius Tullius, the house of Numa Pompilius, the sanctuary of Vesta with the *penates* of the Roman people; through
waving flames the Capitol appeared at intervals; the past and
the spirit of Rome were burning. But Cæsar was there with a
lute in his hand and a theatrical expression on his face, not
thinking of his perishing country, but of his posture and the
prophetic words with which he might describe best the greatness of the catastrophe, rouse most admiration, and receive the
warmest plaudits.

He detested that city, he detested its inhabitants, he loved
only his own songs and verses; hence he rejoiced in heart that
at last he saw a tragedy like that which he was writing. The
poet was happy, the declaimer felt inspired, the seeker for emotions was delighted at the awful sight, and thought with rapt-

ure that even the destruction of Troy was as nothing if compared with the destruction of that giant city. What more
could he desire? There was world-ruling Rome in flames, and
he, standing on the arches of the aqueduct with a golden lute,
conspicuous, purple, admired, magnificent, and poetic. Down
below, somewhere in the darkness, the people are muttering
and storming; let them mutter! Ages will elapse, thousands
of years will pass, but mankind will remember and glorify the
poet who that night sang the fall and the burning of Troy.
What was Homer compared with him? What Apollo himself
with his hollowed-out lute?

Here he raised his hands, and, striking the strings, with
an exaggerated theatrical gesture pronounced the words of
Priam:

"O nest of my fathers, O dear cradle!" His voice in the
open air, with the roar of the conflagration, and the distant
murmur of crowding thousands, seemed marvellously weak,
uncertain, and low, and the sound of the accompaniment like
the buzzing of insects. But senators, dignitaries, and Augustians, assembled on the aqueduct, bowed their heads and listened in silent rapture. He sang long, and his motive was
ever sadder. At moments, when he stopped to catch breath,
the chorus of singers repeated the last verse; then Nero cast
the tragic *syrma* from his shoulder with a gesture learned
from Aliturus, struck the lute, and sang on. When he had
finished the lines composed, he improvised, using grandiose
comparisons in the spectacle unfolded before him. His face
began to change. He was not moved, it is true, by the destruction of his country's capital; but he was delighted and moved
with the pathos of his own words to such a degree that his
eyes filled with tears on a sudden.

At last he dropped the lute to his feet with a clatter, and,
wrapping himself in the syrma, stood as if petrified, like one
of those statues of Niobe which ornamented the courtyard of
the Palatine. Soon a storm of applause broke the silence. But
in the distance this was answered by the howling of multitudes.
No one doubted then that Cæsar had given command to burn
the city, so as to afford himself a spectacle and sing a song
at it.

TACITUS

There followed a dreadful disaster, whether fortuitously or by the wicked contrivance of the prince is not determined, for both are asserted by historians; but of all the calamities which ever befell this city from the rage of fire, this was the most terrible and severe.   It broke out in that part of the Circus which is contiguous to mounts Palatine and Cælius, where, by reason of shops in which were kept such goods as minister aliment to fire, the moment it commenced it acquired strength, and, being accelerated by the wind, it spread at once through the whole extent of the Circus: for neither were the houses secured by enclosures nor the temples environed with walls, nor was there any other obstacle to intercept its progress; but the flame, spreading every way impetuously, invaded first the lower regions of the city, then mounted to the higher; then again ravaging the lower, it baffled every effort to extinguish it, by the rapidity of its destructive course, and from the liability of the city to conflagration, in consequence of the narrow and intricate alleys, and the irregularity of the streets in ancient Rome.

Add to this the wailings of terrified women, the infirm condition of the aged, and the helplessness of childhood; such as strove to provide for themselves and those who labored to assist others; these dragging the feeble, those waiting for them; some hurrying, others lingering; altogether created a scene of universal confusion and embarrassment: and while they looked back upon the danger in their rear, they often found themselves beset before and on their sides; or, if they had escaped into the quarters adjoining, these, too, were already seized by the devouring flames; even the parts which they believed remote and exempt were found to be in the same distress.   At last, not knowing what to shun or where to seek sanctuary, they crowded the streets and lay along in the open fields.   Some, from the loss of their whole substance, even the means of their daily sustenance, others, from affection for their relations whom they had not been able to snatch from the flames, suffered themselves to perish in them, though they had opportunity to escape.   Neither dared any man offer to check the fire, so repeated were the menaces of many who forbade to extinguish it;

and because others openly threw firebrands, with loud declarations "that they had one who authorized them"; whether they did it that they might plunder with the less restraint or in consequence of orders given.

Nero, who was at that juncture sojourning at Antium, did not return to the city till the fire approached that quarter of his house which connected the palace with the gardens of Mæcenas; nor could it, however, be prevented from devouring the house and palace and everything around. But for the relief of the people, thus destitute and driven from their dwellings, he opened the field of Mars and the monumental edifices erected by Agrippa, and even his own gardens. He likewise reared temporary houses for the reception of the forlorn multitude, and from Ostia and the neighboring cities were brought, up the river, household necessaries, and the price of grain was reduced to three sesterces the measure. All which proceedings, though of a popular character, were thrown away, because a rumor had become universally current "that at the very time when the city was in flames, Nero, going on the stage of his private theatre, sang *The Destruction of Troy*, assimilating the present disaster to that catastrophe of ancient times."

At length, on the sixth day, the conflagration was stayed at the foot of Esquiliæ, by pulling down an immense quantity of buildings, so that an open space, and, as it were, void air, might check the raging element by breaking the continuity. But ere the consternation had subsided the fire broke out afresh, with no little violence, but in regions more spacious, and therefore with less destruction of human life; but more extensive havoc was made of the temples and the porticoes dedicated to amusement. This conflagration, too, was the subject of more censorious remark, as it arose in the Æmilian possessions of Tigellinus, and Nero seemed to aim at the glory of building a new city and calling it by his own name; for, of the fourteen sections into which Rome is divided, four were still standing entire, three were levelled with the ground, and in the seven others there remained only here and there a few remnants of houses, shattered and half consumed.

It were no very easy task to recount the number of tenements and temples which were lost; but the following, most venerable for antiquity and sanctity, were consumed: that dedicated by Servius Tullius to the Moon; the temple and great altar consecrated by Evander the Arcadian to Hercules while present; the chapel vowed by Romulus to Jupiter Stator; the palace of Numa with the temple of Vesta, and in it the tutelar gods of Rome. Moreover, the treasures accumulated by so many victories, the beautiful productions of Greek artists, ancient writings of authors celebrated for genius, and till then preserved entire, were consumed; and though great was the beauty of the city, in its renovated form, the older inhabitants remembered many decorations of the ancient which could not be replaced in the modern city. There were some who remarked that the commencement of this fire showed itself on the fourteenth before the calends of July, the day on which the Senones set fire to the captured city. Others carried their investigation so far as to determine that an equal number of years, months, and days intervened between the two fires.

To proceed: Nero appropriated to his own purposes the ruins of his country,[1] and founded upon them a palace; in which the old-fashioned, and, in those luxurious times, common ornaments of gold and precious stones, were not so much the objects of attraction as lands and lakes; in one part, woods like vast deserts; in another part, open spaces and expansive prospects. The projectors and superintendents of this plan were Severus and Celer, men of such ingenuity and daring enterprise as to attempt to conquer by art the obstacles of nature and fool away the treasures of the prince. They had even undertaken to sink a navigable canal from the lake Avernus to the mouth of the Tiber, over an arid shore or through opposing mountains; nor indeed does there occur anything of a humid nature for supplying water except the Pomptine marshes; the rest is either craggy rock or a parched soil; and had it even been possible to break through these obstructions, the toil had

---

[1] According to Suetonius, Nero turned the public calamity to his own private advantage. He promised to remove the bodies that lay amid the ruins, and to clear the ground at his own expense. By that artifice he secured all the remaining property of the unhappy sufferers for his own use. To add to his ill-gotten store, he levied contributions in the provinces, and by those means collected an immense sum.

been intolerable and disproportioned to the object. Nero, however, who longed to achieve things that exceeded credibility,
exerted all his might to perforate the mountains adjoining to
Avernus, and to this day there remain traces of his abortive
project.

But the rest of the old site not occupied by his palace was
laid out, not as after the Gallic fire without discrimination and
regularity, but with the lines of streets measured out, broad
spaces left for transit, the height of the buildings limited, open
areas left, and porticoes added to protect the front of the clustered dwellings: these porticoes Nero engaged to rear at his
own expense, and then to deliver to each proprietor the areas
about them cleared. He, moreover, proposed rewards propor-
tioned to every man's rank and private substance, and fixed a
day within which, if their houses, single and clustered, were
finished, they should receive them. He appointed the marshes
of Ostia for a receptacle of the rubbish, and that the vessels
which had conveyed grain up the Tiber should return laden
with rubbish; that the buildings themselves should be raised a
certain portion of their height without beams, and arched with
stone from the quarries of Gabii or Alba, that stone being proof
against fire; that over the water springs, which had been im-
properly intercepted by private individuals, overseers should be
placed, to provide for their flowing in greater abundance, and
in a greater number of places, for the supply of the public; that
every housekeeper should have in his yard means for extinguish-
ing fire, neither should there be party walls, but every house
should be enclosed by its own walls.[1]

These regulations, which were favorably received, in consideration of their utility, were also a source of beauty to the
new city; yet some there were who believed that the ancient
form was more conducive to health, as from the narrowness of
the streets and the height of the buildings the rays of the sun
were more excluded; whereas now, the spacious breadth of
the streets, without any shade to protect it, was more intensely
heated in warm weather.

Such were the provisions made by human counsels. The

[1] By a law of the Twelve Tables, it was provided that a space of something more than two feet was to be left between all new-built houses.

gods were next addressed with expiations, and recourse had to
the sibyl's books. By admonition from them to Vulcan, Ceres,
and Proserpina, supplicatory sacrifices were made, and Juno
propitiated by the matrons, first in the Capitol, then upon the
nearest shore, where, by water drawn from the sea, the temple
and image of the goddess were besprinkled; the ceremony of
placing the goddess in her sacred chair, and her vigil, were celebrated by ladies who had husbands. But not all the relief
that could come from man, not all the bounties that the prince
could bestow, nor all the atonements which could be presented
to the gods availed to relieve Nero from the infamy of being
believed to have ordered the conflagration. Hence, to suppress
the rumor, he falsely charged with the guilt and punished with
the most exquisite tortures the persons commonly called Christians, who were hated for their enormities.

Christus, the founder of that name, was put to death as a
criminal by Pontius Pilate, procurator of Judea, in the reign of
Tiberius; but the pernicious superstition, repressed for a time,
broke out again, not only through Judea, where the mischief
originated, but through the city of Rome also, whither all
things horrible and disgraceful flow from all quarters as to a
common receptacle and where they are encouraged. Accordingly first those were seized who confessed they were Christians; next on their information a vast multitude were convicted,
not so much on the charge of burning the city as of hating the
human race. And in their deaths they were also made the subjects of sport, for they were covered with the hides of wild
beasts, and worried to death by dogs, or nailed to crosses, or
set fire to, and when day declined, burned to serve for nocturnal lights. Nero offered his own gardens for that spectacle,
and exhibited a Circensien game, indiscriminately mingling
with the common people in the habit of a charioteer, or else
standing in his chariot. Whence a feeling of compassion arose
toward the sufferers, though guilty and deserving to be made
examples of by capital punishment, because they seemed not to
be cut off for the public good, but victims to the ferocity of
one man.

In the mean time, in order to supply money all Italy was
pillaged, the provinces ruined, both the people in alliance with

us and the states which are called free.   Even the gods were
not exempt from plunder on this occasion, their temples in the
city being despoiled, and all the gold conveyed away which the
Roman people, in every age, either in gratitude for triumphs
or in fulfilment of vows, had consecrated, in times of prosperity,
or in seasons of dismay.   Through Greece and Asia, indeed,
the gifts and oblations and even the statues of the deities were
carried off.

PERSECUTION OF THE CHRISTIANS UNDER NERO

A.D. 64-68

FREDERIC WILLIAM FARRAR

Down to the reign of Nero Christians in the Roman Empire were regarded by the ruling powers merely as a Jewish sect, harmless and guilty
of nothing which could call for the interference of the State with their
ways of life or of worship. They were therefore unmolested. But during the reign of the infamous Emperor in whom they saw antichrist and
the actual embodiment of the symbolic monstrosities of the Apocalypse,
the Christians began to be recognized as a separate people, and from
milder persecutions at first, under cover of legal procedure, they were
soon subjected to outrages, tortures, and deaths than which history has
none more revolting and pitiful to record. In Kaulbach's great painting
of Nero's persecution there is enough of portrayal and suggestion to add
a terrible vividness to the ordinary historian's word-pictures. The Emperor, surrounded by his boon companions, stands on his garden terrace
to receive divine honors, while a group of suffering Christians—among
them St. Peter, crucified head down, and St. Paul, passionately protesting against the diabolical work—move to compassion a company of elderly
men and a body of German soldiers who look upon the horrible spectacle
of martyrdom.

This, the first persecution of the Christians, reached its culminating
point of ferocity in A.D. 64, after Nero had been accused of kindling, or
conniving at the work of those who did kindle, the great fire in Rome.
In order to divert attention, even if he could not turn suspicion, from
himself, having charged the Christians with causing the conflagration, he
ordered the atrocities which added a still darker stain to his personal and
imperial record of shameless crime and savage inhumanity. First such
as confessed themselves to be Christians were dealt with, and from
these information was extorted on which vast numbers were convicted,
"not so much on the charge of burning the city as of hating the human
race."

Nero's character and acts have been depicted by many writers and
in famous works of art, but not even the pencil of Kaulbach can make
more keen the realization of those scenes enacted in this persecution

than the thrilling narration of Farrar, which for picturesque eloquence, fired with dramatic intensity, has seldom been surpassed in English literature.

NERO was so secure in his absolutism, he had hitherto found it so impossible to shock the feelings of the people or to exhaust the terrified adulation of the senate, that he was usually indifferent to the pasquinades which were constantly holding up his name to execration and contempt. But now [1] he felt that he had gone too far, and that his power would be seriously imperilled if he did not succeed in diverting the suspicions of the populace. He was perfectly aware that when the people in the streets cursed those who set fire to the city they meant to curse *him*. If he did not take some immediate step, he felt that he might perish, as Gaius had perished before him, by the dagger of the assassin.

It is at this point of his career that Nero becomes a prominent figure in the history of the Church. It was this phase of cruelty which seemed to throw a blood-red light over his whole character and led men to look on him as the very incarnation of the world-power in its most demoniac aspect, as worse than the Antiochus Epiphanes of Daniel's Apocalypse, as the Man of Sin whom—in language figurative indeed, yet awfully true— the Lord should slay with the breath of his mouth and destroy with the brightness of his coming, for Nero endeavored to fix the odious crime of having destroyed the capital of the world upon the most innocent and faithful of his subjects —upon the only subjects who offered heartfelt prayers on his behalf—the Roman Christians. They were the defenceless victims of this horrible charge, for though they were the most harmless, they were also the most hated and the most slandered of living men.

Why he should have thought of singling out the Christians has always been a curious problem, for at this point St. Luke ends the Acts of the Apostles, perhaps purposely dropping the curtain, because it would have been perilous and useless to narrate the horrors in which the hitherto neutral or friendly Roman government began to play so disgraceful a part. Neither Tacitus, nor Suetonius, nor the Apocalypse, helps us to solve this particular problem. The Christians had filled no large

[1] In his behavior at the burning of Rome.

space in the eye of the world. Until the days of Domitian we do not hear of a single noble or distinguished person who had joined their ranks. That the Pudens and Claudia of Rom. xvi. were the Pudens and Claudia of Martial's *Epigrams* seems to me to be a baseless dream. If the "foreign superstition" with which Pomponia Græcina, wife of Aulus Plautius, the conqueror of Britain, was charged, and of which she was acquitted, was indeed, as has been suspected, the Christian religion, at any rate the name of Christianity was not alluded to by the ancient writers who had mentioned the circumstance. Even if Rom. xvi. was addressed to Rome, and not, as I believe, to Ephesus, "they of the household of Narcissus which were in the Lord" were unknown slaves, as also were "they of Cæsar's household."

The slaves and artisans, Jewish and Gentile, who formed the Christian community at Rome, had never in any way come into collision with the Roman government. They must have been the victims rather than the exciters of the messianic tumults—for such they are conjectured to have been—which led to the expulsion of the Jews from Rome by the futile edict of Claudius. Nay, so obedient and docile were they required to be by the very principles on which their morality was based, so far were they removed from the fierce independence of the Jewish zealots, that, in writing to them a few years earlier, the greatest of their leaders had urged upon them a payment of tribute and a submission to the higher powers, not only for wrath, but also for conscience' sake, because the earthly ruler, in his office of repressing evil works, is a minister of God. That the Christians were entirely innocent of the crime charged against them was well known both at the time and afterward. But how was it that Nero sought popularity and partly averted the deep rage which was rankling in many hearts against himself, by torturing men and women, on whose agonies he thought that the populace would gaze not only with a stolid indifference, but even with fierce satisfaction?

Gibbon has conjectured that the Christians were confounded with the Jews, and that the detestation universally felt for the latter fell with double force upon the former. Christians suffered even more than the Jews because of the calumnies so assiduously circulated against them, and from what appeared to the ancients to be the revolting absurdity of their peculiar tenets. "Nero," says Tacitus, "exposed to accusation, and tortured with the most exquisite penalties, a set of men detested for their enormities, whom the common people called ' Christians.' Christus, the founder of this sect, was executed during the reign of Tiberius, by the procurator Pontius Pilate, and the deadly superstition, suppressed for a time, began to burst out once more, not only throughout Judea, where the evil had its root, but even in the city, whither from every quarter all things horrible or shameful are drifted, and find their votaries."

The lordly disdain which prevented Tacitus from making any inquiry into the real views and character of the Christians is shown by the fact that he catches up the most baseless allegations against them. He talks of their doctrines as savage and shameful when they breathed the very spirit of peace and purity. He charges them with being animated by a hatred of their kind when their central tenet was a universal charity. The masses, he says, called them "Christians"; and while he almost apologizes for staining his page with so vulgar an appellation,[1] he merely mentions in passing that, though innocent of the charge of being turbulent incendiaries, on which they were tortured to death, they were yet a set of guilty and infamous sectaries, to be classed with the lowest dregs of Roman criminals.

But the haughty historian throws no light on one difficulty —namely, the circumstances which led to the *Christians* being thus singled out. The Jews were in no way involved in Nero's persecution. To persecute the Jews at Rome would not have

---

[1] There can be little doubt that the name "Christian"—so curiously hybrid, yet so richly expressive—was a nickname due to the wit of the Antiochenes, which exercised itself quite fearlessly even on the Roman emperors. They were not afraid to affix nicknames to Caracalla, and to call Julian Cecrops and Victimarius, with keen satire of his beard. It is clear that the sacred writers avoided the name, because it was employed by their enemies, and by them mingled with terms of the vilest opprobrium. It only became familiar when the virtues of Christians had shed lustre upon it, and when alike in its true form, and in the ignorant mispronunciation "Chrestians," it readily lent itself to valuable allegorical meanings.

been an easy matter. They were sufficiently numerous to be formidable, and had overawed Cicero in the zenith of his fame. Besides this, the Jewish religion was recognized, tolerated, licensed. Throughout the length and breadth of the empire no man, however much he and his race might be detested and despised, could have been burned or tortured for the mere fact of being a Jew. We hear of no Jewish martyrdoms or Jewish persecutions till we come to the times of the Jewish War, and then chiefly in Palestine itself. It is clear that a shedding of blood—in fact, some form or other of human sacrifice—was imperatively demanded by popular feeling as an expiation of the ruinous crime which had plunged so many thousands into the depths of misery. In vain had the sibylline books been once more consulted, and in vain had public prayer been offered, in accordance with their directions to Vulcan and the goddesses of Earth and Hades. In vain had the Roman matrons walked in procession in dark robes, and with their long hair unbound, to propitiate the insulted majesty of Juno, and to sprinkle with sea-water her ancient statue. In vain had largesses been lavished upon the people, and propitiatory sacrifices offered to the gods. In vain had public banquets been celebrated in honor of various deities. A crime had been committed, and Romans had perished unavenged. Blood cried for blood before the sullen suspicion against Nero could be averted or the indignation of heaven appeased.

Nero had always hated, persecuted, and exiled the philosophers, and no doubt, so far as he knew anything of the Christians—so far as he saw among his own countless slaves any who had embraced this superstition, which the *élite* of Rome described as not only new, but "execrable" and "malefic"—he would hate their gravity and purity, and feel for them that raging envy which is the tribute that virtue receives from vice. Moreover, St. Paul, in all probability, had recently stood before his tribunal, and though he had been acquitted on the special charges of turbulence and profanation, respecting which he had appealed to Cæsar, yet during the judicial inquiry Nero could hardly have failed to hear from the emissaries of the Sanhedrin many fierce slanders of a sect which was everywhere spoken against. The Jews were by far the deadliest enemies of the Christians, and two persons of Jewish proclivities were at this time in close proximity to the person of the Emperor. One was the pantomimist Aliturus, the other was Poppæa, the harlot-empress.[1] The Jews were in communication with these powerful favorites, and had even promised Nero that if his enemies ever prevailed at Rome he should have the kingdom of Jerusalem.[2]

It is not even impossible that there may have been a third dark and evil influence at work to undermine the Christians, for about this very time the unscrupulous Pharisee Flavius Josephus had availed himself of the intrigues of the palace to secure the liberation of some Jewish priests. If, as seems certain, the Jews had it in their power during the reign of Nero more or less to shape the whisper of the throne, does not historical induction drive us to conclude with some confidence that the suggestion of the Christians as scapegoats and victims came from them? St. Clement says in his Epistle that the Christians suffered *through jealousy*. *Whose* jealousy? Who can tell what dark secrets lie veiled under that suggestive word? Was Acte a Christian, and was Poppæa jealous of her? That suggestion seems at once inadequate and improbable, especially as Acte was not hurt. But there *was* a deadly jealousy at work against the new religion.

To the pagans Christianity was but a religious extravagance —contemptible, indeed, but otherwise insignificant. To the Jews, on the other hand, it was an object of hatred, which never stopped short of bloodshed when it possessed or could usurp the power, and which, though long suppressed by circum-

[1] According to John of Antioch and the *Chronicon Paschale*, Nero was originally favorable to the Christians, and put Pilate to death, for which the Jews plotted his murder. Poppæa's Judaism is inferred from her refusing to be burned, and requesting to be embalmed; from her adopting the custom of wearing a veil in the streets; from the favor which she showed to Aliturus and Josephus; and from the fact that Josephus speaks of her as a religious woman.

[2] Tiberius Alexander, the nephew of Philo, afterward procurator of Judea, was a person of influence at Rome; but he was a renegade, and would not be likely to hate the Christians. It is, however, remarkable that legend attributed the anger of Nero to the conversion of his mistress and a favorite slave.

stances, displayed itself in all the intensity of its virulence during the brief spasm of the dictatorship of Barcochba. Christianity was hateful to the Jews on *every* ground. It nullified their law. It liberated all Gentiles from the heavy yoke of that law, without thereby putting them on a lower level. It even tended to render those who were born Jews indifferent to the institutions of Mosaism. It was, as it were, a fatal revolt and schism from within, more dangerous than any assault from without. And, worse than all, it was by the Gentiles confounded with the Judaism which was its bitterest antagonist. While it sheltered its existence under the mantle of Judaism, as a *religio licita*, it drew down upon the religion from whose bosom it sprang all the scorn and hatred which were attached by the world to its own special tenets, for however much the Greeks and Romans despised the Jews, they despised still more the belief that the Lord and Saviour of the world was a crucified malefactor who had risen from the dead.

I see in the proselytism of Poppæa, guided by Jewish malice, the only adequate explanation of the first Christian persecution. Hers was the jealousy which had goaded Nero to matricide; hers not improbably was the instigated fanaticism of a proselyte which urged him to imbrue his hands in martyr blood. And she had her reward. A woman of whom Tacitus has not a word of good to say and who seems to have been repulsive even to a Suetonius, is handed down by the renegade Pharisee as "a devout woman"—as a worshipper of God!

And, indeed, when once the Christians were pointed out to the popular vengeance, many reasons would be adduced to prove their connection with the conflagration. Temples had perished—and were they not notorious enemies of the temples? Did not popular rumor charge them with nocturnal orgies and Thyestæan feasts? Suspicions of incendiarism were sometimes brought against Jews; but the Jews were not in the habit of talking, as these sectaries were, about a fire which should consume the world, and rejoicing in the prospect of that fiery consummation.[1] Nay, more, when pagans had bewailed the

[1] St. Peter—apparently thinking of the fire at Rome and its consequences—calls the persecution from which the Christians were suffering when he wrote his First Epistle a "conflagration."

destruction of the city and the loss of the ancient monuments of Rome, had not these pernicious people used ambiguous language, as though they joyously recognized in these events the signs of a coming end? Even when they tried to suppress all outward tokens of exultation, had they not listened to the fears and lamentations of their fellow-citizens with some sparkle in the eyes, and had they not answered with something of triumph in their tones? There was a satanic plausibility which dictated the selection of these particular victims. Because they hated the wickedness of the world, with its ruthless games and hideous idolatries, they were accused of hatred of the whole human race.

The charge of *incivisme,* so fatal in this reign of terror, was sufficient to ruin a body of men who scorned the sacrifices of heathendom and turned away with abhorrence from its banquets and gayeties. The cultivated classes looked down upon the Christians with a disdain which would hardly even mention them without an apology. The *canaille* of pagan cities insulted them with obscene inscriptions and blasphemous pictures on the very walls of the places where they met.[1] Nay, they were popularly known by nicknames, like *Sarmenticii* and *Semaxii* —untranslatable terms of opprobrium derived from the fagots with which they were burned and the stakes to which they were chained. Even the heroic courage which they displayed was described as being sheer obstinacy and stupid fanaticism.

But in the method chosen for the punishment of these saintly innocents Nero gave one more proof of the close connection between effeminate æstheticism and sanguinary callousness. As in old days, "on that opprobrious hill," the temple of Chemosh had stood close by that of Moloch, so now we find the *spoliarium* beside the *fornices*—Lust hard by Hate. The *carnificina* of Tiberius, at Capreæ, adjoined the *sellariæ.* History has given many proofs that no man is more systemati-

[1] Tertullian mentions one of these coarse caricatures—a figure with one foot hoofed, wearing a toga, carrying a book, and with long ass's ears, under which was written, "The God of the Christians, Onokoites." He says that Christians were actually charged with worshipping the head of an ass. The same preposterous calumny, with many others, is alluded to by Minucius Felix. The Christians were hence called *Asinarii.* Analogous calumnies were aimed at the Jews.

cally heartless than a corrupted debauchee. Like people, like prince. In the then condition of Rome, Nero well knew that a nation, " cruel, by their sports to blood inured," would be most likely to forget their miseries and condone their suspicions by mixing games and gayety with spectacles of refined and atrocious cruelty, of which, for eighteen centuries, the most passing record has sufficed to make men's blood run cold.

Tacitus tells us that " those who confessed were first seized, and then on their evidence *a huge multitude* [1] were convicted, not so much on the charge of incendiarism as for their hatred to mankind." Compressed and obscure as the sentence is, Tacitus clearly means to imply by the " confession " to which he alludes the confession of Christianity, and though he is not sufficiently generous to acquit the Christians absolutely of all complicity in the great crime, he distinctly says that they were made the scapegoats of a general indignation. The phrase— " a huge multitude "—is one of the few existing indications of the number of martyrs in the first persecution, and of the number of Christians in the Roman Church. When the historian says that they were convicted on the charge of " hatred against mankind " he shows how completely he confounds them with the Jews, against whom he elsewhere brings the accusation of " hostile feelings toward all except themselves."

Then the historian adds one casual but frightful sentence— a sentence which flings a dreadful light on the cruelty of Nero and the Roman mob. He adds: " And various forms of mockery were added to enhance their dying agonies. Covered with the skins of wild beasts, they were doomed to die by the mangling of dogs, or by being nailed to crosses, or to be set on fire and burned after twilight by way of nightly illumination. Nero offered his own garden for this show, and gave a chariot race, mingling with the mob in the dress of a charioteer, or actually driving about among them. Hence, guilty as the victims were, and deserving of the worst punishments, a feeling of compassion toward them began to rise, as men felt that they were being immolated not for any advantage to the Commonwealth, but to glut the savagery of a single man."

[1] Tertullian says that " Nero was the first who raged with the sword of Cæsar against this sect, which was then specially rising at Rome."

Imagine that awful scene, once witnessed by the silent obe-
lisk in the square before St. Peter's at Rome! Imagine it,
that we may realize how vast is the change which Christianity
has wrought in the feelings of mankind! There, where the
vast dome now rises, were once the gardens of Nero. They
were thronged with gay crowds, among whom the Emperor
moved in his frivolous degradation—and on every side were
men dying slowly on their cross of shame. Along the paths of
those gardens on the autumn nights were ghastly torches,
blackening the ground beneath them with streams of sulphur-
ous pitch, and each of those living torches was a martyr in his
shirt of fire. And in the amphitheatre hard by, in sight of
twenty thousand spectators, famished dogs were tearing to
pieces some of the best and purest of men and women, hide-
ously disguised in the skins of bears or wolves. Thus did Nero
baptize in the blood of martyrs the city which was to be for
ages the capital of the world!

The specific atrocity of such spectacles—unknown to the
earlier ages which they called barbarous—was due to the cold-
blooded selfishness, the hideous realism of a refined, delicate,
æsthetic age. To please these "lisping hawthorn buds," these
debauched and sanguinary dandies, art, forsooth, must know
nothing of morality; must accept and rejoice in a "healthy
animalism"; must estimate life by the number of its few wildest pulsations; must reckon that life is worthless without the
most thrilling experiences of horror or delight! Comedy must
be actual shame, and tragedy genuine bloodshed. When the
play of Afranius, called *The Conflagration*, was put on the
stage, a house must be really burned and its furniture really
plundered. In the mime called *Laureolus* an actor must really
be crucified and mangled by a bear, and really fling himself
down and deluge the stage with blood. When the heroism of
Mucius Scævola was represented, a real criminal must thrust
his hand without a groan into the flame and stand motionless
while it is being burned. Prometheus must be really chained
to his rock, and Dirce in very fact be tossed and gored by the
wild bull; and Orpheus be torn to pieces by a real bear; and
Icarus must really fly, even though he fall and be dashed to
death; and Hercules must ascend the funeral pyre and there

be veritably burned alive; and slaves and criminals must play their parts heroically in gold and purple till the flames envelop them.

It was the ultimate romance of a degraded and brutalized society. The Roman people, "victors once, now vile and base," could now only be amused by sanguinary melodrama. Fables must be made realities, and the criminal must gracefully transform his supreme agonies into amusements for the multitude by becoming a gladiator or a tragedian. Such were the spectacles at which Nero loved to gaze through his emerald eye-glass. And worse things than these—things indescribable, unutterable. Infamous mythologies were enacted, in which women must play their part in torments of shamefulness more intolerable than death. A St. Peter must hang upon the cross in the Pincian gardens, as a real Laureolus upon the stage. A Christian boy must be the Icarus, and a Christian man the Scævola or the Hercules or the Orpheus of the amphitheatre; and Christian women, modest maidens, holy matrons, must be the Danaids or the Proserpine or worse, and play their parts as priestesses of Saturn and Ceres, and in blood-stained dramas of the dead. No wonder that Nero became to Christian imagination the very incarnation of evil; the antichrist; the Wild Beast from the abyss; the delegate of the great red Dragon, with a diadem and a name of blasphemy upon his brow. No wonder that he left a furrow of horror in the hearts of men, and that, ten centuries after his death, the church of Sta. Maria del Popolo had to be built by Pope Pascal II to exorcise from Christian Rome his restless and miserable ghost!

And it struck them with deeper horror to see that the antichrist, so far from being abhorred, was generally popular. He was popular because he presented to the degraded populace their own image and similitude. The frog-like unclean spirits which proceeded, as it were, out of his mouth were potent with these dwellers in an atmosphere of pestilence. They had lost all love for freedom and nobleness; they cared only for doles and excitement. Even when the infamies of a Petronius had been superseded by the murderous orgies of Tigellinus, Nero was still everywhere welcomed with shouts as a god on earth and saluted on all coins as Apollo, as Hercules, as "the savior of the world." The poets still assured him that there was no deity in heaven who would not think it an honor to concede to him his prerogatives; that if he did not place himself well in the centre of Olympus, the equilibrium of the universe would be destroyed. Victims were slain along his path, and altars raised for him—for this wretch, whom an honest slave could not but despise and loathe—as though he was too great for mere human honors. Nay, more, he found adorers and imitators of his execrable example—an Otho, a Vitellius, a Domitian, a Commodus, a Caracalla, a Heliogabalus—to poison the air of the world. The lusts and hungers and furies of the world lamented him, and cherished his memory, and longed for his return.

And yet, though all bad men—who were the majority—admired and even loved him, he died the death of a dog. Tremendous as was the power of imperialism, the Romans often treated their individual emperors as Nero himself treated the Syrian goddess, whose image he first worshipped with awful veneration and then subjected to the most grotesque indignities, for retribution did not linger, and the vengeance fell at once on the guilty Emperor and the guilty city.

"Careless *seems* the Great Avenger: History's pages but record
One death-grapple in the darkness 'twixt false systems and the Word;
Truth forever on the scaffold, wrong forever on the throne,
Yet that scaffold sways the future, and behind the dim unknown
Standeth God within the shadow, keeping watch above his own." [1]

The air was full of prodigies. There were terrible storms; the plague wrought fearful ravages. Rumors spread from lip to lip. Men spoke of monstrous births; of deaths by lightning under strange circumstances; of a brazen statue of Nero melted by the flash; of places struck by the brand of heaven in fourteen regions of the city; of sudden darkenings of the sun. A hurricane devasted Campania; comets blazed in the heavens; earthquakes shook the ground. On all sides were the traces of deep uneasiness and superstitious terror. To all these portents, which were accepted as true by Christians as well as by pagans, the Christians would give a specially terrible significance. They strengthened their conviction that the coming of

[1] James Russell Lowell: *The Present Crisis.*

the Lord drew nigh. They convinced the better sort of pagans that the hour of their deliverance from a tyranny so monstrous and so disgraceful was near at hand.

In spite of the shocking servility with which alike the senate and the people had welcomed him back to the city with shouts of triumph, Nero felt that the air of Rome was heavy with curses against his name. He withdrew to Naples, and was at supper there on March 19, A.D. 68, the anniversary of his mother's murder, when he heard that the first note of revolt had been sounded by the brave C. Julius Vindex, prefect of Farther Gaul. He was so far from being disturbed by the news that he showed a secret joy at the thought that he could now order Gaul to be plundered. For eight days he took no notice of the matter. He was only roused to send an address to the senate because Vindex wounded his vanity by calling him *Ahenobarbus*[1] and "a bad singer." But when messenger after messenger came from the provinces with tidings of menace, he hurried back to Rome. At last, when he heard that Virginius Rufus had also rebelled in Germany, and Galba in Spain, he became aware of the desperate nature of his position.

On receiving this intelligence he fainted away, and remained for some time unconscious. He continued, indeed, his grossness and frivolity, but the wildest and fiercest schemes chased each other through his melodramatic brain. He would slay all the exiles; he would give up all the provinces to plunder; he would order all the Gauls in the city to be butchered; he would have all the senators invited to banquets, and would then poison them; he would have the city set on fire, and the wild beasts of the Amphitheatre let loose among the people; he would depose both the consuls and become sole consul himself, since legend said that only by a consul could Gauls be conquered; he would go with an army to the province, and when he got there would do nothing but weep, and when he had thus moved the rebels to compassion would next day sing with them at a great festival the ode of victory which he must at once compose. Not a single manly resolution lent a moment's dignity to his miserable fall.

[1] " Bronze-beard." Ahenobarbus was the name of a plebeian family to which Nero belonged.

Sometimes he talked of escaping to Ostia and arming the sailors; at others of escaping to Alexandria and earning his bread by his "divine voice." Meanwhile he was hourly subjected to the deadliest insults, and terrified by dreams and omens so sombre that his faith in the astrologers who had promised him the government of the East and the kingdom of Jerusalem began to be rudely shaken. When he heard that not a single army or general remained faithful to him, he kicked over the table at which he was dining, dashed to pieces on the ground two favorite goblets embossed with scenes from the Homeric poems, and placed in a golden box some poison furnished to him by Locusta.

The last effort which he contemplated was to mount the Rostra, beg pardon of the people for his crimes, ask them to try him again, and, at the worst, to allow him the prefecture of Egypt. But this design he did not dare to carry out, from fear that he would be torn to pieces before he reached the Forum. Meanwhile he found that the palace had been deserted by his guards, and that his attendants had robbed his chamber even of the golden box in which he had stored his poison. Rushing out, as though to drown himself in the Tiber, he changed his mind, and begged for some quiet hiding-place in which to collect his thoughts. The freedman Phaon offered him a lowly villa about four miles from the city. Barefooted, and with a faded coat thrown over his tunic, he hid his head and face in a kerchief and rode away with only four attendants. On the road he heard the tumult of the prætorians cursing his name. Amid evil omens and serious perils he reached the back of Phaon's villa, and, creeping toward it through a muddy reed-bed, was secretly admitted into one of its mean slave-chambers by an aperture through which he had to crawl on his hands and feet.

There is no need to dwell on the miserable spectacle of his end, perhaps the meanest and most pusillanimous which has ever been recorded. The poor wretch who, without a pang, had caused so many brave Romans and so many innocent Christians to be murdered could not summon up resolution to die. He devised every operatic incident of which he could think. When even his most degraded slaves urged him to have sufficient manliness to save himself from the fearful infamies which otherwise awaited him, he ordered his grave to be dug, and fragments of marble to be collected for its adornment, and water and wood for his funeral pyre, perpetually whining, "What an artist to perish!"

Meanwhile a courier arrived for Phaon. Nero snatched his despatches out of his hand and read that the senate had decided that he should be punished in the ancestral fashion as a public enemy. Asking what the ancestral fashion was, he was informed that he would be stripped naked and scourged to death with rods, with his head thrust into a fork. Horrified at this, he seized two daggers, and, after theatrically trying their edges, sheathed them again, with the excuse that the fatal moment had not yet arrived! Then he bade Sporus begin to sing his funeral song, and begged some one to show him how to die. Even his own intense shame at his cowardice was an insufficient stimulus, and he whiled away the time in vapid epigrams and pompous quotations. The sound of horses' hoofs then broke on his ears, and, venting one more Greek quotation, he held the dagger to his throat. It was driven home by Epaphroditus, one of his literary slaves. At this moment the centurion who came to arrest him rushed in. Nero was not yet dead, and under pretence of helping him the centurion began to stanch the wound with his cloak. "Too late," he said; "is this your fidelity?" So he died; and the bystanders were horrified with the way in which his eyes seemed to be starting out of his head in a rigid stare. He had begged that his body might be burned without posthumous insults, and this was conceded by Icelus, the freedman of Galbo.

So died the last of the Cæsars! And as Robespierre was lamented by his landlady, so even Nero was tenderly buried by two nurses who had known him in the exquisite beauty of his engaging childhood, and by Acte, who had inspired his youth with a genuine love.

But his history does not end with his grave. He was to live on in the expectation alike of Jews and Christians. The fifth head of the Wild Beast of the Revelation was in some sort to reappear as the eighth; the head with its diadem and its names of blasphemy had been wounded to death, but in the

Apocalyptic sense the deadly wound was to be healed. The Roman world could not believe that the heir of the deified Julian race could be cut off thus suddenly and obscurely and vanish like foam upon the water. The Christians felt sure that it required something more than an ordinary death stroke to destroy the antichrist, and to end the vitality of the Wild Beast from the Abyss, who had been the first to set himself in deadly antagonism against the Redeemer and to wage war upon the saints of God.

THE GREAT JEWISH REVOLT

SIEGE AND DESTRUCTION OF JERUSALEM

A.D. 70

JOSEPHUS

From A.D. 66 events of great moment occurred in Palestine. The Jews were in the throes of revolt against the Roman Government. At the same time the chief factions of the revolutionary party were constantly fighting each other. One of these factions was led by the famous John of Gischala, another by Simon bar Gioras, and a third by Eleazar. These factions of a party which—since the reduction of Judea to a Roman province soon after the death of Herod—had resisted the oppression of the procurators, were now stirred to revolt by the exactions of the procurator Gessius Florus. The revolutionary party, called the Zealots, gained power, and there were many outbreaks in Jerusalem. The counsel of the more prudent spirits was disregarded. At last Roman blood was shed. The nobility and priesthood played into the hands of the Zealots by applying to Florus to put down the revolt. Florus marched against Jerusalem and was badly beaten by the Zealots.

Open war henceforth existed. Josephus, a Jew of the lineage of Aaron, trained according to the best discipline of his race, and who had also been well received at Rome, was placed by his countrymen in command of the province of Galilee. Afterward, as a historian, he described the events of the war.

Vespasian, who was then Rome's greatest general, soon came at the head of sixty thousand Roman soldiers. He attacked Galilee. Josephus, with such followers as he could gather, took position on an almost inaccessible hill in Jotapata, which the Romans for five days stormed in vain, then besieged its brave defenders, afterward repeatedly assaulted; and finally, during the night following the forty-seventh day of the siege, Titus, serving under his father, Vespasian, gained possession of the place. Josephus, with forty of the principal citizens, hid in a cave, but their refuge was discovered through treachery.

Vespasian was anxious to take Josephus alive. He sent the tribune Nicanor, who had been his friend, to the Jewish leader to induce him with fair promises to surrender. Josephus was about to give himself up, but was prevented by his companions. "We will care for the honor of our country," they said. At the same time they offered a sword and "a hand that shall use it against thee." Josephus then proposed that they should all die together, but by the hands of one another, instead of suicide. Lots were cast. He who drew the first offered his neck to him who stood next and so forward. Finally, through marvellous fortune, Josephus and one other alone were left, and here the slaughter ended. The two survivors surrendered to the Romans. Loud cries for the death of Josephus arose, but he was spared by the intercession of Titus. The fall of Jotapata led to the subjugation of Galilee.

When captured, Josephus made to Vespasian the prophecy: "Thou shalt be emperor—thou and thy son after thee," a prediction soon to be fulfilled, for in A.D. 69 Vespasian was proclaimed emperor, and the next year went to Rome, leaving Titus to carry on the war and subdue Jerusalem. Vespasian himself, it is recorded, released Josephus, "cutting off his chains," thus relieving him from all stain of dishonor.

"The capture of Jerusalem by Titus in this campaign," says Hosmer, "is one of the most memorable events in the history of mankind. It caused the expulsion of an entire race from its home. The Roman valor, skill, and persistence were never more conspicuously displayed. No more desperate resistance was ever opposed to the eagle-emblemed mistress of the ancient world. There is no event of ancient history the details of which are more minutely known. The circumstances in all their appalling features are given to us by the eye-witness, Josephus, so that we know them as vividly as we do the events of the career of Grant."

THE legions had orders to encamp at the distance of six furlongs from Jerusalem, at the mount called the Mount of Olives, which lies over against the city on the east side, and is parted from it by a deep valley, interposed between them, which is named Cedron.

Now, when hitherto the several parties in the city had been dashing one against another perpetually, this foreign war, now suddenly come upon them after a violent manner, put the first stop to their contentions one against another; and as the seditious now saw with astonishment the Romans pitching three several camps, they began to think of an awkward sort of concord, and said one to another: "What do we here, and what do we mean, when we suffer three fortified walls to be built to coop us in, that we shall not be able to breathe freely? while the enemy is securely building a kind of city in opposition to us, and while we sit still within our own walls and become spectators only of what they are doing, with our hands idle, and our armor laid by, as if they were about somewhat that was for our good and advantage. We are, it seems (so did they cry out), only courageous against ourselves, while the Romans are likely to gain the city without bloodshed by our sedition." Thus did they encourage one another when they were gotten together and took their armor immediately and ran out upon the Tenth legion and fell upon the Romans with great eagerness, and with a prodigious shout, as they were fortifying their camp. These Romans were caught in different parties, and this in order to perform their several works, and on that account had in great measure laid aside their arms, for they thought the Jews would not have ventured to make a sally upon them; and had they been disposed so to do, they supposed their sedition would have distracted them. So they were put into disorder unexpectedly; when some of them left their works they were about and immediately marched off, while many ran to their arms, but were smitten and slain before they could turn back upon the enemy. The Jews became still more and more in number, as encouraged by the good success of those that first made the attack; and while they had such good fortune, they seemed both to themselves and to the enemy to be many more than they really were.

The disorderly way of their fighting at first put the Romans also to a stand, who had been constantly used to fight skilfully in good order, and with keeping their ranks and obeying the orders that were given them, for which reason the Romans were caught unexpectedly and were obliged to give way to the assaults that were made upon them. Now, when these Romans were overtaken and turned back upon the Jews, they put a stop to their career; yet when they did not take care enough of themselves through the vehemency of their pursuit, they were wounded by them; but as still more and more Jews sallied out of the city, the Romans were at length brought into confusion, and put to flight, and ran away from their camp. Nay, things looked as though the entire legion would have been in danger, unless Titus had been informed of the case they were in, and had sent them succors immediately. So he reproached them for their cowardice and brought those back that were running away, and fell himself upon the Jews on their flank, with those select troops that were with him, and slew a considerable number, and wounded more of them, and put them all to flight, and made them run away hastily down the valley. Now as these

Jews suffered greatly in the declivity of the valley, so when they were gotten over it they turned about and stood over against the Romans, having the valley between them, and there fought with them. Thus did they continue the fight till noon; but when it was already a little after noon, Titus set those that came to the assistance of the Romans with him, and those that belonged to the cohorts, to prevent the Jews from making any more sallies, and then sent the rest of the legion to the upper part of the mountain, to fortify their camp.

This march of the Romans seemed to the Jews to be a flight; and as the watchman who was placed upon the wall gave a signal by shaking his garment, there came out a fresh multitude of Jews, and that with such mighty violence that one might compare it to the running of the most terrible wild beasts. To say the truth, none of those that opposed them could sustain the fury with which they made their attacks; but, as if they had been cast out of an engine, they brake the enemies' ranks to pieces, who were put to flight, and ran away to the mountain; none but Titus himself, and a few others with him, being left in the midst of the acclivity. Now these others, who were his friends, despised the danger they were in and were ashamed to leave their general, earnestly exhorting him to give way to these Jews that are fond of dying, and not to run into such dangers before those that ought to stay before him; to consider what his fortune was, and not, by supplying the place of a common soldier, to venture to turn back upon the enemy so suddenly; and this because he was general in the war, and lord of the habitable earth, on whose preservation the public affairs do all depend.

These persuasions Titus seemed not so much as to hear, but opposed those that ran upon him, and smote them on the face; and when he had forced them to go back, he slew them: he also fell upon great numbers as they marched down the hill, and thrust them forward; while those men were so amazed at his courage and his strength that they could not fly directly to the city, but declined from him on both sides, and pressed after those that fled up the hill; yet did he still fall upon their flank, and put a stop to their fury. In the mean time a disorder and a terror fell again upon those that were fortifying their camp at

the top of the hill, upon their seeing those beneath them running away; insomuch that the whole legion was dispersed while
they thought that the sallies of the Jews upon them were plainly
insupportable, and that Titus was himself put to flight, because
they took it for granted that, if he had stayed, the rest would
never have fled for it. Thus were they encompassed on every
side by a kind of panic fear, and some dispersed themselves one
way, and some another, till certain of them saw their general in
the very midst of an action, and being under great concern for
him, they loudly proclaimed the danger he was in to the entire
legion; and now shame made them turn back, and they reproached one another that they did worse than run away, by
deserting Cæsar. So they used their utmost force against the
Jews, and declining from the straight declivity, they drove them
on heaps into the bottom of the valley. Then did the Jews
turn about and fight them; but as they were themselves retiring, and now, because the Romans had the advantage of the
ground and were above the Jews, they drove them all into the
valley.

As now the war abroad ceased for a while, the sedition
within was revived; and on the feast of unleavened bread,
which was now come, it being the fourteenth day of the month
Xanthicus [Nisan], when it is believed the Jews were first freed
from the Egyptians, Eleazar and his party opened the gates of
this [inmost court of the] Temple, and admitted such of the
people as were desirous to worship God into it. But John
made use of this festival as a cloak for his treacherous designs,
and armed the most inconsiderable of his own party, the greater
part of whom were not purified, with weapons concealed under
their garments, and sent them with great zeal into the Temple,
in order to seize upon it, which armed men, when they were
gotten in, threw their garments away, and presently appeared
in their armor. Upon which there was a very great disorder
and disturbance about the holy house, while the people, who
had no concern in the sedition, supposed that this assault was
made against all without distinction, as the Zealots thought it
was made against themselves only. So these left off guarding
the gates any longer and leaped down from their battlements
before they came to an engagement, and fled away into the

subterranean caverns of the Temple, while the people that stood trembling at the altar and about the holy house were rolled on heaps together and trampled upon, and were beaten both with wooden and with iron weapons without mercy. Such also as had differences with others slew many persons that were quiet, out of their own private enmity and hatred, as if they were opposite to the seditious; and all those that had formerly offended any of these plotters were now known, and were now led away to the slaughter, and when they had done abundance of horrid mischief to the guiltless they granted a truce to the guilty and let those go off that came out of the caverns. These followers of John also did now seize upon this inner temple, and upon all the warlike engines therein, and then ventured to oppose Simon. And thus that sedition, which had been divided into three factions, was now reduced to two.

But Titus, intending to pitch his camp nearer to the city than Scopus, placed as many of his choice horsemen and footmen as he thought sufficient opposite to the Jews to prevent their sallying out upon them, while he gave orders for the whole army to level the distance as far as the wall of the city. So they threw down all the hedges and walls which the inhabitants had made about their gardens and groves of trees, and cut down all the fruit trees that lay between them and the wall of the city, and filled up all the hollow places and the chasms, and demolished the rocky precipices with iron instruments; and thereby made all the place level from Scopus to Herod's monuments, which adjoined to the pool called the Serpent's Pool.

Now at this very time the Jews contrived the following stratagem against the Romans. The bolder sort of the seditious went out at the towers, called the Women's Towers, as if they had been ejected out of the city by those who were for peace, and rambled about as if they were afraid of being assaulted by the Romans, and were in fear of one another, while those that stood upon the wall and seemed to be of the people's side cried out aloud for peace, and entreated they might have security for their lives given them, and called for the Romans, promising to open the gates to them; and as they cried out after that manner they threw stones at their own people, as though they would drive them away from the gates. These also pretended that they were excluded by force, and that they petitioned those that were within to let them in; and rushing upon the Romans perpetually, with violence, they then came back, and seemed to be in great disorder. Now the Roman soldiers thought this cunning stratagem of theirs was to be believed real, and thinking they had the one party under their power, and could punish them as they pleased, and hoping that the other party would open their gates to them, set to the execution of their designs accordingly.

But for Titus himself, he had this surprising conduct of the Jews in suspicion, for whereas he had invited them to come to terms of accommodation, by Josephus, but one day before, he could then receive no civil answer from them; so he ordered the soldiers to stay where they were. However, some of them that were set in the front of the works prevented him, and catching up their arms ran to the gates; whereupon those that seemed to have been ejected at the first retired; but as soon as the soldiers were gotten between the towers on each side of the gate the Jews ran out and encompassed them round, and fell upon them behind, while that multitude which stood upon the wall threw a heap of stones and darts of all kinds at them, insomuch that they slew a considerable number, and wounded many more, for it was not easy for the Romans to escape, by reason those behind them pressed them forward; besides which, the shame they were under for being mistaken, and the fear they were in of their commanders, engaged them to persevere in their mistake; wherefore they fought with their spears a great while, and received many blows from the Jews, though indeed they gave them as many blows again, and at last repelled those that had encompassed them about, while the Jews pursued them as they retired, and followed them, and threw darts at them as far as the monuments of Queen Helena.

Now the warlike men that were in the city, and the multitude of the seditious that were with Simon, were ten thousand, besides the Idumeans. Those ten thousand had fifty commanders, over whom this Simon was supreme. The Idumeans that paid him homage were five thousand, and had eight commanders, among whom those of greatest fame were Jacob, the son of Sosas, and Simon, the son of Cathlas. John, who had seized upon the Temple, had six thousand armed men under twenty commanders; the Zealots also that had come over to him and left off their opposition were two thousand four hundred, and had the same commander that they had formerly, Eleazar, together with Simon, the son of Arinus. Now, while these factions fought one against another, the people were their prey on both sides, and that part of the people who would not join with them in their wicked practices were plundered by both factions.

Simon held the upper city and the great wall as far as Cedron, and as much of the old wall as bent from Siloam to the east, and which went down to the palace of Monobazus, who was king of the Adiabeni, beyond Euphrates; he also held that fountain and the Acra, which was no other than the lower city; he also held all that reached to the palace of Queen Helena, the mother of Monobazus. But John held the Temple and the parts thereto adjoining, for a great way, as also Ophla, and the valley called "the Valley of Cedron"; and when the parts that were interposed between their possessions were burned by them, they left a space wherein they might fight with each other, for this internal sedition did not cease even when the Romans were encamped near their very walls. But although they had grown wiser at the first onset the Romans made upon them, this lasted but awhile, for they returned to their former madness, and separated one from another, and fought it out and did everything that the besiegers could desire them to do, for they never suffered anything that was worse from the Romans than they made each other suffer; nor was there any misery endured by the city, after these men's actions, that could be esteemed new. But it was most of all unhappy before it was overthrown, while those that took it did it a greater kindness; for I venture to affirm that the sedition destroyed the city, and the Romans destroyed the sedition, which it was a much harder thing to do than to destroy the walls; so that we may justly ascribe our misfortunes to our own people, and the just vengeance taken on them to the Romans; as to which matter let everyone determine by the actions on both sides.

Now when affairs within the city were in this posture, Titus went round the city on the outside with some chosen horse-

men and looked about for a proper place where he might make
an impression upon the walls; but as he was in doubt where he
could possibly make an attack on any side—for the place was
no way accessible where the valleys were, and on the other
side the first wall appeared too strong to be shaken by the engines—he thereupon thought it best to make his assault upon
the monument of John, the high-priest, for there it was that
the first fortification was lower, and the second was not joined
to it, the builders neglecting to build strong where the new city
was not much inhabited. Here also was an easy passage to the
third wall, through which he thought to take the upper city and,
through the tower of Antonia, the Temple itself. But at this
time, as he was going round about the city, one of his friends,
whose name was Nicanor, was wounded with a dart on his left
shoulder, as he approached, together with Josephus, too near
the wall, and attempted to discourse to those that were upon
the wall about terms of peace, for he was a person known by
them.

On this account it was that Cæsar, as soon as he knew their
vehemence, that they would not bear even such as approached
them to persuade them to what tended to their own preservation, was provoked to press on the siege. He also, at the same
time, gave his soldiers leave to set the suburbs on fire, and ordered that they should bring timber together, and raise banks
against the city. And when he had parted his army into three
parts, in order to set about those works, he placed those that
shot darts, and the archers in the midst of the banks that were
then raising, before whom he placed those engines that threw
javelins and darts and stones, that he might prevent the enemy from sallying out upon their works and might hinder those
that were upon the wall from being able to obstruct them. So
the trees were now cut down immediately and the suburbs left
naked. But now while the timber was being carried to raise
the banks, and the whole army was earnestly engaged in their
works, the Jews were not, however, quiet. And it happened
that the people of Jerusalem, who had been hitherto plundered
and murdered, were now of good courage, and supposed they
should have a breathing time, while the others were very busy
in opposing their enemies without the city, and that they

should now be avenged on those that had been the authors of their miseries, in case the Romans did but get the victory.

However, John stayed behind, out of his fear of Simon, even while his own men were earnest in making a sally upon their enemies without. Yet did not Simon lie still, for he lay near the place of the siege; he brought his engines of war and disposed of them at due distances upon the wall, both those which they took from Cestius formerly, and those which they got when they seized the garrison that lay in the tower Antonia. But though they had these engines in their possession, they had so little skill in using them that they were in great measure useless to them; but a few there were who had been taught by deserters how to use them, which they did use, though after an awkward manner. So they cast stones and arrows at those that were making the banks; they also ran out upon them by companies and fought with them.

Now those that were at work covered themselves with hurdles spread over their banks, and their engines were opposed to them when they made their excursions. The engines, that all the legions had ready prepared for them, were admirably contrived; but still more extraordinary ones belonged to the Tenth legion: those that threw darts and those that threw stones were more forcible and larger than the rest, by which they not only repelled the excursions of the Jews, but drove those away that were upon the walls also. Now the stones that were cast were of the weight of a talent, and were carried two furlongs and farther. The blow they gave was no way to be sustained, not only by those that stood first in the way, but by those that were beyond them for a great space.

As for the Jews, they at first watched the coming of the stone, for it was of a white color, and could therefore not only be perceived by the great noise it made, but could be seen also before it came, by its brightness. Accordingly, the watchmen that sat upon the towers gave them notice when the engine was let go, and the stone came from it, and cried out aloud, in their own country language, "The son cometh!" so those that were in its way stood off, and threw themselves down upon the ground; by which means, and by their thus guarding themselves, the stone fell down and did them no harm. But the

Romans contrived how to prevent that, by blacking the stone, who then could aim at them with success when the stone was not discerned beforehand as it had been till then; and so they destroyed many of them at one blow. Yet did not the Jews, under all this distress, permit the Romans to raise their banks in quiet, but they shrewdly and boldly exerted themselves, and repelled them both by night and by day.

And now, upon the finishing the Roman works, the workmen measured the distance there was from the wall, and this by lead and a line which they threw to it from their banks, for they could not measure it any other wise, because the Jews would shoot at them, if they came to measure it themselves. And when they found that the engines could reach the wall they brought them thither. Then did Titus set his engines, at proper distances, so much nearer to the wall that the Jews might not be able to repel them, and gave orders they should go to work; and when, thereupon, a prodigious noise echoed round about from three places, and that on a sudden there was a great noise made by the citizens that were within the city, and no less a terror fell upon the seditious themselves. Whereupon both sorts, seeing the common danger they were in, contrived to make a like defence. So those of different factions cried out one to another that they acted entirely as in concert with their enemies, whereas they ought, however, notwithstanding God did not grant them a lasting concord in their present circumstances, to lay aside their enmities one against another and to unite together against the Romans. Accordingly, Simon gave those that came from the Temple leave, by proclamation, to go upon the wall; John also himself, though he could not believe Simon was in earnest, gave them the same leave.

So on both sides they laid aside their hatred and their peculiar quarrels, and formed themselves into one body. They then ran round the walls, and having a vast number of torches with them threw them at the machines, and shot darts perpetually upon those that impelled those engines which battered the wall —nay, the bolder sort leaped out by troops upon the hurdles that covered the machines, and pulled them to pieces, and fell upon those that belonged to them, and beat them, not so much by any skill they had, as principally by the boldness of their attacks.

However, Titus himself still sent assistance to those that were the hardest beset, and placed both horsemen and archers on the several sides of the engines, and thereby beat off those that brought the fire to them. He also thereby repelled those that shot stones or darts from the towers, and then set the engines to work in good earnest; yet did not the wall yield to these blows, excepting where the battering ram of the Fifteenth legion moved the corner of a tower, while the wall itself continued unhurt, for the wall was not presently in the same danger with the tower, which was extant far above it; nor could the fall of that part of the tower easily break down any part of the wall itself together with it.

And now the Jews intermitted their sallies for a while, but when they observed the Romans dispersed all abroad at their works, and in their several camps—for they thought the Jews had retired out of weariness and fear—they all at once made a sally at the tower Hippicus, through an obscure gate, and at the same time brought fire to burn the works, and went boldly up to the Romans, and to their very fortifications themselves, where, at the cry they made, those that were near them came presently to their assistance, and those farther off came running after them. And here the boldness of the Jews was too hard for the good order of the Romans, and as they beat those whom they first fell upon, so they pressed upon those that were now gotten together. So this fight about the machines was very hot, while the one side tried hard to set them on fire, and the other side to prevent it. On both sides there was a confused cry made, and many of those in the forefront of the battle were slain.

However, the Jews were now too hard for the Romans by the furious assaults they made like madmen, and the fire caught hold of the works, and both all those works, and the engines themselves, had been in danger of being burned, had not many of those select soldiers that came from Alexandria opposed themselves to prevent it, and had they not behaved themselves with greater courage than they themselves supposed they could have done, for they outdid those in this fight that had greater reputation than themselves. This was the state of things till Cæsar took the stoutest of his horsemen and attacked the enemy, while he himself slew twelve of those that were in the forefront of the Jews, which death of these men, when the rest of the multitude saw, they gave way, and he pursued them, and drove them all into the city, and saved the works from the fire.   Now it happened at this fight that a certain Jew was taken alive who, by Titus' order, was crucified before the wall, to see whether the rest of them would be affrighted and abate of their obstinacy.   But after the Jews were retired, John,[1] who was commander of the Idumeans, and was talking to a certain soldier of his acquaintance before the wall, was wounded by a dart shot at him by an Arabian, and died immediately, leaving the greatest lamentation to the Jews, and sorrow to the seditious, for he was a man of great eminence, both for his actions and his conduct also.

Now, on the next night, a surprising disturbance fell upon the Romans; for whereas Titus had given orders for the erection of three towers of fifty cubits high, that, by setting men upon them at every bank, he might from thence drive those away who were upon the wall, it so happened that one of these towers fell down about midnight, and as its fall made a very great noise, fear fell upon the army, and they, supposing that the enemy was coming to attack them, ran all to their arms. Whereupon a disturbance and a tumult arose among the legions, and as nobody could tell what had happened, they went on after a disconsolate manner; and seeing no enemy appear, they were afraid one of another, and every one demanded of his neighbor the watchword with great earnestness as though the Jews had invaded their camp.   And now were they like people under a panic fear, until Titus was informed of what had happened, and gave orders that all should be acquainted with it; and then, though with some difficulty, they got clear of the disturbance they had been under.

Now these towers were very troublesome to the Jews, who otherwise opposed the Romans very courageously, for they shot at them out of their lighter engines from those towers, as they did also by those that threw darts, and the archers, and those that flung stones.   For neither could the Jews reach those

[1] Not to be confounded with John of Gischala, leader of one of the three factions.

that were over them, by reason of their height; and it was not practicable to take them, nor to overturn them, they were so heavy, nor to set them on fire, because they were covered with plates of iron. So they retired out of the reach of the darts, and did no longer endeavor to hinder the impression of their rams, which, by continually beating upon the wall, did gradually prevail against it; so that the wall already gave way to the Nico, for by that name did the Jews themselves call the greatest of their engines, because it conquered all things. And now they were for a long while grown weary of fighting and of keeping guards, and were retired to lodge in the night-time at a distance from the wall. It was on other accounts also thought by them to be superfluous to guard the wall, there being besides that two other fortifications still remaining, and they being slothful, and their counsels having been ill-concerted on all occasions; so a great many grew lazy and retired. Then the Romans mounted the breach, where Nico had made one, and all the Jews left the guarding that wall and retreated to the second wall; so those that had gotten over that wall opened the gates and received all the army within it. And thus did the Romans get possession of this first wall, on the fifteenth day of the siege, which was the seventh day of the month Artemisius (Jyar), when they demolished a great part of it, as well as they did of the northern parts of the city, which had been demolished also by Cestius formerly.

And now Titus pitched his camp within the city, at that place which was called "the Camp of the Assyrians," having seized upon all that lay as far as Cedron, but took care to be out of the reach of the Jews' darts. He then presently began his attacks, upon which the Jews divided themselves into several bodies, and courageously defended that wall, while John [1] and his faction did it from the tower of Antonia, and from the northern cloister of the Temple, and fought the Romans before the monuments of King Alexander; and Simon's army also took for their share the spot of ground that was near John's monument,[2] and fortified it as far as to that gate where water

[1] John of Gischala.
[2] Probably that of John Hyrcanus I, a Maccabæan, prince of Judea, B.C. 135–105.

was brought in to the tower Hippicus. However, the Jews made violent sallies, and that frequently also, and in bodies together out of the gates, and there fought the Romans; and when they were pursued all together to the wall, they were beaten in those fights, as wanting the skill of the Romans. But when they fought them from the walls they were too hard for them; the Romans being encouraged by their power, joined to their skill, as were the Jews by their boldness, which was nourished by the fear they were in, and that hardiness which is natural to our nation under calamities; they were also encouraged still by the hope of deliverance, as were the Romans by their hopes of subduing them in a little time.

Nor did either side grow weary; but attacks and fightings upon the wall, and perpetual sallies out in bodies, were there all the day long; nor were there any sort of warlike engagements that were not then put in use. And the night itself had much ado to part them, when they began to fight in the morning—nay, the night itself was passed without sleep on both sides, and was more uneasy than the day to them, while the one was afraid lest the wall should be taken, and the other lest the Jews should make sallies upon their camps; both sides also lay in their armor during the night-time, and thereby were ready at the first appearance of light to go to the battle. Now among the Jews the ambition was who should undergo the first dangers, and thereby gratify their commanders. Above all, they had a great veneration and dread of Simon; and to that degree was he regarded by every one of those that were under him, that at his command they were very ready to kill themselves with their own hands.

What made the Romans so courageous was their usual custom of conquering and disuse of being defeated, their constant wars, and perpetual warlike exercises, and the grandeur of their dominion. And what was now their chief encouragement —Titus, who was present everywhere with them all—for it appeared a terrible thing to grow weary while Cæsar was there, and fought bravely as well as they did—was himself at once an eye-witness of such as behaved themselves valiantly, and he was to reward them also. It was, besides, esteemed an advantage at present to have anyone's valor known by Cæsar; on which account many of them appeared to have more alacrity than strength to answer it. And now, as the Jews were about this time standing in array before the wall, and that in a strong body, and while both parties were throwing their darts at each other, Longinus, one of the equestrian order, leaped out of the army of the Romans, and leaped into the very midst of the army of the Jews; and as they dispersed themselves upon this attack, he slew two of their men of the greatest courage; one of them he struck in his mouth as he was coming to meet him, the other was slain by him by that very dart which he drew out of the body of the other, with which he ran this man through his side as he was running away from him; and when he had done this, he first of all ran out of the midst of his enemies to his own side.

So this man signalized himself for his valor, and many there were who were ambitious of gaining the like reputation. And now the Jews were unconcerned at what they suffered themselves from the Romans, and were only solicitous about what mischief they could do them; and death itself seemed a small matter to them, if at the same time they could but kill any one of their enemies. But Titus took care to secure his own soldiers from harm, as well as to have them overcome their enemies. He also said that inconsiderate violence was madness, and that this alone was the true courage that was joined with good conduct. He therefore commanded his men to take care, when they fought their enemies, that they received no harm from them at the same time, and thereby show themselves to be truly valiant men.

And now Titus brought one of his engines to the middle tower of the north part of the wall, in which a certain crafty Jew, whose name was Castor, lay in ambush, with ten others like himself, the rest being fled away by reason of the archers. These men lay still for a while, as in great fear, under their breastplates; but when the tower was shaken, they arose, and Castor did then stretch out his hand, as a petitioner, and called for Cæsar, and by his voice moved his compassion, and begged of him to have mercy upon them; and Titus, in the innocency of his heart, believing him to be in earnest, and hoping that the Jews did now repent, stopped the working of the battering ram, and forbade them to shoot at the petitioners, and bid Castor say what he had a mind to say to him. He said that he would come down, if he would give him his right hand for his security.

To which Titus replied that he was well pleased with such his agreeable conduct, and would be well pleased if all the Jews would be of his mind, and that he was ready to give the like security to the city. Now five of the ten dissembled with him, and pretended to beg for mercy, while the rest cried out aloud that they would never be slaves to the Romans, while it was in their power to die in a state of freedom. Now while these men were quarrelling for a long while the attack was delayed; Castor also sent to Simon, and told him that they might take some time for consultation about what was to be done, because he would elude the power of the Romans for a considerable time. And at the same time that he sent thus to him, he appeared openly to exhort those that were obstinate to accept of Titus' hand for their security; but they seemed very angry at it, and brandished their naked swords upon the breastworks, and struck themselves upon their breast, and fell down as if they had been slain. Hereupon Titus, and those with him, were amazed at the courage of the men; and as they were not able to see exactly what was done, they admired at their great fortitude and pitied their calamity.

During this interval a certain person shot a dart at Castor, and wounded him in his nose; whereupon he presently pulled out the dart, and showed it to Titus, and complained that this was unfair treatment; so Cæsar reproved him that shot the dart, and sent Josephus, who then stood by him, to give his right hand to Castor. But Josephus said that he would not go to him, because these pretended petitioners meant nothing that was good; he also restrained those friends of his who were zealous to go to him. But still there was one Eneas, a deserter, who said he would go to him. Castor also called to them, that somebody should come and receive the money which he had with him; this made Eneas the more earnestly to run to him with his bosom open. Then did Castor take up a great stone and threw it at him, which missed him, because he guarded himself against it; but still it wounded another soldier that was coming to him. When Cæsar understood that this was a delusion, he perceived that mercy in war is a pernicious thing, because such cunning tricks have less place under the exercise of greater severity. So he caused the engine to work more strongly than before, on account of his anger at the deceit put upon him. But Castor and his companions set the tower on fire when it began to give way, and leaped through the flame into a hidden vault that was under it, which made the Romans further suppose that they were men of great courage, as having cast themselves into the fire.

Now Cæsar took this wall there on the fifth day after he had taken the first; and when the Jews had fled from him he entered into it with a thousand armed men, and those of his choice troops, and this at a place where were the merchants of wool, the braziers, and the market for cloth, and where the narrow streets led obliquely to the wall. Wherefore, if Titus had either demolished a larger part of the wall immediately, or had come in, and, according to the law of war, had laid waste what was left, his victory would not, I suppose, have been mixed with any loss to himself. But now, out of the hope he had that he should make the Jews ashamed of their obstinacy by not being willing, when he was able, to afflict them more than he needed to do, he did not widen the breach of the wall, in order to make a safer retreat upon occasion, for he did not think they would lay snares for him that did them such a kindness. When therefore, he came in, he did not permit his soldiers to kill any of those they caught, nor to set fire to their houses neither—nay, he gave leave to the seditious, if they had a mind, to fight without any harm to the people, and promised to restore the people's effects to them, for he was very desirous to preserve the city for his own sake, and the Temple for the sake of the city.

As to the people, he had them of a long time ready to comply with his proposals; but as to the fighting men, this humanity of his seemed a mark of his weakness, and they imagined that he made these proposals because he was not able to take the rest of the city. They also threatened death to the people, if they should any one of them say a word about a surrender. They, moreover, cut the throats of such as talked of a peace, and then attacked those Romans that were come within the

wall.   Some of them they met in the narrow streets, and some
they fought against from their houses, while they made a sudden sally out at the upper gates, and assaulted such Romans as
were beyond the wall, till those that guarded the wall were so
affrighted that they leaped down from their towers and retired
to their several camps: upon which a great noise was made by
the Romans that were within, because they were encompassed
round on every side by their enemies; as also by them that
were without, because they were in fear for those that were left
in the city.   Thus did the Jews grow more numerous perpetually, and had great advantages over the Romans, by their full
knowledge of those narrow lanes; and they wounded a great
many of them, and fell upon them, and drove them out of the
city.

Now these Romans were at present forced to make the best
resistance they could, for they were not able, in great numbers,
to get out at the breach in the wall, it was so narrow.   It is also
probable that all those that were gotten within had been cut to
pieces, if Titus had not sent them succors, for he ordered the
archers to stand at the upper ends of these narrow lanes, and
he stood himself where was the greatest multitude of his enemies, and with his darts he put a stop to them; as with him did
Domitius Sabinus also, a valiant man, and one that in this battle
appeared so to be.   Thus did Cæsar continue to shoot darts at
the Jews continually and to hinder them from coming upon his
men, and this until all his soldiers had retreated out of the
city.

And thus were the Romans driven out, after they had possessed themselves of the second wall.   Whereupon the fighting
men that were in the city were lifted up in their minds and
were elevated upon this their good success, and began to think
that the Romans would never venture to come into the city any
more; and that if they kept within it themselves they should
not be any more conquered, for God had blinded their minds
for the transgressions they had been guilty of, nor could they
see how much greater forces the Romans had than those that
were now expelled, no more than they could discern how a famine was creeping upon them, for hitherto they had fed themselves out of the public miseries and drank the blood of the

city. But now poverty had for a long time seized upon the better part, and a great many had died already for want of necessaries, although the seditious indeed supposed the destruction of the people to be an easement to themselves, for they desired that none others might be preserved but such as were against a peace with the Romans, and were resolved to live in opposition to them, and they were pleased when the multitude of those of a contrary opinion were consumed, as being then freed from a heavy burden. And this was their disposition of mind with regard to those that were within the city, while they covered themselves with their armor, and prevented the Romans, when they were trying to get into the city again, and made a wall of their own bodies over against that part of the wall that was cast down.

Thus did they valiantly defend themselves for three days; but on the fourth day they could not support themselves against the vehement assaults of Titus, but were compelled by force to fly whither they had fled before; so he quietly possessed himself again of that wall and demolished it entirely. And when he had put a garrison into the towers that were on the south parts of the city, he contrived how he might assault the third wall.

A resolution was now taken by Titus to relax the siege for a little while, and to afford the seditious an interval for consideration, and to see whether the demolishing of their second wall would not make them a little more compliant, or whether they were not somewhat afraid of a famine, because the spoils they had gotten by rapine would not be sufficient for them long; so he made use of this relaxation in order to compass his own designs. Accordingly, as the usual appointed time when he must distribute subsistence money to the soldiers was now come, he gave orders that the commanders should put the army into battle array, in the face of the enemy, and then give every one of the soldiers his pay.

The Romans spent four days in bringing this subsistence money to the several legions. But on the fifth day, when no signs of peace appeared to come from the Jews, Titus divided his legions and began to raise banks, both at the tower of Antonia and at John's monument. Now his designs were to take

the upper city at that monument, and the Temple at the tower
of Antonia, for if the Temple were not taken, it would be dangerous to keep the city itself; so at each of these parts he raised
him banks, each legion raising one. As for those that wrought
at John's monument, the Idumeans, and those that were in
arms with Simon, made sallies upon them, and put some stop
to them; while John's party, and the multitude of Zealots with
them, did the like to those that were before the tower of Antonia.

These Jews were now too hard for the Romans, not only in
direct fighting, because they stood upon the higher ground, but
because they had now learned to use their own engines, for
their continual use of them one day after another did by degrees improve their skill about them, for of one sort of engines
for darts they had three hundred, and forty for stones; by the
means of which they made it more tedious for the Romans to
raise their banks. But then Titus, knowing that the city
would be either saved or destroyed for himself, did not only
proceed earnestly in the siege, but did not omit to have the Jews
exhorted to repentance; so he mixed good counsel with his
works for the siege. And being sensible that exhortations are
frequently more effectual than arms, he persuaded them to surrender the city, now in a manner already taken, and thereby to
save themselves, and sent Josephus to speak to them in their
own language, for he imagined they might yield to the persuasion of a countryman of their own.

As Josephus was speaking thus with a loud voice, the seditious would neither yield to what he said, nor did they deem it
safe for them to alter their conduct; but as for the people, they
had a great inclination to desert to the Romans. Accordingly,
some of them sold what they had, and even the most precious
things that had been laid up as treasures by them, for a very
small matter, and swallowed down pieces of gold, that they
might not be found out by the robbers; and when they had
escaped to the Romans, went to stool, and had wherewithal to
provide plentifully for themselves, for Titus let a great number
of them go away into the country, whither they pleased. And
the main reasons why they were so ready to desert were these:
That now they should be freed from those miseries which they

had endured in that city, and yet should not be in slavery to the Romans. However John and Simon, with their factions, did more carefully watch these men's going out than they did the coming in of the Romans; and if any one did but afford the least shadow of suspicion of such an intention, his throat was cut immediately.

But as for the richer sort, it proved all one to them whether they stayed in the city or attempted to get out of it, for they were equally destroyed in both cases, for every such person was put to death under this pretence, that they were going to desert, but in reality that the robbers might get what they had. The madness of the seditious did also increase together with their famine, and both those miseries were every day inflamed more and more, for there was no corn which anywhere appeared publicly, but the robbers came running into and searched men's private houses; and then, if they found any, they tormented them, because they had denied they had any; and if they found none, they tormented them worse, because they supposed they had more carefully concealed it. The indication they made use of whether they had any or not was taken from the bodies of these miserable wretches, which, if they were in good case, they supposed they were in no want at all of food; but if they were wasted away, they walked off without searching any further; nor did they think it proper to kill such as these, because they saw they would very soon die of themselves for want of food. Many there were indeed who sold what they had for one measure. It was of wheat, if they were of the richer sort; but of barley, if they were poorer. When these had so done, they shut themselves up in the inmost rooms of their houses, and ate the corn they had gotten. Some did it without grinding it, by reason of the extremity of the want they were in, and others baked bread of it, according as necessity and fear dictated to them. A table was nowhere laid for a distinct meal, but they snatched the bread out of the fire, half-baked, and ate it very hastily.

It was now a miserable case, and a sight that would justly bring tears into our eyes, how men stood as to their food, while the more powerful had more than enough, and the weaker were lamenting [for want of it]. But the famine was too hard for

all other passions, and it is destructive to nothing so much as
to modesty, for what was otherwise worthy of reverence was in
this case despised; insomuch that children pulled the very morsels that their fathers were eating out of their very mouths,
and what was still more to be pitied, so did the mothers do as
to their infants; and when those that were most dear were perishing under their hands, they were not ashamed to take from
them the very last drops that might preserve their lives; and
while they ate after this manner, yet were they not concealed
in so doing; but the seditious everywhere came upon them
immediately and snatched away from them what they had gotten from others, for when they saw any house shut up this was
to them a signal that the people within had gotten some food;
whereupon they broke open the doors and ran in and took pieces
of what they were eating almost up out of their very throats,
and this by force: the old men who held their food fast were
beaten; and if the women hid what they had within their hands,
their hair was torn for so doing; nor was there any commiseration shown either to the aged or to the infants, but they lifted
up children from the ground as they hung upon the morsels
they had gotten and shook them down upon the floor. But
still they were more barbarously cruel to those that had prevented their coming in, and had actually swallowed down what
they were going to seize upon, as if they had been unjustly de-
frauded of their right.

They also invented terrible methods of torments to discover
where any food was, and they were these: to stop up the passages of the privy parts of the miserable wretches, and to drive
sharp stakes up their fundaments; and a man was forced to
bear what it is terrible even to hear, in order to make him con-
fess that he had but one loaf of bread, or that he might discover a handful of barley meal that was concealed; and this was
done when these tormentors were not themselves hungry, for
the thing had been less barbarous had necessity forced them to
it; but this was done to keep their madness in exercise, and as
making preparation of provisions for themselves for the following days. These men went also to meet those that had crept
out of the city by night, as far as the Roman guards, to gather
some plants and herbs that grew wild; and when those people

thought they had got clear of the enemy, they snatched from them what they had brought with them, even while they had frequently entreated them, and that by calling upon the tremendous name of God, to give them back some part of what they had brought, though these would not give them the least crumb, and they were to be well contented that they were only spoiled and not slain at the same time.

It is impossible to go distinctly over every instance of these men's iniquity. I shall therefore speak my mind here at once briefly: That neither did any other city ever suffer such miseries, nor did any age ever breed a generation more fruitful in wickedness than this was, from the beginning of the world. Finally, they brought the Hebrew nation into contempt, that they might themselves appear comparatively less impious with regard to strangers. They confessed what was true, that they were the slaves, the scum, and the spurious and abortive offspring of our nation, while they overthrew the city themselves, and forced the Romans, whether they would or no, to gain a melancholy reputation, by acting gloriously against them, and did almost draw that fire upon the Temple which they seemed to think came too slowly; and indeed when they saw that Temple burning from the upper city, they were neither troubled at it nor did they shed any tears on that account, while yet these passions were discovered among the Romans themselves.

So now Titus' banks were advanced a great way, notwithstanding his soldiers had been very much distressed from the wall. He then sent a party of horsemen and ordered they should lay ambushes for those that went out into the valleys to gather food. Some of these were indeed fighting men, who were not contented with what they got by rapine; but the greater part of them were poor people, who were deterred from deserting by the concern they were under for their own relations, for they could not hope to escape away, together with their wives and children, without the knowledge of the seditious; nor could they think of leaving these relations to be slain by the robbers on their account; nay, the severity of the famine made them bold in thus going out; so nothing remained but that, when they were concealed from the robbers, they should be taken by the enemy; and when they were going to be taken they were forced to defend themselves for fear of be-ing punished; as after they had fought they thought it too late to make any supplications for mercy; so they were first whipped and then tormented with all sorts of tortures before they died, and were then crucified before the wall of the city. This mis-erable procedure made Titus greatly to pity them, while they caught every day five hundred Jews; nay, some days they caught more; yet it did not appear to be safe for him to let those that were taken by force go their way, and to set a guard over so many he saw would be to make such as guarded them useless to him. The main reason why he did not forbid that cruelty was this: that he hoped the Jews might perhaps yield at that sight, out of fear lest they might themselves afterward be liable to the same cruel treatment. So the soldiers, out of the wrath and hatred they bore the Jews, nailed those they caught, one after one way, and another after another, to the crosses, by way of jest, when their multitude was so great that room was wanting for the crosses, and crosses wanting for the bodies.

But so far were the seditious from repenting at this sad sight that, on the contrary, they made the rest of the multi-tude believe otherwise, for they brought the relations of those that had deserted upon the wall, with such of the populace as were very eager to go over upon the security offered them, and showed them what miseries those underwent who fled to the Romans; and told them that those who were caught were supplicants to them, and not such as were taken prisoners. This sight kept many of those within the city who were so eager to desert, till the truth was known; yet did some of them run away immediately as unto certain punishment, esteeming death from their enemies to be a quiet departure, if compared with that by famine. So Titus commanded that the hands of many of those that were caught should be cut off, that they might not be thought deserters, and might be credited on ac-count of the calamity they were under, and sent them in to John and Simon, with this exhortation, that they would now at length leave off (their madness), and not force him to destroy the city, whereby they would have those advantages of repent-ance, even in their utmost distress, that they would preserve their own lives, and so find a city of their own, and that Temple

which was their peculiar. He then went round about the banks
that were cast up, and hastened them, in order to show that his
words should in no long time be followed by his deeds. In answer to which the seditious cast reproaches upon Cæsar himself,
and upon his father also, and cried out, with a loud voice, that
they contemned death, and did well in preferring it before slavery; that they would do all the mischief to the Romans they
could while they had breath in them; and that for their own
city, since they were, as he said, to be destroyed, they had no
concern about it, and that the world itself was a better temple
to God than this. That yet this Temple would be preserved by
Him that inhabited therein, whom they still had for their assistant in this war, and did therefore laugh at all his threatenings,
which would come to nothing, because the conclusion of the
whole depended upon God only. These words were mixed with
reproaches, and with them they made a mighty clamor.

In the mean time Antiochus Epiphanes came to the city,
having with him a considerable number of other armed men,
and a band called the Macedonian band about him, all of the
same age, tall, and just past their childhood, armed, and instructed after the Macedonian manner, whence it was that they
took that name. Antiochus with his Macedonians made a sudden assault upon the wall; and, indeed, for his own part, his
strength and skill were so great that he guarded himself from
the Jewish darts, and yet shot his darts at them, while yet the
young men with him were almost all sorely galled, for they had
so great a regard to the promises that had been made of their
courage, that they would needs persevere in their fighting, and
at length many of them retired, but not till they were wounded;
and then they perceived that true Macedonians, if they were to
be conquerors, must have Alexander's good fortune also.

Now as the Romans began to raise their banks on the
twelfth day of the month Artemisius [Jyar], so had they much
ado to finish them by the twenty-ninth day of the same month,
after they had labored hard for seventeen days continually, for
there were now four great banks raised, one of which was at
the tower Antonia. This was raised by the Fifth legion, over
against the middle of that pool which was called Struthius.
Another was cast up by the Twelfth legion at the distance of

about twenty cubits from the other. But the labors of the Tenth legion, which lay a great way off these, were on the north quarter, and at the pool called Amygdalon; as was that of the Fifteenth legion about thirty cubits from it, and at the high-priest's monument. And now, when the engines were brought, John had from within undermined the space that was over against the tower of Antonia, as far as the banks themselves, and had supported the ground over the mine with beams laid across one another, whereby the Roman works stood upon an uncertain foundation.

Then did he order such materials to be brought in as were daubed over with pitch and bitumen, and set them on fire; and as the cross-beams that supported the banks were burning, the ditch yielded on the sudden, and the banks were shaken down, and fell into the ditch with a prodigious noise. Now at the first there arose a very thick smoke and dust, as the fire was choked with the fall of the bank; but as the suffocated materials were now gradually consumed, a plain flame brake out; on which sudden appearance of the flame a consternation fell upon the Romans, and the shrewdness of the contrivance discouraged them; and indeed this accident coming upon them at a time when they thought they had already gained their point, cooled their hopes for the time to come. They also thought it would be to no purpose to take the pains to extinguish the fire, since if it were extinguished the banks were swallowed up already [and become useless to them].

Two days after this Simon and his party made an attempt to destroy the other banks, for the Romans had brought their engines to bear there, and began already to make the wall shake. And here one Tephtheus, of Garsis, a city of Galilee, and Megassarus, one who was derived from some of Queen Mariamne's servants, and with them one from Adiabene, he was the son of Nabateus, and called by the name of Chagiras, from the ill-fortune he had, the word signifying "a lame man," snatched some torches and ran suddenly upon the engines. Nor were there during this war any men that ever sallied out of the city who were their superiors, either in their boldness or in the terror they struck into their enemies, for they ran out upon the Romans, not as if they were enemies, but friends, without fear or delay; nor did they leave their enemies till they had rushed violently through the midst of them, and set their machines on fire. And though they had darts thrown at them on every side and were on every side assaulted with their enemies' swords, yet did they not withdraw themselves out of the dangers they were in till the fire had caught hold of the instruments; but when the flame went up the Romans came running from their camp to save their engines.

Then did the Jews hinder their succors from the wall, and fought with those that endeavored to quench the fire, without any regard to the danger their bodies were in. So the Romans pulled the engines out of the fire, while the hurdles that covered them were on fire; but the Jews caught hold of the battering rams through the flame itself and held them fast, although the iron upon them was become red hot; and now the fire spread itself from the engines to the banks, and prevented those that came to defend them; and all this while the Romans were encompassed round about with the flame; and, despairing of saving their works from it, they retired to their camp. Then did the Jews become still more and more in number by the coming of those that were within the city to their assistance; and as they were very bold upon the good success they had had, their violent assaults were almost irresistible—nay, they proceeded as far as the fortifications of the enemies' camp, and fought with their guards.

Now there stood a body of soldiers in array before that camp, which succeeded one another by turns in their armor; and as to those, the law of the Romans was terrible, that he who left his post there, let the occasion be whatsoever it might be, he was to die for it; so that body of soldiers, preferring rather to die in fighting courageously than as a punishment for their cowardice, stood firm; and at the necessity these men were in of standing to it, many of the others that had run away, out of shame, turned back again; and when they had set the engines against the wall they put the multitude from coming more of them out of the city (which they could the more easily do) because they had made no provision for preserving or guarding their bodies at this time; for the Jews fought now hand-to-hand with all that came in their way, and, without any caution, fell against the points of their enemies' spears, and attacked them bodies against bodies, for they were now too hard for the Romans, not so much by their other warlike actions, as by these courageous assaults they made upon them; and the Romans gave way more to their boldness than they did to the sense of the harm they had received from them.

And now Titus was come from the tower of Antonia, whither he was gone to look out for a place for raising other banks, and reproached the soldiers greatly for permitting their own walls to be in danger, when they had taken the walls of their enemies, and sustained the fortune of men besieged, while the Jews were allowed to sally out against them, though they were already in a sort of prison. He then went round about the enemy with some chosen troops and fell upon their flank himself; so the Jews, who had been before assaulted in their faces, wheeled about to Titus and continued the fight.

The armies also were now mixed one among another, and the dust that was raised so far hindered them from seeing one another, and the noise that was made so far hindered them from hearing one another, that neither side could discern an enemy from a friend. However, the Jews did not flinch, though not so much from their real strength as from their despair of deliverance. The Romans also would not yield, by reason of the regard they had to glory and to their reputation in war, and because Cæsar himself went into the danger before them; insomuch that I cannot but think the Romans would in the conclusion have now taken even the whole multitude of the Jews, so very angry were they at them, had these not prevented the upshot of the battle, and retired into the city. However, seeing the banks of the Romans were demolished, these Romans were very much cast down upon the loss of what had cost them so long pains, and this in one hour's time. And many indeed despaired of taking the city with their usual engines of war only.

And now did Titus consult with his commanders what was to be done. Those that were of the warmest tempers thought he should bring the whole army against the city and storm the wall. The opinion of Titus was, that if they aimed at quickness joined with security they must build a wall round about the

whole city, and he gave orders that the army should be distributed to their several shares of this work. Titus began the
wall from the camp of the Assyrians, where his own camp was
pitched, and drew it down to the lower parts of Cenopolis;
thence it went along the valley of Cedron to the Mount of
Olives; it then bent toward the south, and encompassed the
mountain as far as the rock called Peristereon, and that other
hill which lies next it, and is over the valley which reaches to
Siloam; whence it bended again to the west, and went down to
the valley of the Fountain, beyond which it went up again at
the monument of Ananus, the high-priest, and encompassing
that mountain where Pompey had formerly pitched his camp,
it returned back to the north side of the city, and was carried
on as far as a certain village called "The House of the Ere-
binthi"; after which it encompassed Herod's monument, and
there, on the east, was joined to Titus' own camp, where it
began.

Now the length of this wall was forty furlongs, one only
abated. Now at this wall without were erected thirteen places
to keep garrison in, whose circumferences, put together,
amounted to ten furlongs; the whole was completed in three
days; so that what would naturally have required some months
was done in so short an interval as is incredible. When Titus
had therefore encompassed the city with this wall and put garrisons into proper places, he went round the wall, at the first
watch of the night, and observed how the guard was kept; the
second watch he allotted to Alexander; the commanders of
legions took the third watch. They also cast lots among themselves who should be upon the watch in the night-time, and
who should go all night long round the spaces that were interposed between the garrisons.

So all hope of escaping was now cut off from the Jews, together with their liberty of going out of the city. Then did
the famine widen its progress and devoured the people by
whole houses and families; the upper rooms were full of women
and children that were dying by famine, and the lanes of the
city were full of the dead bodies of the aged; the children also
and the young men wandered about the market-places like shadows, all swelled with the famine, and fell down dead, whereso-

ever their misery seized them. As for burying them, those
that were sick themselves were not able to do it; and those
that were hearty and well were deterred from doing it by the
great multitude of those dead bodies, and by the uncertainty
there was how soon they should die themselves, for many died
as they were burying others, and many went to their coffins
before that fatal hour was come. Nor was there any lamentations made under these calamities, nor were heard any mournful complaints; but the famine confounded all natural passions, for those who were just going to die looked upon those
that were gone to rest before them with dry eyes and open
mouths.

A deep silence also, and a kind of deadly night, had seized
upon the city; while yet the robbers were still more terrible
than these miseries were themselves, for they brake open those
houses which were no other than graves of dead bodies, and
plundered them of what they had; and carrying off the cover-
ings of their bodies went out laughing, and tried the points of
their swords in their dead bodies; and, in order to prove what
metal they were made of, they thrust some of those through
that still lay alive upon the ground; but for those that entreated
them to lend them their right hand and their sword to despatch
them, they were too proud to grant their requests, and left
them to be consumed by the famine. Now every one of these
died with their eyes fixed upon the Temple, and left the seditious alive behind them. Now the seditious at first gave orders
that the dead should be buried out of the public treasury, as
not enduring the stench of their dead bodies. But afterward,
when they could not do that, they had them cast down from
the walls into the valleys beneath.

However, when Titus, in going his rounds along those valleys, saw them full of dead bodies, and the thick putrefaction
running about them, he gave a groan; and, spreading out his
hands to heaven, called God to witness that this was not his
doing; and such was the sad case of the city itself. But the
Romans were very joyful, since none of the seditious could
now make sallies out of the city, because they were themselves
disconsolate, and the famine already touched them also. These
Romans besides had great plenty of corn and other necessaries

out of Syria and out of the neighboring provinces; many of whom would stand near to the wall of the city and show the people what great quantities of provisions they had and so make the enemy more sensible of their famine, by the great plenty, even to satiety, which they had themselves.

In the mean time Josephus, as he was going round the city, had his head wounded by a stone that was thrown at him; upon which he fell down as giddy. Josephus soon recovered of his wound and came out and cried out aloud, that it would not be long ere they should be punished for this wound they had given him. He also made a fresh exhortation to the people to come out upon the security that would be given them. This sight of Josephus encouraged the people greatly and brought a great consternation upon the seditious.

Hereupon some of the deserters, having no other way, leaped down from the wall immediately, while others of them went out of the city with stones, as if they would fight them; but thereupon they fled away to the Romans. But here a worse fate accompanied these than what they had found within the city; and they met with a quicker despatch from the too great abundance they had among the Romans than they could have done from the famine among the Jews, for when they came first to the Romans they were puffed up by the famine and swelled like men in a dropsy; after which they all on the sudden overfilled those bodies that were before empty, and so burst asunder, excepting such only as were skilful enough to restrain their appetites, and by degrees took in their food into bodies unaccustomed thereto.

Yet did another plague seize upon those that were thus preserved, for there was found among the Syrian deserters a certain person who was caught gathering pieces of gold out of the excrements of the Jews' bellies, for the deserters used to swallow such pieces of gold, as we told you before, when they came out, and for these did the seditious search them all; for there was a great quantity of gold in the city, insomuch that as much was now sold [in the Roman camp] for twelve Attic [drachmas] as was sold before for twenty-five. But when this contrivance was discovered in one instance, the fame of it filled their several camps, that the deserters came to them full of gold.   So the multitude of the Arabians, with the Syrians, cut up those that came as supplicants, and searched their bellies. Nor does it seem to me that any misery befell the Jews that was more terrible than this, since in one night's time about two thousand of these deserters were thus dissected.

When Titus came to the knowledge of this wicked practice, he threatened that he would put such men to death if any of them were discovered to be so insolent as to do so again. Moreover, he gave it in charge to the legions, that they should make a search after such as were suspected, and should bring them to him.   But it appeared that the love of money was too great for all their dread of punishment, and a vehement desire of gain is natural to men, and no passion is so venturesome as covetousness.   Otherwise such passions have certain bounds and are subordinate to fear.   But in reality it was God who condemned the whole nation and turned every course that was taken for their preservation to their destruction.   This, therefore, which was forbidden by Cæsar under such a threatening, was ventured upon privately against the deserters, and these barbarians would go out still and meet those that ran away before any saw them, and looking about them to see that no Roman spied them, they dissected them and pulled this polluted money out of their bowels, which money was still found in a few of them, while yet a great many were destroyed by the bare hope there was of thus getting by them, which miserable treatment made many that were deserting to return back again into the city.

And, indeed, why do I relate these particular calamities? while Manneus, the son of Lazarus, came running to Titus at this very time and told him that there had been carried out through that one gate, which was intrusted to his care, no fewer than a hundred and fifteen thousand eight hundred and eighty dead bodies in the interval between the fourteenth day of the month Xanthicus (Nisan), when the Romans pitched their camp by the city, and the first day of the month Panemus (Tamuz).   This was itself a prodigious multitude; and though this man was not himself set as a governor at that gate, yet was he appointed to pay the public stipend for carrying these bodies out, and so was obliged of necessity to number them, while the rest were buried by their relations, though all their burial was but this, to bring them away and cast them out of the city.

After this man there ran away to Titus many of the eminent citizens and told him the entire number of the poor that were dead, and that no fewer than six hundred thousand were thrown out at the gates, though still the number of the rest could not be discovered; and they told him further that when they were no longer able to carry out the dead bodies of the poor they laid their corpses on heaps in very large houses and shut them up therein; as also that a medimno of wheat was sold for a talent; and that when, a while afterward, it was not possible to gather herbs, by reason the city was all walled about, some persons were driven to that terrible distress as to search the common sewers and old dunghills of cattle, and to eat the dung which they got there, and what they of old could not endure so much as to see they now used for food. When the Romans barely heard all this they commiserated their case; while the seditious, who saw it also, did not repent, but suffered the same distress to come upon themselves, for they were blinded by that fate which was already coming upon the city, and upon themselves also.

And now the Romans, although they were greatly distressed in getting together their materials, raised their banks in one-and-twenty days, after they had cut down all the trees that were in the country that adjoined to the city, and that for ninety furlongs round about. And when the banks were finished, they afforded a foundation for fear both to the Romans and to the Jews, for the Jews expected that the city would be taken unless they could burn those banks, as did the Romans expect that, if these were once burned down they should never be able to take it, for there was a mighty scarcity of materials, and the bodies of the soldiers began to fail with such hard labors, as did their souls faint with so many instances of ill-success.

The Romans had an advantage, in that their engines for sieges coöperated with them in throwing darts and stones as far as the Jews, when they were coming out of the city; whereby the man that fell became an impediment to him that was next to him, as did the danger of going farther make them less zeal-ous in their attempts; and for those that had run under the darts some of them were terrified by the good order and close-ness of the enemies' ranks before they came to a close fight, and others were pricked with their spears and turned back again. At length they reproached one another for their cow-ardice, and retired without doing anything. This attack was made upon the first day of the month Panemus (Tamuz).

So when the Jews were retreated the Romans brought their engines, although they had all the while stones thrown at them from the tower of Antonia, and were assaulted by fire and sword, and by all sorts of darts, which necessity afforded the Jews to make use of, for although these had great dependence on their own wall, and a contempt of the Roman engines, yet did they endeavor to hinder the Romans from bringing them. Now these Romans struggled hard, on the contrary, to bring them, as deeming that this zeal of the Jews was in order to avoid any impression to be made on the tower of Antonia, be-cause its wall was but weak and its foundations rotten. How-ever, that tower did not yield to the blows given it from the engines; yet did the Romans bear the impressions made by the enemies' darts which were perpetually cast at them, and did not give way to any of those dangers that came upon them from above, and so they brought their engines to bear. But then, as they were beneath the other, and were sadly wounded by the stones thrown down upon them, some of them threw their shields over their bodies, and partly with their hands and partly with their bodies and partly with crows they under-mined its foundations, and with great pains they removed four of its stones. Then night came upon both sides, and put an end to this struggle for the present. However, that night the wall was so shaken by the battering rams in that place where John had used his stratagem before, and had undermined their banks, that the ground then gave way and the wall fell down suddenly.

When this accident had unexpectedly happened, the minds of both parties were variously affected, for though one would expect that the Jews would be discouraged, because this fall of their wall was unexpected by them, and they had made no provision in that case, yet did they pull up their courage, because the tower of Antonia itself was still standing; as was the unexpected joy of the Romans at this fall of the wall soon quenched by the sight they had of another wall, which John and his party had built within it.

Upon the fifth day of the month Panemus (Tamuz), twelve of those men that were on the forefront and kept watch upon the banks got together and called to them the standard-bearer of the Fifth legion, and two others of a troop of horsemen, and one trumpeter; these went without noise, about the ninth hour of the night, through the ruins, to the tower of Antonia; and when they had cut the throats of the first guards of the place, as they were asleep, they got possession of the wall and ordered the trumpeter to sound his trumpet. Upon which the rest of the guard got up on the sudden and ran away before anybody could see how many they were that were gotten up, for partly from the fear they were in and partly from the sound of the trumpet which they heard they imagined a great number of the enemy were gotten up. But as soon as Cæsar heard the signal he ordered the army to put on their armor immediately, and came thither with his commanders, and first of all ascended, as did the chosen men that were with him. And as the Jews were flying away to the Temple they fell into that mine which John had dug under the Roman banks. Then did the seditious of both the bodies of the Jewish army, as well that belonging to John as that belonging to Simon, drive them away; and indeed were no way wanting as to the highest degree of force and alacrity; for they esteemed themselves entirely ruined if once the Romans got into the Temple, as did the Romans look upon the same thing as the beginning of their entire conquest.

So a terrible battle was fought at the entrance of the Temple, while the Romans were forcing their way, in order to get possession of that Temple, and the Jews were driving them back to the tower of Antonia; in which battle the darts were on both sides useless, as well as the spears, and both sides drew their swords and fought it out hand-to-hand. Now during this struggle the positions of the men were undistinguished on both sides, and they fought at random, the men being intermixed

one with another and confounded, by reason of the narrowness
of the place; while the noise that was made fell on the ear
after an indistinct manner, because it was so very loud. Great
slaughter was now made on both sides, and the combatants
trod upon the bodies and the armor of those that were dead,
and dashed them to pieces. Accordingly, to which side soever
the battle inclined, those that had the advantage exhorted one
another to go on, as did those that were beaten make great
lamentation. But still there was no room for flight nor for
pursuit, but disorderly revolutions and retreats, while the
armies were intermixed one with another; but those that were
in the first ranks were under the necessity of killing or being
killed, without any way for escaping, for those on both sides
that came behind forced those before them to go on, without
leaving any space between the armies.

At length the Jews' violent zeal was too hard for the Romans' skill, and the battle already inclined entirely that way;
for the fight had lasted from the ninth hour of the night till
the seventh hour of the day, while the Jews came on in crowds,
and had the danger the Temple was in for their motive; the
Romans having no more here than a part of their army, for those
legions, on which the soldiers on that side depended, were not
come up to them. So it was at present thought sufficient by
the Romans to take possession of the tower of Antonia.

In the mean time the rest of the Roman army had, in seven
days' time, overthrown [some] foundations of the tower of Antonia, and had made a ready and broad way to the Temple.
Then did the legions come near the first court and began to
raise their banks. The one bank was over against the northwest corner of the inner temple; another was at that northern
edifice which was between the two gates; and of the other two,
one was at the western cloister of the outer court of the Temple; the other against its northern cloister. However these
works were thus far advanced by the Romans, not without
great pains and difficulty, and particularly by being obliged to
bring their materials from the distance of a hundred furlongs.

They had further difficulties also upon them; sometimes
by their over-great security they were in that they should overcome the Jewish snares laid for them, and by that boldness of

the Jews which their despair of escaping had inspired them withal.

In the mean time the Jews were so distressed by the fights they had been in, as the war advanced higher and higher, and creeping up to the holy house itself, that they, as it were, cut off those limbs of their body which were infected, in order to prevent the distemper's spreading further, for they set the northwest cloister, which was joined to the tower of Antonia, on fire, and after that brake off about twenty cubits of that cloister, and thereby made a beginning in burning the sanctuary; two days after which, or on the twenty-fourth day of the forenamed month [Panemus or Tamuz], the Romans set fire to the cloister that joined to the other, when the fire went fifteen cubits farther. The Jews, in like manner, cut off its roof; nor did they entirely leave off what they were about till the tower of Antonia was parted from the Temple, even when it was in their power to have stopped the fire—nay, they lay still while the Temple was first set on fire, and deemed this spreading of the fire to be for their own advantage. However, the armies were still fighting one against another about the Temple, and the war was managed by continual sallies of particular parties against one another.

Now of those that perished by famine in the city the number was prodigious, and the miseries they underwent were unspeakable, for if so much as the shadow of any kind of food did anywhere appear a war was commenced presently, and the dearest friends fell a-fighting one with another about it, snatching from each other the most miserable supports of life. Nor would men believe that those who were dying had no food, but the robbers would search them when they were expiring, lest anyone should have concealed food in his bosom and counterfeited dying; nay, these robbers gaped for want, and ran about stumbling and staggering along like mad dogs, and reeling against the doors of the houses like drunken men; they would also, in the great distress they were in, rush into the very same houses two or three times in one and the same day. Moreover, their hunger was so intolerable that it obliged them to chew everything, while they gathered such things as the most sordid animals would not touch, and endured to eat them;

nor did they at length abstain from girdles and shoes; and the very leather which belonged to their shields they pulled off and gnawed; the very wisps of old hay became food to some; and some gathered up fibres and sold a very small weight of them for four Attic [drachmas].

But why do I describe the shameless impudence that the famine brought on men in their eating inanimate things, while I am going to relate a matter of fact, the like to which no history relates, either among the Greeks or barbarians? It is horrible to speak of it and incredible when heard. I had indeed willingly omitted this calamity of ours, that I might not seem to deliver what is so portentous to posterity, but that I have innumerable witnesses to it in my own age; and besides, my country would have had little reason to thank me for suppressing the miseries that she underwent at this time.

There was a certain woman that dwelt beyond Jordan, her name was Mary; her father was Eleazar, of the village Bethezob, which signifies "the House of Hyssop." She was eminent for her family and her wealth, and had fled away to Jerusalem with the rest of the multitude, and was with them besieged therein at this time. The other effects of this woman had been already seized upon, such I mean as she had brought with her out of Perea, and removed to the city. What she had treasured up besides, as also what food she had contrived to save, had been also carried off by the rapacious guards, who came every day running into her house for that purpose. This put the poor woman into a very great passion, and by the frequent reproaches and imprecations she cast at these rapacious villains she had provoked them to anger against her; but none of them, either out of the indignation she had raised against herself, or out of commiseration of her case, would take away her life; and if she found any food, she perceived her labors were for others, and not for herself; and it was now become impossible for her any way to find any more food, while the famine pierced through her very bowels and marrow, when also her passion was fired to a degree beyond the famine itself; nor did she consult with anything but with her passion and the necessity she was in. She then attempted a most unnatural thing; and snatching up her son, who was a child sucking at her breast, she said: "O thou miserable infant! for whom shall I preserve thee in this war, this famine, and this sedition? As to the war with the Romans, if they preserve our lives we must be slaves. This famine also will destroy us even before that slavery comes upon us. Yet are these seditious rogues more terrible than both the other. Come on: be thou my food, and be thou a fury to these seditious varlets, and a by-word to the world, which is all that is now wanting to complete the calamities of us Jews."

As soon as she had said this she slew her son, and then roasted him, and eat the one half of him, and kept the other half by her concealed. Upon this the seditious came in presently, and smelling the horrid scent of this food, they threatened her that they would cut her throat immediately if she did not show them what food she had gotten ready. She replied that she had saved a very fine portion of it for them, and withal uncovered what was left of her son. Hereupon they were seized with a horror and amazement of mind, and stood astonished at the sight, when she said to them: "This is mine own son, and what hath been done was mine own doing! Come, eat of this food, for I have eaten of it myself! Do not you pretend to be either more tender than a woman or more compassionate than a mother; but if you be so scrupulous and do abominate this my sacrifice, as I have eaten the one half, let the rest be reserved for me also." After which those men went out trembling, being never so much affrighted at anything as they were at this, and with some difficulty they left the rest of that meat to the mother. Upon which the whole city was full of this horrid action immediately; and while everybody laid this miserable case before their own eyes, they trembled, as if this unheard-of action had been done by themselves. So those that were thus distressed by the famine were very desirous to die, and those already dead were esteemed happy, because they had not lived long enough either to hear or to see such miseries.

This sad instance was quickly told to the Romans, some of whom could not believe it, and others pitied the distress which the Jews were under; but there were many of them who were hereby induced to a more bitter hatred than ordinary against our nation. But for Cæsar, he excused himself before God as to this matter, and said that he had proposed peace and liberty to the Jews, as well as an oblivion of all their former insolent practices; but that they, instead of concord, had chosen sedition; instead of peace, war; and before satiety and abundance, a famine. That they had begun with their own hands to burn down that Temple which we have preserved hitherto, and that therefore they deserved to eat such food as this was. That, however, this horrid action of eating an own child ought to be covered with the overthrow of their very country itself, and men ought not to leave such a city upon the habitable earth to be seen by the sun wherein mothers are thus fed, although such food be fitter for the fathers than for the mothers to eat of, since it is they that continue still in a state of war against us, after they have undergone such miseries as these. And at the same time that he said this, he reflected on the desperate condition these men must be in; nor could he expect that such men could be recovered to sobriety of mind after they had endured those very sufferings, for the avoiding whereof it only was probable they might have repented.

And now two of the legions had completed their banks on the eighth day of the month Lous [Ab]. Whereupon Titus gave orders that the battering rams should be brought and set over against the western edifice of the inner temple; for before these were brought, the firmest of all the other engines had battered the wall for six days together without ceasing, without making any impression upon it; but the vast largeness and strong connection of the stones were superior to that engine and to the other battering rams also. Other Romans did indeed undermine the foundations of the northern gate, and after a world of pains removed the outermost stones, yet was the gate still upheld by the inner stones, and stood still unhurt; till the workmen, despairing of all such attempts by engines and crows, brought their ladders to the cloisters.

Now the Jews did not interrupt them in so doing; but when they were gotten up, they fell upon them and fought with them; some of them they thrust down and threw them backward headlong; others of them they met and slew; they also beat many of those that went down the ladders again, and slew them with their swords before they could bring their shields to protect them; nay, some of the ladders they threw down from above when they were full of armed men. A great slaughter was made of the Jews also at the same time, while those that bare the ensigns fought hard for them, as deeming it a terrible thing, and what would tend to their great shame, if they permitted them to be stolen away. Yet did the Jews at length get possession of these engines, and destroyed those that had gone up the ladders, while the rest were so intimidated by what those suffered who were slain that they retired; although none of the Romans died without having done good service before his death. Of the seditious, those that had fought bravely in the former battles did the like now, as besides them did Eleazar, the brother's son of Simon the tyrant. But when Titus perceived that his endeavors to spare a foreign temple turned to the damage of his soldiers and made them be killed, he gave order to set the gates on fire.

But then, on the next day, Titus commanded part of his army to quench the fire and to make a road for the more easy marching up of the legions, while he himself gathered the commanders together. Titus proposed to these that they should give him their advice what should be done about the holy house. Now some of these thought it would be the best way to act according to the rules of war [and demolish it], because the Jews would never leave off rebelling while that house was standing; at which house it was that they used to get all together. Others of them were of opinion that in case the Jews would leave it, and none of them would lay their arms up in it, he might save it; but that in case they got upon it and fought any more, he might burn it; because it must then be looked upon not as a holy house, but as a citadel; and that the impiety of burning it would then belong to those that forced this to be done, and not to them.

But Titus said that "although the Jews should get upon that holy house and fight us thence, yet ought we not to revenge ourselves on things that are inanimate, instead of the men themselves"? and that he was not in any case for burning down so vast a work as that was, because this would be a mischief to the Romans themselves, as it would be an ornament to their government while it continued. So Fronto and Alexander and Cerealis grew bold upon that declaration, and agreed to the opinion of Titus. Then was this assembly dissolved, when Titus had given orders to the commanders that the rest of their forces should lie still; but that they should make use of such as were most courageous in this attack. So he commanded that the chosen men that were taken out of the cohorts should make their way through the ruins and quench the fire.

Now it is true that on this day the Jews were so weary and under such consternation that they refrained from any attacks. But on the next day they gathered their whole force together, and ran upon those that guarded the outward court of the Temple very boldly, through the east gate, and this about the second hour of the day. These guards received their attack with great bravery, and by covering themselves with their shields before, as if it were with a wall, drew their squadron close together; yet was it evident that they could not abide there very long, but would be overborne by the multitude of those that sallied out upon them, and by the heat of their passion. However, Cæsar seeing, from the tower of Antonia, that this squadron was likely to give way, sent some chosen horsemen to support them. Hereupon the Jews found themselves not able to sustain their onset, and, upon the slaughter of those in the forefront, many of the rest were put to flight. But as the Romans were going off, the Jews turned upon them and fought them; and as those Romans came back upon them, they retreated again, until about the fifth hour of the day they were overborne, and shut themselves up in the inner [court of the] Temple.

So Titus retired into the tower of Antonia and resolved to storm the Temple the next day, early in the morning, with his whole army, and to encamp round about the holy house. But as for that house, God had, for certain, long ago doomed it to the fire; and now that fatal day was come, according to the revolution of ages. It was the tenth day of the month Lous [Ab] upon which it was formerly burned by the king of Babylon; although these flames took their rise from the Jews themselves, and were occasioned by them, for upon Titus' retiring the seditious lay still for a little while, and then attacked the Romans again when those that guarded the holy house fought with those that quenched the fire that was burning the inner [court of the] Temple; but these Romans put the Jews to flight and proceeded as far as the holy house itself. At which time one of the soldiers, without staying for any orders and without any concern or dread upon him at so great an undertaking and being hurried on by a certain divine fury, snatched somewhat out of the materials that were on fire, and being lifted up by another soldier he set fire to a golden window through which there was a passage to the rooms that were round about the holy house on the north side of it.

As the flames went upward the Jews made a great clamor such as so mighty an affliction required and ran together to prevent it; and now they spared not their lives any longer nor suffered anything to restrain their force, since that holy house was perishing for whose sake it was that they kept such a guard about it.

And now Cæsar was no way able to restrain the enthusiastic fury of the soldiers, and the fire proceeded on more and more. He went into the holy place of the Temple with his commanders and saw it, with what was in it, which he found to be far superior to what the relations of foreigners contained, and not inferior to what we ourselves boasted of and believed about it. But as the flame had not as yet reached to its inward parts, but was still consuming the rooms that were about the holy house, and Titus supposing what the fact was, that the house itself might yet be saved, came in haste and endeavored to persuade the soldiers to quench the fire, and gave order to Liberalius the centurion, and one of those spearmen that were about him, to beat the soldiers that were refractory with their staves and to restrain them; yet were their passions too hard for the regards they had for Cæsar, and the dread they had of him who forbade them, as was their hatred of the Jews, and a certain vehement inclination to fight them, too hard for them also. Moreover, the hope of plunder induced many to go on, as having this opinion, that all the places within were full of money, and as seeing that all round about it was made of gold. And besides, one of those that went into the place prevented Cæsar,

when he ran so hastily out to restrain the soldiers, and threw
the fire upon the hinges of the gate, in the dark; whereby the
flame burst out from within the holy house itself immediately,
when the commanders retired, and Cæsar with them, and when
nobody any longer forbade those that were without to set fire
to it.   And thus was the holy house burned down without Cæsar's approbation.

While the holy house was on fire everything was plundered
that came to hand, and ten thousand of those that were caught
were slain; nor was there a commiseration of any age, or any
reverence of gravity, but children, and old men, and profane
persons, and priests were all slain in the same manner; so that
this war went round all sorts of men, and brought them to destruction, and as well those that made supplication for their
lives as those that defended themselves by fighting.   The
flame was also carried a long way, and made an echo, together
with the groans of those that were slain; and because this hill
was high, and the works at the Temple were very great, one
would have thought the whole city had been on fire.   Nor can
one imagine anything either greater or more terrible than this
noise, for there was at once a shout of the Roman legions, who
were marching all together, and a sad clamor of the seditious,
who were now surrounded with fire and sword.

The people also that were left above were beaten back upon
the enemy, and under a great consternation, and made sad
moans at the calamity they were under; the multitude also that
was in the city joined in this outcry with those that were upon
the hill.   And besides, many of those that were worn away by
the famine and their mouths almost closed, when they saw the
fire of the holy house they exerted their utmost strength and
brake out into groans and outcries again.   Perea did also return
the echo, as well as the mountains round about [the city], and
augmented the force of the entire noise.   Yet was the misery
itself more terrible than this disorder, for one would have
thought that the hill itself, on which the Temple stood, was
seething hot, as full of fire on every part of it, that the blood
was larger in quantity than the fire, and those that were slain
more in number than those that slew them, for the ground did
nowhere appear visible for the dead bodies that lay on it; but

the soldiers went over heaps of those bodies, as they ran upon
such as fled from them.

And now it was that the multitude of the robbers were
thrust out [of the inner court of the Temple] by the Romans,
and had much ado to get into the outward court, and from
thence into the city, while the remainder of the populace fled
into the cloister of that outer court. As for the priests, some of
them plucked up from the holy house the spikes that were
upon it, with their bases, which were made of lead, and shot
them at the Romans instead of darts. But then as they gained
nothing by so doing, and as the fire burst out upon them, they
retired to the wall that was eight cubits broad, and there they
tarried.

And now the Romans, judging that it was in vain to spare
what was round about the holy house, burned all those places,
as also the remains of the cloisters and the gates, two excepted:
the one on the east side and the other on the south; both
which, however, they burned afterward. They also burned
down the treasury chambers, in which was an immense quantity of money and an immense number of garments and other
precious goods there reposited; and, to speak all in a few
words, there it was that the entire riches of the Jews were
heaped up together, while the rich people had there built themselves chambers (to contain such furniture). The soldiers also
came to the rest of the cloisters that were in the outer (court
of the) Temple, whither the women and children, and a great
mixed multitude of the people, fled, in number about six thousand. But before Cæsar had determined anything about these
people, or given the commanders any orders relating to them,
the soldiers were in such a rage that they set that cloister on
fire; by which means it came to pass that some of these were
destroyed by throwing themselves down headlong, and some
were burned in the cloisters themselves. Nor did any one of
them escape with his life.

And now the Romans, upon the flight of the seditious into
the city, and upon the burning of the holy house itself and of
all the buildings round about it, brought their ensigns to the
Temple and set them over against its eastern gate; and there
did they offer sacrifices to them, and there did they make

Titus imperator with the greatest acclamations of joy. And now all the soldiers had such vast quantities of the spoils which they had gotten by plunder that in Syria a pound weight of gold was sold for half its former value.

But as for the tyrants themselves and those that were with them, when they found that they were encompassed on every side, and, as it were, walled round, without any method of escaping, they desired to treat with Titus by word of mouth. Accordingly, such was the kindness of his nature and his desire of preserving the city from destruction, joined to the advice of his friends, who now thought the robbers were come to a temper, that he placed himself on the western side of the outer (court of the) Temple, for there were gates on that side above the Xystus, and a bridge that connected the upper city to the Temple. This bridge it was that lay between the tyrants and Cæsar, and parted them; while the multitude stood on each side; those of the Jewish nation about Simon and John, with great hopes of pardon; and the Romans about Cæsar, in great expectation how Titus would receive their supplication.

So Titus charged his soldiers to restrain their rage and to let their darts alone, and appointed an interpreter between them, which was a sign that he was the conqueror, and first began the discourse, and said: "I hope you, sirs, are now satiated with the miseries of your country, who have not had any just notions either of our great power or of your own great weakness, but have, like madmen, after a violent and inconsiderate manner, made such attempts as have brought your people, your city, and your holy house to destruction. You have been the men that have never left off rebelling since Pompey first conquered you, and have since that time made open war with the Romans. . . . And now, vile wretches, do you desire to treat with me by word of mouth? To what purpose is it that you would save such a holy house as this was which is now destroyed? What preservation can you now desire after the destruction of your Temple? Yet do you stand still at this very time in your armor; nor can you bring yourselves so much as to pretend to be suppliants even in this your utmost extremity. O miserable creatures! what is it you depend on? Are not your people dead? is not your holy house gone? is not your city in my power? and are not your own very lives in my hands? And do you still deem it a part of valor to die? However, I will not imitate your madness. If you throw down your arms and deliver up your bodies to me, I grant you your lives; and I will act like a mild master of a family; what cannot be healed shall be punished, and the rest I will preserve for my own use."

To that offer of Titus they made this reply: That they could not accept of it, because they had sworn never to do so; but they desired they might have leave to go through the wall that had been made about them, with their wives and children; for that they would go into the desert and leave the city to him.

At this Titus had great indignation, that when they were in the case of men already taken captives, they should pretend to make their own terms with him, as if they had been conquerors. So he ordered this proclamation to be made to them: That they should no more come out to him as deserters, nor hope for any further security, for that he would henceforth spare nobody, but fight them with his whole army; and that they must save themselves as well as they could, for that he would from henceforth treat them according to the laws of war. So he gave orders to the soldiers both to burn and to plunder the city; who did nothing indeed that day; but on the next day they set fire to the repository of the archives, to Acra, to the council house, and to the place called Ophlas; at which time the fire proceeded as far as the palace of Queen Helena, which was in the middle of Acra; the lanes also were burned down, as were also those houses that were full of the dead bodies of such as were destroyed by famine.

On the same day it was that the sons and brethren of Izates the King, together with many others of the eminent men of the populace, got together there, and besought Cæsar to give them his right hand for their security. Upon which, though he was very angry at all that were now remaining, yet did he not lay aside his old moderation, but received these men. At that time, indeed, he kept them all in custody, but still bound the King's sons and kinsmen, and led them with him to Rome, in order to make them hostages for their country's fidelity to the Romans.

And now the seditious rushed into the royal palace, into which many had put their effects, because it was so strong, and drove the Romans away from it. They also slew all the people that had crowded into it, who were in number about eight thousand four hundred, and plundered them of what they had.

On the next day the Romans drove the robbers out of the lower city and set all on fire as far as Siloam. These soldiers were indeed glad to see the city destroyed. But they missed the plunder, because the seditious had carried off all their effects, and were retired into the upper city, for they did not yet at all repent of the mischiefs they had done, but were insolent, as if they had done well; for, as they saw the city on fire, they appeared cheerful, and put on joyful countenances, in expectation, as they said, of death to end their miseries. Accordingly, as the people were now slain, the holy house was burned down, and the city was on fire, there was nothing further left for the enemy to do. Yet did not Josephus grow weary, even in this utmost extremity, to beg of them to spare what was left of the city; he spake largely to them about their barbarity and impiety, and gave them his advice in order to their escape, though he gained nothing thereby more than to be laughed at by them; and as they could not think of surrendering themselves up, because of the oath they had taken, nor were strong enough to fight with the Romans any longer upon the square, as being surrounded on all sides, and a kind of prisoners already, yet were they so accustomed to kill people that they could not restrain their right hands from acting accordingly.

So they dispersed themselves before the city and laid themselves in ambush among its ruins, to catch those that attempted to desert to the Romans. Accordingly, many such deserters were caught by them and were all slain, for these were too weak, by reason of their want of food, to fly away from them; so their dead bodies were thrown to the dogs. Now every other sort of death was thought more tolerable than the famine, insomuch that, though the Jews despaired now of mercy, yet would they fly to the Romans, and would themselves, even of their own accord, fall among the murderous rebels also. Nor was there any place in the city that had no dead bodies in it, but what was entirely covered with those that were killed either by the famine or the rebellion; and all was full of the dead bodies of such as had perished, either by that sedition or by the famine.

So now the last hope which supported the tyrants and that crew of robbers who were with them was in the caves and caverns underground; whither, if they could once fly, they did not expect to be searched for; but endeavored that, after the whole city should be destroyed and the Romans gone away, they might come out again and escape from them. This was no better than a dream of theirs, for they were not able to lie hid either from God or from the Romans. However, they depended on these underground subterfuges, and set more places on fire than did the Romans themselves; and those that fled out of their houses thus set on fire into the ditches they killed without mercy, and pillaged them also; and if they discovered food belonging to anyone they seized upon it and swallowed it down, together with their blood also — nay, they were now come to fight one with another about their plunder; and I cannot but think that, had not their destruction prevented it, their barbarity would have made them taste of even the dead bodies themselves.

Now when Cæsar perceived that the upper city was so steep that it could not possibly be taken without raising banks against it, he distributed the several parts of that work among his army, and this on the twentieth day of the month Lous [Ab].

It was at this time that the commanders of the Idumeans got together privately and took counsel about surrendering up themselves to the Romans. Accordingly, they sent five men to Titus and entreated him to give them his right hand for their security. So Titus, thinking that the tyrants would yield, if the Idumeans, upon whom a great part of the war depended, were once withdrawn from them, after some reluctancy and delay complied with them, and gave them security for their lives, and sent the five men back. But as these Idumeans were preparing to march out, Simon perceived it, and immediately slew the five men that had gone to Titus, and took their commanders and put them in prison, of whom the most eminent was Jacob, the son of Sosas; but as for the multitude of the Idumeans, who did not at all know what to do, now their commanders were taken from them, he had them watched, and secured the walls by a more numerous garrison. Yet could not that garrison resist those that were deserting, for although a great number of them were slain, yet were the deserters many more in number. These were all received by the Romans, because Titus himself grew negligent as to his former orders for killing them, and because the very soldiers grew weary of killing them, and because they hoped to get some money by sparing them, for they left only the populace, and sold the rest of the multitude, with their wives and children, and every one of them at a very low price, and that because such as were sold were very many, and the buyers were few; and although Titus had made proclamation beforehand that no deserter should come alone by himself, that so they might bring out their families with them, yet did he receive such as these also.

However, he set over them such as were to distinguish some from others, in order to see if any of them deserved to be punished. And indeed the number of those that were sold was immense; but of the populace above forty thousand were saved, whom Cæsar let go whither every one of them pleased.

But now at this time it was that one of the priests, the son of Thebuthus, whose name was Jesus, upon his having security given him, by the oath of Cæsar, that he should be preserved upon condition that he should deliver to him certain of the precious things that had been deposited in the Temple, came out of it and delivered him from the wall of the holy house two candlesticks, like to those that lay in the holy house, with tables, and cisterns, and vials, all made of solid gold and very heavy. He also delivered to him the veils and the garments, with the precious stones, and a great number of other precious vessels that belonged to their sacred worship.

The treasurer of the Temple also, whose name was Phineas, was seized on, and showed Titus the coats and girdles of the priests, with a great quantity of purple and scarlet, which were there deposited for the uses of the veil, as also a great deal of cinnamon and cassia, with a large quantity of other sweet spices, which used to be mixed together and offered as incense to God every day. A great many other treasures were also delivered to him, with sacred ornaments of the Temple not a few, which things thus delivered to Titus obtained of him for this man the same pardon that he had allowed to such as deserted of their own accord.

And now were the banks finished on the seventh day of the month Gorpieus (Elul) in eighteen days' time, when the Romans brought their machines against the wall. But for the seditious, some of them, as despairing of saving the city, retired from the wall to the citadel. Others of them went down into the subterranean vaults, though still a great many of them defended themselves against those that brought the engines for the battery; yet did the Romans overcome them by their number and by their strength; and, what was the principal thing of all, by going cheerfully about their work, while the Jews were quite dejected and become weak. Now as soon as a part of the wall was battered down, and certain of the towers yielded to the impression of the battering rams, those that opposed themselves fled away, and such a terror fell upon the tyrants as was much greater than the occasion required, for before the enemy got over the breach they were quite stunned, and were immediately for flying away. And now one might see these men, who had hitherto been so insolent and arrogant in their wicked practices, to be cast down and to tremble, insomuch that it would pity one's heart to observe the change that was made in those vile persons.

Accordingly, they ran with great violence upon the Roman wall that encompassed them, in order to force away those that guarded it, and to break through it and get away. But when they saw that those who had formerly been faithful to them had gone away—as indeed they were fled whithersoever the great distress they were in persuaded them to flee—as also when those that came running before the rest told them that the western wall was entirely overthrown, while others said the Romans were gotten in, and others that they were near and looking out for them, which were only the dictates of their fear, which imposed upon their sight, they fell upon their face and greatly lamented their own mad conduct; and their nerves were so terribly loosed that they could not flee away. And here one may chiefly reflect on the power of God exercised upon these wicked wretches, and on the good fortune of the Romans, for these tyrants did now wholly deprive themselves of the security they had in their own power, and came down from those very towers of their own accord, wherein they could have never been taken by force, nor indeed by any other way than by famine. And thus did the Romans, when they had taken such great pains about weaker walls, get by good fortune what they could never have gotten by their engines, for three of these towers were too strong for all mechanical engines whatsoever.

So they now left these towers of themselves, or rather they were ejected out of them by God himself, and fled immediately to that valley which was under Siloam, where they again recovered themselves out of the dread they were in for a while, and ran violently against that part of the Roman wall which lay on that side; but as their courage was too much depressed to make their attacks with sufficient force, and their power was now broken with fear and affliction, they were repulsed by the guards, and dispersing themselves at distances from each other, went down into the subterranean caverns.

So the Romans being now become masters of the walls, they both placed their ensigns upon the towers and made joyful acclamations for the victory they had gained, as having found the end of this war much lighter than its beginning, for when they had gotten upon the last wall, without any bloodshed, they could hardly believe what they found to be true; but seeing nobody to oppose them, they stood in doubt what such an unusual solitude could mean. But when they went in numbers into the lanes of the city with their swords drawn they slew those whom they overtook without mercy, and set fire to the houses whither the Jews were fled, and burned every soul in them, and laid waste a great many of the rest; and when they were come to the houses to plunder them they found in them entire families of dead men; and the upper rooms full of corpses, that is, of such as died by the famine. They stood in horror at this sight, and went out without touching anything.

Although they had this commiseration for such as were de-

stroyed in that manner, yet had they not the same for those
that were still alive, but they ran every one through whom
they met, and obstructed the very lanes with their dead bodies,
and made the whole city run with blood, to such a degree indeed that the fire of many of the houses was quenched with
these men's blood.   And truly so it happened, that though the
slayers left off. at the evening, yet did the fire greatly prevail
in the night; and as all was burning, came that eighth day of
the month Gorpieus [Elul] upon Jerusalem, a city that had
been liable to so many miseries during this siege, that, had it
always enjoyed as much happiness from its first foundation, it
would certainly have been the envy of the world.   Nor did it
on any other account so much deserve these sore misfortunes
as by producing such a generation of men as were the occasion
of this its overthrow.

Now when Titus was come into this (upper) city, he admired not only some other places of strength in it, but particularly those strong towers which the tyrants in their mad conduct had relinquished, for when he saw their solid altitude, and
the largeness of their several stones, and the exactness of their
joints, as also how great was their breadth and how extensive
their length, he expressed himself after the manner following:
" We have certainly had God for our assistant in this war, and
it was no other than God who ejected the Jews out of these
fortifications, for what could the hands of men or any machines
do toward overthrowing these towers?"   At which time he
had many such discourses to his friends; he also let such go
free as had been bound by the tyrants, and were left in the
prisons.   To conclude, when he entirely demolished the rest
of the city and overthrew its walls, he left these towers as a
monument of his good fortune, which had proved his auxiliaries, and enabled him to take what could not otherwise have
been taken by him.

And now, since his soldiers were already quite tired with
killing men, and yet there appeared to be a vast multitude still
remaining alive, Cæsar gave orders that they should kill none
but those that were in arms and opposed them, but should take
the rest alive.   But, together with those whom they had orders
to slay, they slew the aged and the infirm; but for those that

were in their flourishing age and who might be useful to them they drove them together into the Temple and shut them up within the walls of the court of the women, over which Cæsar set one of his freedmen, as also Fronto, one of his own friends, which last was to determine everyone's fate, according to his merits.

So this Fronto slew all those that had been seditious and robbers, who were impeached one by another; but of the young men he chose out the tallest and most beautiful and reserved them for the triumph, and as for the rest of the multitude that were above seventeen years old he put them into bonds and sent them to the Egyptian mines. Titus also sent a great number into the provinces as a present to them, that they might be destroyed upon their theatres by the sword and by the wild beasts; but those that were under seventeen years of age were sold for slaves. Now during the days wherein Fronto was distinguishing these men there perished, for want of food, eleven thousand, some of whom did not taste any food, through the hatred their guards bore to them, and others would not take in any when it was given them. The multitude also was so very great that they were in want even of corn for their sustenance.

Now the number of those that were carried captive during this whole war was collected to be ninety-seven thousand; as was the number of those that perished during the whole siege eleven hundred thousand, the greater part of whom was indeed of the same nation [with the citizens of Jerusalem], but not belonging to the city itself. They were come up from all the country to the feast of unleavened bread and were on a sudden shut up by an army, which, at the very first, occasioned so great a straitness among them that there came a pestilential destruction upon them, and soon afterward such a famine as destroyed them more suddenly.

That this city could contain so many people in it is manifest by that number of them which was taken under Cestius, who, being desirous of informing Nero of the power of the city, who otherwise was disposed to contemn that nation, entreated the high-priests, if the thing were possible, to take the number of their whole multitude. So these high-priests, upon the coming of that feast which is called the Passover, when they slay their sacrifices, from the ninth hour till the eleventh, but so that a company not less than ten belong to every sacrifice (for it is not lawful for them to feast singly by themselves), and many of them were twenty in a company, found the number of sacrifices was two hundred and fifty-six thousand five hundred, which, upon the allowance of no more than ten that feast together, amounts to two millions seven hundred thousand and two hundred persons that were pure and holy; for as to those that have the leprosy, or the gonorrhœa, or women that have their monthly courses, or such as are otherwise polluted, it is not lawful for them to be partakers of this sacrifice; nor indeed for any foreigners neither, who come hither to worship.

Now this vast multitude is indeed collected out of remote places, but the entire nation was now shut up by fate as in prison, and the Roman army encompassed the city when it was crowded with inhabitants. Accordingly, the multitude of those that therein perished exceeded all the destructions that either men or God ever brought upon the world; for, to speak only of what was publicly known, the Romans slew some of them, some they carried captives, and others they made a search for underground, and when they found where they were they broke up the ground and slew all they met with. There were also found slain there above two thousand persons, partly by their own hands and partly by one another, but chiefly destroyed by the famine; but then the ill-savor of the dead bodies was most offensive to those that lighted upon them, insomuch that some were obliged to get away immediately, while others were so greedy of gain that they would go in among the dead bodies that lay on heaps and tread upon them, for a great deal of treasure was found in these caverns, and the hope of gain made every way of getting it to be esteemed lawful.

Many also of those that had been put in prison by the tyrants were now brought out, for they did not leave off their barbarous cruelty at the very last; yet did God avenge himself upon upon them both in a manner agreeable to justice. As for John, he wanted food, together with his brethren, in these caverns, and begged that the Romans would now give him their right hand for his security, which he had often proudly rejected before; but for Simon, he struggled hard with the distress he was in, till he was forced to surrender himself. So he was reserved for the triumph, and to be then slain, as was John condemned to perpetual imprisonment. And now the Romans set fire to the extreme parts of the city, and burned them down, and entirely demolished its walls.

And thus was Jerusalem taken, in the second year of the reign of Vespasian, on the eighth day of the month Gorpeius (Elul). It had been taken five times before, though this was the second time of its desolation, for Shishak, the king of Egypt, and after him Antiochus, and after him Pompey, and after them Sosius and Herod, took the city, but still preserved it; but before all these the king of Babylon conquered it and made it desolate, one thousand four hundred and sixty-eight years and six months after it was built.

But he who first built it was a potent man among the Canaanites, and is in our own tongue called (Melchisedek), the righteous king, for such he really was. On which account he was (there) the first priest of God, and first built a temple (there), and called the city Jerusalem, which was formerly called Salem. However, David, the king of the Jews, ejected the Canaanites, and settled his own people therein.

It was demolished entirely by the Babylonians, four hundred and seventy-seven years and six months after him. And from King David, who was the first of the Jews who reigned therein, to this destruction under Titus, were one thousand one hundred and seventy-nine years; but from its first building till this last destruction were two thousand one hundred and seventy-seven years; yet hath not its great antiquity, nor its vast riches, nor the diffusion of its nation over all the habitable earth, nor the greatness of the veneration paid to it on a religious account, been sufficient to preserve it from being destroyed. And thus ended the siege of Jerusalem.

DESTRUCTION OF POMPEII

A.D. 79

PLINY   LYTTON

Among the historic calamities of the world none has gathered about itself more of human interest, whether in connection with the study of ancient cities and customs or in the calling forth of sympathy through the magical treatment of imaginative literature, than the destruction of Pompeii and Herculaneum by the eruption of Mount Vesuvius, which occurred at the beginning of the reign of Titus. The eruption was accompanied by an earthquake, and the combination of natural commotions caused the complete ruin and burial of the two cities.

One of the most vivid descriptions of the catastrophe is that given in the account of Dion Cassius. Among those who perished in the disaster was the elder Pliny, the celebrated naturalist; and the most famous narrative of the eruption is that here given of Pliny the Younger, nephew of the other, in the two letters which he wrote to Tacitus in order to supply that historian with accurate details.

Lytton's well-known *Last Days of Pompeii*, although a work of imagination, deals with this subject in a manner which almost simulates the realistic tale of an actual observer; and his account, linking the calamity itself with the revelations of the earlier explorers of the buried city, after so many centuries had passed, well deserves a place in connection with the story of the older and more circumstantial writer.

One of the earliest important discoveries at Pompeii, made in 1771, was that of the "Villa of Diomedes," named from the tomb of Marcus Arrius Diomedes across the street. Since then every decade has seen some progress in the work of excavation, and among other buildings brought to light are the "House of Pansa," the "House of the Tragic Poet," the "House of Sallustius," the "Castor and Pollux," a double house, and the "House of the Vettii"—the last, a recent discovery, being left with all its furnishings as found. Many interesting objects have been discovered lately, and a complete picture can now be presented of a small Italian city and its life in the first century A.D. Valuable finds are wall paintings, illustrative of decorative art; floor mosaics, etc., which may be seen in the Royal Museum of Naples. Another of the most recent discoveries is that of the temple of Venus Pompeiana in the southern corner of the city; others are the remains of persons who, carrying valuables, perished in a wayside inn where they had sought refuge. At the present time about one-half of the city has been excavated, and the cir-

207

cuit of the walls has been found to be about two miles. The uncovering of the whole city will probably require many years. Excavations now being made in the adjacent country promise results as interesting as those already obtained within the city limits.

PLINY

YOUR request that I would send you an account of my uncle's death, in order to transmit a more exact relation of it to posterity, deserves my acknowledgments; for, if this accident shall be celebrated by your pen, the glory of it, I am well assured, will be rendered forever illustrious. And notwithstanding he perished by a misfortune, which as it involved at the same time a most beautiful country in ruins, and destroyed so many populous cities, seems to promise him an everlasting remembrance; notwithstanding he has himself composed many and lasting works; yet I am persuaded, the mentioning of him in your immortal writings will greatly contribute to render his name immortal.

Happy I esteem those to be to whom by provision of the gods has been granted the ability either to do such actions as are worthy of being related or to relate them in a manner worthy of being read; but peculiarly happy are they who are blessed with both these uncommon talents: in the number of which my uncle, as his own writings and your history will evidently prove, may justly be ranked. It is with extreme willingness, therefore, that I execute your commands; and should indeed have claimed the task if you had not enjoined it. He was at that time with the fleet under his command at Misenum.

On the 24th of August, about one in the afternoon, my mother desired him to observe a cloud which appeared of a very unusual size and shape. He had just taken a turn in the sun,[1] and, after bathing himself in cold water, and making a

[1] The Romans used to lie or walk naked in the sun, after anointing their bodies with oil, which was esteemed as greatly contributing to health, and therefore daily practised by them. This custom, however, of anointing themselves, is inveighed against by the satirists as in the number of their luxurious indulgences; but since we find the elder Pliny here, and the amiable Spurinna in a former letter, practising this method, we cannot suppose the thing itself was esteemed unmanly, but only when it was attended with some particular circumstances of an over-refined delicacy.

light luncheon, gone back to his books: he immediately arose and went out upon a rising ground from whence he might get a better sight of this very uncommon appearance. A cloud, from which mountain was uncertain at this distance (but it was found afterward to come from Mount Vesuvius [1]) was ascending, the appearance of which I cannot give you a more exact description of than by likening it to that of a pine tree, for it shot up to a great height in the form of a very tall trunk, which spread itself out at the top into a sort of branches; occasioned, I imagine, either by a sudden gust of air that impelled it, the force of which decreased as it advanced upward, or the cloud itself, being pressed back again by its own weight, expanded in the manner I have mentioned; it appeared sometimes bright and sometimes dark and spotted, according as it was either more or less impregnated with earth and cinders.

This phenomenon seemed to a man of such learning and research as my uncle extraordinary and worth further looking into. He ordered a light vessel to be got ready, and gave me leave, if I liked, to accompany him. I said I had rather go on with my work; and it so happened he had himself given me something to write out. As he was coming out of the house, he received a note from Rectina, the wife of Bassus, who was in the utmost alarm at the imminent danger which threatened her; for her villa lying at the foot of Mount Vesuvius, there was no way of escape but by sea; she earnestly entreated him therefore to come to her assistance.

He accordingly changed his first intention, and what he had begun from a philosophical, he now carried out in a noble and generous, spirit. He ordered the galleys to put to sea, and went himself on board with an intention of assisting not only Rectina, but the several other towns which lay thickly strewn along that beautiful coast. Hastening then to the place from whence others fled with the utmost terror, he steered his course direct to the point of danger, and with so much calmness and presence of mind as to be able to make and dictate his observations upon the motion and all the phenomena of that dreadful scene. He was now so close to the mountain that the cinders, which grew thicker and hotter the nearer he approached, fell

---

[1] About six miles distant from Naples.

into the ships, together with pumice-stones and black pieces of burning rock: they were in danger too not only of being aground by the sudden retreat of the sea, but also from the vast fragments which rolled down from the mountain and obstructed all the shore. Here he stopped to consider whether he should turn back again; to which the pilot advising him, "Fortune," said he, "favors the brave; steer to where Pomponianus is." Pomponianus was then at Stabiæ, separated by a bay, which the sea, after several insensible windings, forms with the shore. He had already sent his baggage on board; for though he was not at that time in actual danger, yet being within sight of it, and indeed extremely near, if it should in the least increase, he was determined to put to sea as soon as the wind, which was blowing dead in-shore, should go down. It was favorable, however, for carrying my uncle to Pomponianus, whom he found in the greatest consternation: he embraced him tenderly, encouraging and urging him to keep up his spirits, and, the more effectually to soothe his fears by seeming unconcerned himself, ordered a bath to be got ready, and then, after having bathed, sat down to supper with great cheerfulness, or at least —what is just as heroic—with every appearance of it.

Meanwhile broad flames shone out in several places from Mount Vesuvius, which the darkness of the night contributed to render still brighter and clearer. But my uncle, in order to soothe the apprehensions of his friend, assured him it was only the burning of the villages, which the country people had abandoned to the flames. After this he retired to rest, and it is most certain he was so little disquieted as to fall into a sound sleep, for his breathing, which, on account of his corpulence, was rather heavy and sonorous, was heard by the attendants outside.

The court which led to his apartment being now almost filled with stones and ashes, if he had continued there any time longer, it would have been impossible for him to have made his way out. So he was awoke and got up, and went to Pomponianus and the rest of his company, who were feeling too anxious to think of going to bed. They consulted together whether it would be most prudent to trust to the houses—which now rocked from side to side with frequent and violent concussions as though shaken from their very foundations—or fly to